aka bpNichol

a preliminary biography / frank davey

ecw press

Published by ECW Press
2120 Queen Street East, Suite 200, Toronto, Ontario, Canada M4E 1E2
416-694-3348 / info@ecwpress.com

LIBRARY AND ARCHIVES CANADA CATALOGUING IN PUBLICATION

Davey, Frank, 1940-
Aka bpNichol : a preliminary biography / Frank Davey.

ISBN 978-1-77041-019-0
ALSO ISSUED AS: 978-177090-259-6 (PDF); 978-1-77090-260-2 (EPUB)

1. Nichol, B. P., 1944-1988. 2. Poets, Canadian (English)—
20th century—Biography. I. Title.

PS8527.I32Z63 2012   C811'.54   C2012-902711-1

Editor for the press: Emily Schultz
Cover design: David Gee
Cover image: Marilyn Westlake
Interior images: From the Collection of Frank Davey: 2, 9, 17, 20, 40, 66, 79, 85, 90, 112, 132, 141, 143, 152, 170, 200, 223; Dezso Huba: 42; bill bissett: 77; Grant Goodbrand: 92, 182; Marilyn Westlake: 234, 252, 277; Stan Bevington: 289
Type: Troy Cunningham
Printing: Trigraphik | LBF   5   4   3   2   1

This book has been published with the help of a grant from the Canadian Federation for the Humanities and Social Sciences, through the Awards to Scholarly Publications Program, using funds provided by the Social Sciences and Humanities Research Council of Canada.

The publication of aka bpNichol has been generously supported by the Canada Council for the Arts which last year invested $20.1 million in writing and publishing throughout Canada, and by the Ontario Arts Council, an agency of the Government of Ontario. We also acknowledge the financial support of the Government of Canada through the Canada Book Fund for our publishing activities, and the contribution of the Government of Ontario through the Ontario Book Publishing Tax Credit. The marketing of this book was made possible with the support of the Ontario Media Development Corporation.

  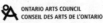

PRINTED AND BOUND IN CANADA

CONTENTS

acknowledgements

I thank Barrie Nichol for being such a pack rat, Eleanor Nichol for ensuring that so much of what he created and gathered has been so well preserved, and for assisting me in the early part of my research, and his sister Deanna for offering me her still vivid early memories. His Therafields colleagues Grant Goodbrand, Philip McKenna, and Sharon McIsaac, his brother Don, and his fellow Four Horsemen collaborators Paul Dutton and Steve McCaffery generously helped me solve various narrative mysteries. Sharon Barbour, Lori Emerson, and Stan Bevington were also at the ready to help me mull through Barrie's more complicated moments. David Rosenberg was repeatedly ready with encouragement, advice, and eagerness to read chapter drafts. Of great assistance as well were some of Barrie's earliest friends, Andy Phillips, Arnold Shives, and Dezso Huba, all of whom offered details that could otherwise have been lost to oral history. I also have to thank Arnold Shives and bill bissett for being such loyal correspondents with Barrie at various times during the 1960s. Barrie had difficulty writing letters in those years, and without their friendship and engagement with Barrie's ideas and projects much of his early thoughts about writing would also have been lost. I thank Sharon Barbour, bill bissett, David Robinson, Stephen Scobie, D.r. Wagner, and the late Nicholas Zurbrugg (via Tony Zurbrugg acting for his estate) for permitting me to quote from their letters to Barrie, and Loren Lind for permitting me to quote from his important unpublished 1965 interview with him. Thanks also to Arnold Shives, Paul Dutton, and Gerry Shikatani for permitting me to quote their unpublished recollections of Barrie, and again to

Eleanor Nichol for helping me browse through the scrapbooks, photos, Therafields publications, and other memorabilia still in her basement. And a big thanks to Maria Hindmarch for listening to all my research anecdotes during my visit to Vancouver and being such a thoughtful host and excitable Canucks fan.

I must also thank the Ontario Arts Council for the Writers' Reserve grant that helped me travel to gather the material for the book, and Tony Power, Eric Swanick, and Keith Gilbert of Simon Fraser University's Special Collections for their kind assistance. I was a daily visitor to their department for more than a month, during which they often found items for me that I might not have known were there. I also thank York University's Clara Thomas Archives for generous access to bill bissett's papers. I should probably apologize as well to the hundreds of Barrie's friends I didn't manage to contact. This book could only be so long, and is undoubtedly preliminary to others whose authors will devote more years to them. I urge you all to record your memories of Barrie, and offer any letters you may have received from him to a public collection before they also fall "beyond the reach of talking." Finally a huge thank-you to longtime bpNichol reader Jack David of ECW Press for undertaking to publish this story.

My main regret is that Eleanor ("Ellie") Nichol, on reading partway through an early version of this book in manuscript, felt unable to support its publication by granting permission for me to quote or include photographs of previously unpublished Nichol material, including most of the material in his numerous notebooks and extensive correspondence. Although she was initially enthusiastic about the project, she had also assumed that a "literary biography" would make many fewer references to his private life and suggest fewer links between it and his writing. Her unhappiness may have also caused others who had been important to Barrie, such as Rob Hindley-Smith, to be unavailable for interview.

Frank Davey
May 2012

introduction

*I am highly suspicious of well-documented biographies,
just as I am skeptical about historical records and events.
If, on the other hand, the biographer would write about
his subject purely from his imagination, from what he
<u>thinks</u> his subject was or is, that is another matter.*

— Henry Miller, letter to Jay Martin,
quoted in Martin's *Always Merry and Bright*

Barrie Nichol records this Henry Miller passage in 1979 in his "Houses
of the Alphabet" notebook. It's one of many moments in his notebooks
that display his concern both with the genre of biography and with the
question of how he will be remembered. The earliest such moment occurs
in his very first notebook, in which, on July 15, 1965, after looking back
over its contents, he worried that they might be mostly "shit" and, from
the viewpoint of a future "theoretical" biographer, worthless. Barrie was
then only 21 years old, virtually unpublished, and already anticipating
being memorialized in a book such as the present one. A decade later he
would chuckle whenever he or someone else mentioned British novelist
B.S. Johnson's *Aren't You Rather Young to Be Writing Your Memoirs*, but
would continue recording his thoughts, dreams, ideas for novels, poems
or drawings, and conversations with his parents in his notebooks anyway.

The present "theoretical biographer" met Barrie Nichol in Toronto in

late 1970 — toward the end of the half-decade in which Barrie met most of
his important friends and collaborators. I knew him then as "bpNichol," a
young visual poet. We had argued in the pages of my journal *Open Letter*
some years earlier — 1966 — over whether I ought to view visual poetry
as "relevant to what I understand as poetry." We'd differed somewhat
vigorously — causing Victor Coleman to quip in a letter to the journal
that Frank was sure that people were saying "ugh and the like" before
they could draw, and that bpNichol was defending visual poetry "like
the civil servant *will* defend his job."[1] Four years later I was newly in
Toronto and writing a small book about Earle Birney, who had created
a number of visual poems. Even if I didn't want to create such things,
I needed to understand them. bpNichol, with whom I had not been in
contact since 1966, was now the author of the box of visual poems *Still
Water* and anthologist of another boxful, *The Cosmic Chef: An Evening of
Concrete*, as well as the creator of the more conventionally confessional
booklet "Journeying and the Returns" — itself part of yet another box
of stuff, ambiguously labelled *bp*. I phoned bp — or more likely Barrie
— and asked for help, and he suggested we have lunch in a little box of a
Hungarian restaurant on Bloor Street near Spadina.

Lunch went on for quite a while: by 1972 he was the most active con-
tributing editor of *Open Letter*, by 1976 we were together as the two most
active editors of Coach House Press, and by 1977 I was writing books like
Edward and Patricia in the midst of "artists' marathons" that Barrie was con-
ducting at the lay psychoanalytical foundation Therafields, of which he was
vice-president. Lunch had stretched to include numerous pots of Earl Grey
in my living room, numerous lobsters at the biannual Coach House wayz-
goose, and numerous mugs of honey-sweetened coffee and "Lisa bread"
in the Therafields barn in Mono Township. I saw Barrie in most of his
various circles — Coach House, the Four Horsemen sound poetry group,
the international sound poets,[2] the "'pataphysicians,"[3] his writing classes
at York University, and Therafields. He was still the one of many names
— Barrie, bp, beep, beeper, beepers, bar, Bear, Professor Nichol. My son
Mike, who much preferred the sciences to the arts, came to admire and
trust Barrie/bp so much that in May 1988 he enrolled in what was probably
Barrie's last high school sound poetry workshop. Unlike Boswell, I was not
taking notes in any of these places, or planning to need such.

It was Barrie who was the more preoccupied with biography — or for him both autobiography and much of its larger context, origin. Throughout his life he would search for forms that might be appropriate for telling his "story" — creating numerous quasi-autobiographical texts, from the published *Captain Poetry Poems*, "Journeying and the Returns," *Monotones*, *The Other Side of the Room*, *The Martyrology*, *Two Novels*, *The True Eventual Story of Billy the Kid* (which he once considered part of his ongoing semi-autobiographical "The Plunkett Papers"), *Journal*, and *Selected Organs: Parts of an Autobiography* to the unpublished and unfinished "The Life and Search of Jonathan Quest" (begun 1964), "The Plunkett Papers" (begun 1969), "An Autobiography" (begun 1972), "The Autobiography of Phillip Workman by bpNichol" (begun 1972), "John Cannyside" (begun 1968), "John Cannyside an Epic Poem" (begun 1972), "bpNichol by John Cannyside" (drafted 1974–86), "Organ Music" (drafted 1980–88), and "Desiring to Become" (planned 1979–88), an autobiographical text probably to be based on family photographs that he asked his mother to gather for him in March 1979.[4] Sometimes he told his stories in the first person, as in "Journeying and the Returns" and *Selected Organs*, sometimes in the third, as in "The Autobiography of Phillip Workman," where he gave his persona his own middle name and his mother's maiden name. Sometimes he gave himself a metaphoric persona, like Billy the Kid, the kid who thought his "dick" was not only short but also "short for richard" like bp was now short for Barrie Phillip. Sometimes, as in "For Jesus Lunatick" in *Two Novels*, he blurred persons and narrative lines together in dream landscapes that echoed the confusions caused by psychological "transference" — again using his middle name Phillip for the main character. In the various drafts of "bpNichol by John Cannyside" he used the conventions of postmodern metafiction to create a work in which "bpNichol" was merely a fictionalizable character that he and several other rival characters could competitively vie to define. In *The Martyrology* he would send "bpNichol" to pun and wordgame multiple paths through language in search of more biography of Barrie Nichol — letting bp occupy the first-person "i" and leaving to Barrie the ambiguous "you."

In nearly all of Barrie's 34 notebooks one can find evidence of preoccupation with the several questions of autobiography: origin, or how did I come to be; shaping events, or how did I become what I am; and

identity, or who am I anyway; and with how to find the appropriate forms
in which to address these. In his first notebook, as he set out to begin a
new life in Toronto, he wrote the startling announcement that he wanted
to write a novel that would take him all of his lifetime and would finish
only with his death — adding that all authors — Kerouac, Lowry, Kafka,
Burroughs — write autobiographically even when they change the names
of the personages. How could one write about anything else? he won-
dered. Then he added the even more startling comment that he didn't
even want to write a novel, that all he wanted to create was a huge image
of his life stuffed into a book (entry April 1, 1964). Change "novel" or
"book" in this passage to "epic poem" and one has precisely what Barrie
will have done by his death in 1988.

In May 1972 while drafting for a second time that year parts of "An
Autobiography," he wrote to himself in his "Notebook IV" (which was
actually the eighth notebook of various sizes that he had begun and pre-
served by this date) that the biggest irony of autobiography was that the
writer could never write his own story completely, that he was inevitably
destined to die with the project uncompleted. In this note he moved back
and forth between referring to his "i"-narrator in the first person and in
the third; "i" would die before its life was narrated, he wrote, although
"we," he suggested, could relate what it could not. "i" here was simul-
taneously both Barrie Nichol and a fiction, with the quick shifts of the
pronouns also suggesting that the "i" that he was experiencing as his own
mind might also be a kind of fiction.

Again, his prescience was, and is, unsettling — not only about his
leaving his story uncompleted but also about how others — his "we" —
could continue to tell it. At this point he knew, as a now self-consciously
inventive writer, both that his subjectivities, his "i's," were multiple and
fictional, and that their stories were still, whatever their multipleness, part
of his own personal "i" story. He knew that because "i" was destined to
die, any fictional third-person "i" that "i" created would die also — but
that inversely only the death of his various subjectivities could satisfacto-
rily "finish" his and their stories. He also wrote here, however, about how
interchangeable these subjectivities could be, how the "phillip" he was
calling himself in "An Autobiography" was also he whose middle name is
Phillip — Barrie Phillip Nichol. He was calling himself phillip, he wrote,

while not being phillip although phillip was still a part of his own name. Thus he was who he was not, he wrote, even though he was as he was saying he was — i.e. both "phillip" and not "phillip." Then he crossed out this impressively convoluted passage and many lines around it, possibly because they had crossed for him a limit of metafictional "undecidability," or perhaps because he worried that overall they had become tiresomely clever ("Notebook iv" 6).

In his "Notebook Begun February 21, 1974" (the 15th surviving one overall) — started when he had become adept at half-concealing auto-biographical material beneath such formal, metafictional play, at playing a kind of identity peekaboo with his readers — he wrote to himself that he was realizing that the proportion of autobiography in his current draft of his novel, *Journal*, was even greater than he had earlier thought. He told himself that this had happened because long ago, when he was an elementary schoolchild, he had embraced writing as a substitute for the mother he could not satisfyingly embrace in person. He had shifted all his longing into his writing and away from her, he wrote, and thus was creating in *Journal* an imaginary woman whom he could envision himself touching and caressing — someone who was in his Oedipally possessed imagination a "good" mother. In a nearby entry he observed that *Journal* now contained a significant number of revised parts that he had originally written for the manuscript titled "An Autobiography."

On a visit to his sister Deanna in 1979 Barrie recorded that she told him that he wrote in order to communicate with their father, because to him books were more important than other things — including, evidently, relations with people. She had joked that it was hard to get their father to put a book down in order to do things with him (entry February 25, 1979). It is on this notebook page that Barrie conceived of his never-written autobiography "Desiring to Become." Earlier in a short note to himself in his "4th Short Notebook Begun April 15, 1975" (the 20th note-book, and the second that he has titled the "4th Short"[5]), he had written that it felt as if no one, including his mother and Deanna, had ever wanted to listen to what he had to say. And consequently, he concluded, he had begun exploring "forms" — always looking for better and more effective ways to articulate.

Barrie had understood very early, it seems, that autobiography both

aka{ barrie / phillip }Nichol

is and isn't autobiography, that it is at best a plausible invention, a fiction that makes sense of memories that are themselves at best plausible interpretations of events a person has experienced or witnessed or believed themselves to have witnessed, or that create substitute versions of disappointing past experiences. We are all autobiographers, in the sense that our lives require us to construct a sense of "self," an understanding of who we are, how we came to be so, who we were and are in what contexts and what relationships,[6] and who we might be able to become — an answer to a question that both a fiction writer or a psychoanalyst might ask: "Who do you think you are?" Barrie appears to have begun writing fantasy versions of an autobiography in childhood. In adulthood, looking for that best way to express things, he wrote various versions of his life in other genres — the joke (*The True Eventual Story of Billy the Kid*), the comic book (*The Captain Poetry Poems*), the lyric (*The Other Side of the Room),* the epic poem (*The Martyrology*), the nouveau roman (*Two Novels, Journal*), the postmodern detective novel ("John Cannyside"), simultaneously trying both to communicate his life story and to disguise it as illusion, fantasy, "art." He was recurrently conscious of this creative split. In that 1979 note about "Desiring to Become" he theorized that he perhaps wrote voluminously both to communicate his story to his father and to protect it from his mother who, when he was 10, had — traumatically for him — thrown out the manuscript of his first work of fiction. He reflected that this double sense of purpose — to write things that his mother couldn't destroy and that his father might be interested in reading — might also have given him an idiosyncratic understanding of the form/content dichotomy, and be now causing his early life to be reflected in both the content of his writing and its often rushed-to-publication form. Multiple copies are much less easy for a mother to destroy than a single copy, and much easier for a father to discover. "AutobIography" is not a fiction and yet is constructed, and edited, he had scribbled in 1975 on a slip of International Hotel of Calgary notepaper, after quoting Rimbaud's "je est un autre." He was about to tell a University of Calgary class that the "je" they were listening to was often "un autre," even to himself.[7]

Biography can be also no more than a plausible construction — a hypothetical story that interprets an incomplete set of data, memories, perspectives, and facts. In undertaking this one Frank Davey becomes not

only another part of bpNichol's much envisioned "we" that he expected
might continue to tell what his "i," once dead, could never tell, but
also another biography-competitor, along with John Cannyside, Phillip
Workman, bpNichol, whatever Nichol biographers volunteer later, and
the various Barrie Nichol friends and relatives, including Ellie Nichol,
who have developed their own differing understandings of who Barrie
was and who he saw others — such as his mother — as being. Some of
these, particularly among his poetry and psychotherapy colleagues, may
think that I have misconstrued the relationship between his neo-Freudian
understandings and his poetry — possibly worrying that any such con-
nection could render the poetry abreactive, less creative, or *merely* auto-
biographical. Others may think that I have done violence to some of his
writing, not so much by reading it as merely autobiographical — which I
hope I have not done — as by repeatedly reading it *for* autobiography —
which I believe was one of the readings Barrie Nichol both desired and
feared. At least from his father. "Barrie Nichol," that is. "Go for it," he
used to tell me.

aka{ barrie
      phillip }Nichol

1. Birth, Death, and Life, 1944-48

The 'i' is me and isn't me.

— Nichol in Niechoda, *A Sourcery*, 178

At Vancouver's mock-Tudor Grace Hospital in late September 1944, the birth of Glen and Avis Nichol's fifth child, soon to be named Barrie Phillip, was apparently uneventful. The hospital photographer took the routine photo and inserted it into a small folder that bore a sepia engraving of the hospital. In a few days the newborn's mother would paste both folder and photo into a "baby book" and record his weight (9 pounds, 14 ounces) and length (22 inches). Under "Remarks" she would whimsically write that she didn't need to remark, that of course she and the rest of the family thought he was wonderful. On the next page she recorded the gifts he had received and commented that he'd done really well, especially considering that he was the family's fifth child. This was bpNichol's first book, and like quite a few others it would be unfinished. Avis's final health entry — on the fourth page — reported that he'd received his first vegetables at four months; several earlier lines, including the one for when he received his first "solid food," she left unfilled. Although the book allowed a parent five years of narrative, almost all of the remaining pages were also left blank, and with them their spaces for when baby first crawled, walked, or talked.

Such barely begun baby books are not unusual. New parents — especially ones with other children — have numerous demands on their time. In the Nichols' case three other children vied for their attention — their eldest, Donna, born in Saskatoon in September 1933, had died at six weeks, much to Avis's continuing distress. Then had come Bob in 1935, Don in 1937, and Deanna in 1940. Their day-to-day well-being was mostly their mother's responsibility. Deanna recalls that their father, like many Canadian men of his time, understood his main family duty as the bringing home of a paycheque. He worked in the freight department of the Canadian National Railway, and was regularly promoted and transferred, under company policy, to a different city approximately every four or so years. To refuse a transfer was to refuse the promotion. The family had started out in Saskatoon, where Donna, Bob, and Don had been born, moved to Regina in 1937, to Port Arthur (now part of Thunder Bay) in 1939, and to the working-class Vancouver suburb of Burnaby in 1941. Avis thus did not have a large number of local friends, although her mother, now a widow, did live with them in Burnaby for part of the war years. Two cousins, with whom she enjoyed outings, also lived nearby.

GRACE HOSPITAL
VANCOUVER, B. C.

GRACE HOSPITAL, VANCOUVER, BRITISH COLUMBIA

Years later Barrie would hint in his novel *Journal* that he believed that he may not have been a "wanted" child. While this usage of "want" implies an exaggeration, it does seem unlikely that he was planned. With Deanna's birth in 1940 the Nichols had a "complete" boys-and-girl family — one that Donna's unfortunate death had made more difficult to achieve. Donna, moreover, had remained a haunting family presence through her mother's frequent recollections, which she continued to routinely ver-balize even after the birth of Deanna's children in the 1960s. Donna was so present in the family during Barrie's childhood that into early adulthood he would have the illusion that somewhere she was alive, and possibly dictating much of his writing to him from "beyond." In one of his early notebooks he wrote of her as a fellow artist and implicit twin. Quite possibly he saw Donna as more present to his mother than he was himself. Barrie also seems to have come to associate his mother with death. In a 1968 notebook he would write a passage for his unpublished book "The Plunkett Papers" — in it either misremembering or reconstructing Donna's death as happening in 1934, and at six months rather than six weeks. He would add that he had once found her tiny shoes in a box, and that they'd been smaller than the palm of his hand, and added also the apparent non sequitur that his mother once had a pet rabbit that slept in her bed and that smothered one night when she unknowingly rolled over on it. Presumably this event occurred while his mother was a child. Death had been following him, was obsessing him, he would write. In the spring of 1977, possibly during a visit with both his parents and his sister Deanna in Victoria, he would develop a theory of how his mother's persistent grief at Donna's death had dominated her view of her later children ("The Way Notebook," January 31, 1977). In 1982 he would include this detail in *The Martyrology, Book 5,* Chain 3, writing how his mother continued

> crying after Donna's death
> nothing left to remember her by
> echoed her in Deanna's name
> the next & last girl to be born
> & Don
>   when he came into this world

Curiously, Barrie almost followed Donna into his own early death. Sometime after he was three months old, around the family dinnertime, he stopped breathing and turned blue. Avis shouted to Glen to call a doctor. Glen replied that it was too late, that Barrie was already dead. Recounted frequently by Avis, the words became part of the family history. Somehow he was revived — Deanna later came to believe that he may have had a convulsion. Barrie wrote about the incident several times in his journals and partly fictionalized "autobiographies," sometimes

aka{ barrie phillip }Nichol

recalling it as happening when he was three months old, sometimes when six months, sometimes when eight months. In his "Notebook Begun March 13, 1971" he drafted a possible *Martyrology, Book 3* section to be called "Future Music," and wrote that when he was "maybe" eight months of age his father believed he was dead and thought it futile to call a doctor. In his "Notebook #3" on April 18, 1972, he created his first draft of "The Autobiography of Phillip Workman by bpNichol," and had Phillip recall that his mother told him that he almost died when he was "maybe" three months old, that his body turned blue, that he appeared to be choking, that he couldn't breathe, and that even while his mother was phoning the doctor his father was shouting that there was no point in phoning, that he was already dead. In his "Notebook Begun February 21, 1974" he recorded a dream on March 18, 1975, and wrote that it seemed to be about material that he tried to avoid thinking about, the time when he was around six months of age and turned blue, no longer interested in living. The inability of his parents to explain the incident seems to have mythologized it for Barrie, and led him to suspect that his early childhood had been so unhappy that he had tried to die by forcing himself to stop breathing — a child at three, six, or eight months already suicidal. These notebook passages would lead in 1977 to a more poetic narration, which he included in Chain 3 of *The Martyrology, Book 5* in 1982, and which appears to declare attempted suicide a certainty. The apparently unexplainable "reason" for the incident was, he wrote, "inside me":

> my sister Donna died
> six weeks old
>   as i almost died
> six months old
> Rupert Street in Vancouver
> choking to death for no reason
> the no reason was inside me

Here he got her age correct, and possibly his own, but got, or made, the place of his near-death wrong. At the time (whether he was three months, six months, or eight months old) the family was still living in a large rented house at 2661 Blenheim Avenue (now renamed Burlington Avenue) in

Burnaby. His father did not buy their house at 4936 Rupert Street a few blocks away in Vancouver until January 1947. A few pages later Barrie linked himself and Donna as having shared "a fear of living" and suggested that his not dying may have been a turning back from suicide:

> we shared that fear of living
> you died at six weeks
> i almost died at six months
> in that moment glimpsing you
> we shared some common experience
> i turned away
> back into the world

For Barrie this almost-dying incident appears to have become in his early years a self-defining moment. He was someone who had been allowed to choose between living and dying. Both the option of death and death's inevitability would always be in his consciousness. But so too would be the conviction that when one chooses life one is choosing the fullest possible engagement with it — with family, history, language, art, music, and above all imagination. Only such a wide, intense, and fruitful life could satisfy him — or enable him to avoid depression.

In these various notebooks he recorded only two vivid early childhood memories. In the first, which he recorded in his April 18, 1972, draft of "The Autobiography of Phillip Workman by bpNichol," he was crawling on the grass in their Burnaby garden, not yet able to walk or talk. It was a warm spring or summer day. He had a slight panic that he may have crawled too far from his mother, and looked back through a trellis to reassure himself that she was there. She was, her face turned toward him, and framed by profusely flowering vines, morning glory or possibly sweet pea, but her eyes seemingly vacant and focussed on things miles beyond him. Her hair was long and blonde, he wrote, as it was in photographs from that time, but in her eyes he recalled sensing things he was once unable to describe — vague sadness, unfocussed anger. Her gaze disturbed him and would come to haunt him. He wrote that those memories were reminding him as well of a dream he had later of crawling down an extremely long hallway and finding his mother in an old kitchen weeping at the table. He added that he thought the dream was not memory but a vision of what he had wordlessly understood that day in the garden.

Substantially rewritten, this garden scene would reappear in the closing pages of his novel *Journal*.

> i'm speaking mommy & you arent listening   so many times i would stand at the foot of the garden calling your name quietly so that you wouldn't hear me   i wanted you to hear me   for so many years i wanted you to hear so badly & i couldnt speak   i'd call your name to myself tired now finally frightened but never stopping always calling quietly at the foot of the garden as the sun went down over the trellis (74)

Here the child is able to talk, but reluctant to do so in case his talking might confirm the terrifying possibility that his mother is indeed unable or unwilling to hear.

Was Barrie's mother as sad, distant, and vaguely angry as "bpNichol" describes these mothers as being? It's impossible to know, and quite possible that she wasn't. But this seems to have been his childhood perception of her — one that lodged in his unconscious and caused him many years of unhappiness. Twenty-five years later he would tell his sister Deanna, who had questioned the accuracy of his memories, that he must have been an "unusually sensitive child."[1]

In the second early childhood memory he was sharing a bathtub with his mother. Barrie treated this memory as a gothic nightmare in 1969 in "For Jesus Lunatick" (*Two Novels* 32–33), and as an opportunity for humour in "The Vagina" (*Selected Organs: Parts of An Autobiography*), first drafted in April 18, 1980. In the latter he attributed his childhood desire to have a vagina to these shared baths, which sometimes appear to have included his slightly older sister as well. In his correspondence files is the carbon of a 1979 letter he has jokingly addressed to Deanna as his former bathtub mate (January 30, 1979).[2] But in 1972, in the first draft of "The Autobiography of Phillip Workman by bpNichol," his bath narrative was both darker and explicit. He wrote of how, when with him in the bathtub, "Phillip's" mother changes from seeming vague and remote to being overpoweringly present and how that drastic contrast splits his feelings and his understanding of her reality. She seems to be two irreconcilable women, he wrote. Seated between her legs in the warm steam of the bath, he makes himself into second persona in an attempt to cope with her enveloping vastness. But this tactic merely fractures his fragile sense of self, making him afterward a different person, a "puppet," with each woman he meets. He cannot reconcile his various consequent selves any more than he could envision the two "or three" versions of his mother as a whole person. Moreover, he wrote, he never knows which woman, which version of his mother, he is about to meet, and thus which version of himself he must summon. Large parts of the adult Barrie Nichol were foreshadowed in this long passage — his understanding of, and fascination with, variability and alternativity, his awareness that he can have multiple self-constructed identities and parlay these into alternate semi-fictional versions of himself, his ability to imagine hypothetical "'pata-physical" realities.

One reason that the 1972 Barrie Nichol semi-concealed this painful memory under the semi-pseudonym "Phillip Workman" is that he knew, as a psychoanalytical therapist, that this was *his* memory, his memory as "a sensitive child," and not necessarily what someone else who viewed or experienced these events would have thought was happening. (In a notebook entry dated March 17, 1965, he recorded having already read psychoanalyst Edmund Bergler's *Parents Not Guilty of Their Children's Neuroses*.) Another reason is that he wanted his parents, should they happen to read this text, to assume it was a fiction. As he reworked this "Autobiography" he would further fictionalize it and radicalize its prose — perhaps consciously, or unconsciously, hoping that this could discourage someone like his mother from reading it. In 1987, when preparing his prose-poem sequence "Organ Music" for publication, he would omit the poem "The Lily," with its "long" section about his father's post-coital penis, out of concern that his father might read it; he had to rename the truncated manuscript "Selected Organs."

This evidently embarrassing mention of his father is a rare explicitly autobiographical reference to him, although there are numerous disturbingly metaphoric descriptions of a sexual "father" named "Frank" in *Journal* (33–43) in which a narrator named "Phillip" desperately laments his unrequited Oedipal desire for his mother — descriptions clearly written

aka{ barrie / phillip }Nichol

by a Nichol who was, as Stephen Scobie would write in 1982, "deeply aware of Freud" (86).

One reason for his father's absence in Barrie's recollections may well be that the two had little early interaction — frighteningly little, perhaps, from the son's perspective. Deanna's memory of their father is as a man who "was not into little kids too much," and who "liked us a lot better when we became adults." Her mother, she says, "was always making excuses for him — I look at it that way now — she was always explaining why Dad might be in a bad mood." According to Deanna, she often described how hard it was for him to concentrate while working in an open room where there were "all these stenos going type-type-type-type-type all day long while he had to be thinking about whatever it was he was doing. 'So therefore when your dad gets home he wants peace and quiet.'" Deanna further recalls, "I didn't know that other people talked at the dinner table because quiet was the way it was supposed to be." She recounts that when they lived on Rupert Street her mother "once in a while would rebel and say she was going downtown" with her cousins and the children would exclaim "don't go, because dad will have to cook for us." The only thing he could cook was porridge, which he always over-salted. She also recalls that once

> Mom said to Dad, "It's time you did something with the children, so take them to Stanley Park, and buy them some 7-Up and ice cream" — you know, she's telling him how to do it. I still remember how — of course it all had to be done in a hurry, with Dad, and so you had to hurry up and eat the ice cream, hurry up and drink the 7-Up. And then we went into the aquarium, and I still remember seeing this octopus and then vomiting on the floor — poor Dad. And then Dad of course was so embarrassed. I don't know who cleaned it up. But it was not a good experience, for Dad or for us, particularly. Yeah, Dad was not into little kids too much.

But she does not recall such incidents as being unusual for the time or traumatic for the children. Rather they are amusing and endearing.

There is a third, even darker, more oblique and chilling reference to Barrie's early childhood baths in Nichol's writings, in his notebook entry for May 6, 1965 — an entry that does not appear to be even partly fictionalized. He framed this entry as a darkness in him, not in his parents. The passage suggests not only enduring confusion because of his long-ago longings for his mother, but also Oedipal guilt at having possibly offended or angered a remote and troublingly silent father. He wrote that he had been having repeated fantasies of cutting off his own penis, and that these fantasies had been disturbing him so much that he was having strong urges to kill himself by jumping in front of a moving car. A few weeks ago, he wrote, he had the fantasy or dream of not only cutting off his penis but of poking at the raw stump, which resembled a sausage, with a pencil so that deep red blood would come from the hole. He had taken the dream to a session with his psychotherapist, Lea Hindley-Smith, but wrote that they had been unable to get — no pun probably intended — to the "root" of it. He would like to see her again, but was for some reason nervous about phoning her, and so was now standing beside a busy street again thinking about walking blindly into traffic. He lamented that none of his friends seemed to think him

THE COVER OF BRIAN DEDORA AND BPNICHOL'S *A B.C. CHILDHOOD*, 1982, WITH NICHOL'S PHOTO ON THE LEFT.

troubled because he appeared so cheerful about things. He wrote that he wondered whether the dream had something to do with his mother and father, or with the baths he took in childhood with his mother and sister. Was he wanting to cut off his penis in order to look more like them? "FUCK!!" he wrote in capital letters and wished all were over.

aka{ barrie phillip }Nichol

2. *H* a Section

remembering . . .
spilling the peanuts my father bought
                         all down the aisle of the train,
1954, or dad yelling at me, 1948,
because I was running back & forth to the water cooler

— bpNichol in *Continental Trance*, 16

I knew that 'H' comes after 'G' and that 'I' was next,
so that if I was at 'I' I had gone too far.

— Nichol in Multineddu
"An Interview with bpNichol
in Torino, May 6 & 8, 1987," 34

In the spring of 1948 Glen Nichol was transferred by the railway to Winnipeg where he unexpectedly and unwittingly gave his son Barrie a gift that he would increasingly treasure. Glen bought a newly built house in the south of the city near the west bank of the Red River. It was not, on the surface, the most practical of gifts. Given the likelihood of his being transferred, the Nichols would usually rent their accommodations. Moreover the spring of 1948 had been one of worst periods of serious flooding along the Red. Glen's chosen house was part of a novel experimental residential development, Wildwood Park,[1] built on a series of paved looping laneways within a sharp bend of the river. The fronts of the houses faced each other across unfenced parkland — their own village green — with the rear or service entrances facing narrow laneways. There were sidewalks across the fronts but none along the lanes. The plan was intended by the designer to encourage a village-like sense of community. Each laneway loop was called a "section" and named alphabetically. The Nichols' new house was in Section *H*.

Glen actually did intend the house as a gift — as a surprise for Avis. He was apparently not on the 1948 train on which Barrie recalls, in *Continental Trance*, being chastised for too frequently running to the water fountain, but had gone to Winnipeg in advance to find and set up the new home. In a 1972 draft of "The Autobiography of Phillip Workman by bpNichol," written 10 years before *Continental Trance*, it was Barrie's mother who accompanied his siblings and him from Vancouver to their new Winnipeg home, and who angered him by making him stop dumping paper cup-fuls of water into the fountain and watching them disappear. Having told her and the children almost nothing about their new home, Glen Nichol picked them up at the Winnipeg CN rail station and drove them directly to it. Avis was delighted — like many in the postwar period she was entranced by "the new." A new house, with new furniture and appliances in an ultramodern subdivision, was much better than she had hoped for. The one-and-a-half-storey house had three bedrooms, one of which was shared by Bob and Don, and another by Deanna and Barrie.

Despite the hundreds of drawings, cartoons, and visual poems based on the letter *H* that Barrie would go on to create, and Avis's pleasure in her ultramodern surroundings, the family's years in Wildwood Park would not be especially happy. As at each new move, the children's schooling and friendships had been disrupted. Avis also had to develop new friendships and was now far from relatives. She was also far from shopping areas and unable to drive. A neighbourhood friend would sometimes offer a ride, but often Avis would have to go by bus to buy groceries and take a taxi back home.

For young Barrie, however, the most important aspect of Wildwood Park would be how it was making intensely physical his encounters with language. Those alphabetically named streets would render the alphabet non-transparent for him — making each letter a recurrently self-referential sign. While most people routinely "see through" the letters of words to the sound or idea or object to which their culture has agreed that they refer, for Barrie those letters would also be tangible material things in themselves. "So when I was first learning to find my way home to H-section," he will tell an interviewer in 1987, "I was also learning to find my way through the alphabet. I knew that 'H' comes after 'G' and that 'I' was next, so that if I was at 'I' I had gone too far." He continued, "I was always very aware of letters, and so on, and of the 'S' at 'house.' . . . I've always had a kind of, I suppose, idiosyncratic, very particular relationship to the idea of the alphabet, the idea of language" (Multineddu 34). In fact he would come to regard alphabetic characters as designs, or pieces of visual sculpture, or visual drama — 'H' as the linking of an 'I' and an 'I' — far beyond their conventional roles as signs for phonemes or building blocks for words and sentences.

Wildwood, with its spacious common parklands, would also be for many years the most rural of Barrie's homes, the one with the most plant and animal life, the one where it was easiest to watch clouds. What made it isolating for his mother would make it a place of solitary and complex imaginings for him. It would be the probable inspiration for the images of "Cloudtown" in his continuing poem *The Martyrology*, and for those images of lost pastoral gardens there and in his other early works. Barrie/bpNichol would claim so in *The Martyrology, Book 5*, Chain 9, saying of his "saints"

>   . . . i saw these same faces
> early in my first phrase's speaking
> (age 6) summer mornings i'd escape
> before my family'd awake
> H section   Wildwood Park
> singing my heart
> straight up at that Winnipeg prairie sky
>   at you Lord
>   at the saints i knew lived there
> leaving my head till 16

aka{ barrie / phillip }Nichol

> one day
> looked up at that cloud range
> a kind of joy took me
> perception you were all still there
> if only i could once again sing to you.

It may have taken him a while to "again sing," for there is no surviving textual evidence that Barrie wrote of saints in 1960–61 when he was 16, or before 1965 when he begins writing the early sequences of *Scraptures*. However, in a 1974 interview he provided a more detailed and plausible account of the saints' early childhood origin. "And the saints! I mean the saints essentially came out of that whole perception of when I was a kid and thought that real people lived up in the clouds."

> I looked up between the clouds. I always thought it was like the edges of a lake and that we were living at the bottom of the ocean and the real folks were up there. That's where I thought we were going to go someday. Heaven. I always thought heaven was the clouds, because those are the drawings you get: in the United Church you get a little Sunday school paper and everybody's walking around on clouds. ("Interview: with Pierre Coupey et al," Miki 2002 149)

He would give Flavio Multineddu a similar explanation in a 1987 interview:

> . . . as a little kid I had a whole fantasy world up in the clouds: that people lived up there and they were watching us all the time. This was my child imagination of God: that God lived up there and that the devil lived down in the ground, and I had this feeling of these eyes looking down over the edges of clouds. (19)

Here at Wildwood was indeed where Barrie experienced his first formal instructions in theology. He and Deanna attended a nearby United Church Sunday school because the Presbyterian church was much further away.

> I was raised Presbyterian with lots of time in the United Church because

there weren't that many Presbyterian churches around and because my parents both loved to golf on Sundays and therefore did not really have a strong case for pushing me to church, though they felt guilty. [. . .] I grew up with Sunday school comics in which great sweating Corinthians battled I can't remember who, but it was all done like Superhero comics, and heaven was a place of clouds and of people in funny white robes. ("Talking About the Sacred in Writing," Miki 2002 335)

There is considerable irony here in Barrie's absorbing theological imagery from comic books provided by the United Church — a church created in a 1925 merging of Methodists, Congregationalists, and Presbyterians — when in the English 17th century Presbyterians often led the mobs of "iconoclasts" who destroyed the medieval statues and stained glass portraits of saints at almost every English cathedral. And there's a little additional irony in that stained glass often being described by historians as the precursor of modern religious comic books.[2]

At Wildwood Park, Barrie also learned from his mother a version of the once commonplace child's prayer, which he recorded in a 1971 notebook as Part 9 of "The Book of Oz," and later included, with small changes, in *The Martyrology, Book 3*.

'God bless mother & father
dj bob & dea
grandma & grandma
all my cousins aunts & uncles
all my friends
all the plants & animals
forever & ever
amen'

But except for the compilers of the four gospels, Barrie would have been unlikely to have heard mention of the specific word "saint" in either the United Church or in his Presbyterian-descended family. However, the valley of the Red River did harbour quite a few saints — the settlements of St. Anne, St. Clements, St. Paul, St. Boniface, and St. Pierre, as well as

aka{ barrie / phillip }Nichol

the potentially blessed Stonewall and Steinbach. In *The Martyrology, Book 5*, Chain 3, Barrie recalled one of these —

> H origins
> remembered names
>
> Fort Rouge
>
> St Boniface
> he of the happy face
> eternal smile
> saints that were there
> over the river in
> my childhood
> the presbyterian boy who
> eschewed the ritual view

However, any "happy face" images young Barrie may have been developing of an Oz-like parkland sparkling beneath an ever-changing heavenly Cloudtown were soon to be drastically interrupted. By late March 1950 it was evident that the melting of heavy winter snows was threatening to overwhelm the dikes along the Red River. Massive efforts to repair and strengthen those dikes and add walls of sandbags began and continued through April. But by May 11, eight of the dikes protecting Winnipeg had failed, one-quarter of the city had been submerged, and around 100,000 people had been evacuated — the largest Canadian evacuation to that date. At its bend in the river, Wildwood Park was one of the most vulnerable areas. In late April seepage through the dikes had already flooded the common lawns. The yards of many of the houses had become worksites for crews fighting the rising waters. In his 1972 draft of "An Autobiography of Phillip Workman by bpNichol" ("Notebook III") Barrie detailed a 1949–50 winter of much snow followed by intense spring rains and the Red River steadily rising. He described himself standing on a dike that workmen were building amid continuing rain and river seepage. Some houses closer to the river, he wrote, had already been evacuated, and he figured their house was next. He added that they would leave three days later for Calgary and be gone for six months, and that while they were gone someone would place a wooden donkey in the window of a second-storey room that the waters rose to. The account shows again how directly autobiographical his "Phillip Workman" narrative can be. On May 11, the Wildwood dike was the first Winnipeg dike to fail, and by the end the day most of the Park's houses were flooded up to their eaves, with their sheds and garages floating free.

The Nichols, however, did not all go to Calgary, nor did any go directly there. Glen remained at his job in Winnipeg; Bob, the rowdy and adventurous son, went to one of Avis's uncles' farms in Plunkett, Saskatchewan; Avis took Don, Deanna, and Barrie to stay with her sister and her family in Saskatoon. Her brother Bill in Regina, however, insisted that they would be more comfortable with him, his wife Ethel, and their two young daughters, who lived in a spacious Quonset hut. So after a short and pleasant stay in Saskatoon, Avis and the three children moved on. But in Regina, Avis soon became unhappy, and resolved to continue onward to Calgary where they could

WILDWOOD PARK, MANITOBA,
AT THE PEAK OF THE 1950 FLOOD.

stay with Glen's mother. She explained later to Deanna that — prevented from doing housework, which she found pleasure in — she had been bored, and that also her brother's quiet young girls and her own children did not get along. But she herself was also not getting along with Ethel who appeared unhappy to be hosting them.

In a 1971 draft of a text titled "Plains Poems" — much of which he included in *The Martyrology, Book 3* — Barrie recorded a more poetic, but

Oedipally troubled, memory of that journey. Its metaphor was part of the "i wish i had a ship would carry me" metaphor of *Book 3*, Part v. In the draft he wrote that one is one's ship, forever seeking harbour or hoping to return "home" while the aurora borealis shimmers and the river, the red river, flows and rises against its dikes. He is abruptly a small boy of six watching in the rain while the river rises and men stack sandbags. He writes of Okeanos seeming angered, going by boat from his home, fleeing Lethe and the Styx, and travelling by train to Calgary where it was also raining, and of wanting someone, a "you," to make love to him. Okeanos as the angry father, and his mother as the boy's desired "harbour," seem almost too predictable — which may be why the passage did not survive his editing.

It was not until August that the Nichols were all able to reunite at Wildwood. The house had needed extensive repairs. The furniture and appliances of the first floor and basement had to be removed and replaced. The yard and parkland had been littered with debris, including the corpses of livestock that had been drowned on the farms to the south, and had had to be cleaned and restored. Once again, Glen Nichol had a "new" house and furnishings ready for his family when they arrived at the Winnipeg rail station. But in less than two years, the Canadian National Railway again moved him to another location.

In these two years one hugely formative event befell Barrie. It was his chance visiting of another child and encountering a Dick Tracy comic strip. He wrote his fullest narrative of this encounter in his April 1972 draft of "The Autobiography of Phillip Workman by bpNichol," Part II, Section IV. It's a section that is seemingly more carefully written, and more literary, than most and is framed as a message by Phillip to his mother. But considering that Nichol's collection of Dick Tracy comics would, by his death, fill a small room, its various specifics — the visit, the rain, the Dick Tracy images, the feelings of being lost in darkness — seem very likely accurate. In the voice of a mature adult looking back at a troubled childhood, he wrote that it was because of encountering the Dick Tracy comic strip that he came to choose, at six years of age, to withdraw psychologically from the "noise" of his life with his family that he could not respond to.

On a rainy day he had gone to make a first visit to a new friend. The friend showed him a book of Tracy comic strips; in one Tracy and his dog crawled into a dark sewer pipe in which Junior had become lost. Barrie wrote that this story was becoming difficult to write because he had identified with that lost boy, that he too had felt lost in darkness. He had been amazed and thrilled to think that there could be someone who might try to rescue a boy like him when no one else would. He had found himself loving Dick Tracy. Later in Port Arthur, he wrote, his fixation on the yellow-hatted Dick Tracy had become even clearer and more memorable. You have to do whatever you can, he commented, to make your life endurable, if you have a desire to live.

What this passage appears to recall is Barrie Nichol's very first turn outward from his family — outward, but not necessarily away — and toward at least two basic elements of his adulthood. The most obvious element is the comic strip, which would later become not only a room-sized collection but one of a number of narrative solutions he would frequently deploy, and the most likely basis of his visual poetry. The second is the determination expressed to do whatever you can to make your life endurable. It's a determination that would see him make decisive and sharp life changes, and become increasingly creative and productive — all the way to September 1988. Notable also are various expressions of agency that appear new to his memories: that he *chose* to withdraw from his family, that he identified with Junior, that he *loved*. As well, there is a positively perceived male figure — possibly the first of his imagination. Some fragments from this passage recur in *The Martyrology, Book 3*, "Interlude: The Book of OZ":

i remember winter nights in my room
the bed dj & i shared
i had a friend
torn as he was from the funny papers
crazy jutting jaw   stupid yellow hat
i talked with him.[3]

There was also in these last two years in *H* section of Wildwood a smaller but similarly significant development for Barrie. Deanna recalls that her bedroom companion began composing oral stories, mostly fantasy adventures, and narrating them to her before they fell asleep. Their mother regularly sent them to bed at 7 p.m., ensuring quiet for Glen and less work for herself, but leaving Barrie and Deanna with much time to fill. One of the stories he called "The Little Man with the Big Head who Came over the Hill." Much later Deanna would remind him of it, and he would make a cartoon of the little man for one of her young children. But these oral stories soon came to an end. Early in 1953 oldest brother Bob left home and joined the Canadian navy; the family would not see him again until 1965. The parents moved Barrie into Bob's old space in the room he had shared with Don. Scholarly in contrast to Bob's angry rebelliousness, Don had never gotten along well with Bob, and had privately seen himself as the more suited to the role of elder brother. He was much happier to have Barrie as his roommate. With Bob he had been an unhappy rival, with Barrie he could be cheerful mentor. Still sent to bed at 7 p.m., Barrie impressed his new roommate not by improvising oral stories but by taking a dictionary to bed so that he could acquire new words before sleeping.

CANADIAN NATIONAL RAILWAY'S GRAIN ELEVATORS IN PORT ARTHUR,
ONTARIO — THE LARGEST IN THE WORLD IN THE 1920S.

3. Port Arthur, 1953-57

*. . . all writing, by the very act of writing, transforms
the "I" into an Other.*

— Stephen Scobie,
bpNichol: What History Teaches, 125

The Nichols had lived in Port Arthur,[1] the Canadian National Railway's
major transfer site for the shipment of grain, in 1939–40, and Avis had not
liked it. Possibly she found its mountain and lake geography confining,
Deanna speculates, after having spent all of her life in Saskatchewan. She
also had found her inability to drive more confining there than it had been
in Vancouver or Winnipeg, and so was especially unhappy to be leaving
her still new house at Wildwood Park. Moreover Glen had resolved never
again to own a house, having being transferred out of his Rupert Street
one after a year and a half of ownership and out of Wildwood after four
years, four months of which had been lost to the flood. Avis passed on her
dismay to Barrie and Deanna, who attempted to glare an "evil eye" at
their real estate agent each time he drove into *H* section, in hope that they
could stop the house from being sold. Both children liked their new room
arrangements and were wary about losing them.

Eight-year-old Barrie and 12-year-old Deanna had recently also begun
going to Saturday afternoon movies together, mostly musical comedies,
and begun reading screen magazines and writing to movie stars. Often

they would receive replies, although they suspected most of these were signed by secretaries. Barrie was especially fond of Jane Powell, Howard Keel, Rex Allen, Ginger Rogers, and Fred Astaire, and had begun collecting photos of the various screen "couples" that they formed. They worried about not being close to a theatre in their new home.

By late June the house in *H* section had been sold, and the family was on its way to an older one-and-one-half storey wooden house at 441 Marks Street in Port Arthur. Barrie again shared a room with Don, who entered Grade 11 in Port Arthur, successfully resisting school board attempts to promote him to Grade 12 because of the somewhat more advanced Manitoba school curriculum (11 grades plus senior matriculation). An accomplished draftsman and cartoonist, Don began producing clever cartoons for his new school's newspaper and yearbook. His work was popular with the other students. Created with a pen and India ink, his images were dense, complex, and usually satiric. They quickly caught the envious eye of his younger brother, and led Barrie to attempt his own structurally simpler drawings. But Don's, he was sure, were much better. With Don's help he created a Dick Tracy movie-in-a-box, assembling Tracy strips together on rollers, which they had mounted in a cardboard box so that the images could pass across the open side.

Dick Tracy had been becoming an increasingly important part of Barrie's fantasy life. He briefly recalled this part of his childhood to Irene Niechoda in a 1987 interview when she asked him about "The Dark Walker" reference in *The Martyrology, Book 1*, and in doing so indirectly confirmed how literally autobiographical much of his unpublished "An Autobiography" and "The Autobiography of Phillip Workman" probably are.

> As I write this note what suddenly strikes me is the THE DARK WALKER was in every sense Dick Tracy who i used to imagine walking the streets of Port Arthur with me when i was a kid. It is difficult to chart the effect that Chester Gould's [the creator of the Dick Tracy strip] stark characterizations had on my consciousness. There was an immediate impression: cold, distance, & underlying violence imprinting itself in my mind. Tracy, Catchem & Pat Patton were so much a part of my life that it became difficult at times to separate myself from them.

He went on to repeat to her the "Autobiography of Phillip Workman" passage in which Phillip (or Barrie, or Barrie Phillip) first encountered Tracy, in a strip in which he was rescuing the young Junior.

> And a lot of his stories focus around kids; that's an ongoing motif that he's always dealing with. I used to really identify with him. In fact, I still remember the first strip of his I ever saw, which had to do with a kid who was lost in the sewers, among the pipes, with a dog. I actually found it. It was a 1949, I think, comic strip. (Niechoda 1992 98–99)

He described his Port Arthur nighttime Tracy fantasies in more detail, and with much more emotion, in his "Notebook IV" (begun May 1, 1972) drafts of "An Autobiography." He described them as being dreams of not dreaming, dreams of having a substantial and meaningful life, and from which he would wake in confusion, not sure what world he was in. He was embracing the imagination "too strongly," he wrote. He would lie awake in his room waiting to hear Tracy's footsteps in the street below his window, then see him stop to light a cigarette — despite never having seen him smoke in the comics pages. He would hear Tracy speak to him. Barrie would climb through his window and down the side of his house so he could walk beside Tracy and talk. Then he abruptly broke his narrative — announcing that all this was a lie — not the fantasy itself but the things fantasized, the climbing from the window and walking the nighttime streets of Port Arthur. He lamented what he'd had to do, lamented having had to let the fantasy "devour" him. He wrote of how odd it was that someone so wary of being engulfed in another person's fantasies — presumably a reference to his mother — should have submerged himself so dangerously in ones of his own making.

Despite his seemingly productive activities with Don, in this 1972 retrospective Barrie portrayed himself as having withdrawn from conscious engagement with everyday life into an ongoing comic strip narrative. It was once again a retrospective addressed to his mother, and again one that by addressing her implicated her — in attempting to escape her fantasies, he suggested, he had trapped himself in his own. He went on to describe his immersion in the Tracy fantasy as a kind of psychic suicide, an attraction not to the contradictory romance of complete annihilation, he suggested, but to an imitation self-annihilation, an annihilation of consciousness. It was both a self-betrayal and a betrayal of the "we" to which a social person is obligated to contribute. Years later in *The Martyrology* he would translate Dick Tracy, Junior, Catchem, Blossom Tight, and his other fantasy figures into "saints," but toward the end of *Book II* say much the same thing about the horror of his self-committment to them:

> fuck you all saints
> dream world of half remembered death
> i loved you all
> > it nearly killed me
> there is another world i've lived in all my life
> took my own mind for a wife when just a kid
> & hid there

What is especially notable about Barrie's various attempts to write these narratives of his early life is the extent to which these were narratives of fantasy — actual fantasy — rather than narratives of actual events. The impression he gave here of his life after 1953 was of a zombie state in which he often participated in school and home events without noticing that he was participating, or without investing any emotion in his participation. He wrote of having experienced extreme anger — he was not specific about this — and of then having turned inward, of having "split" himself in order to invent a new "we" of himself and Dick Tracy, and of how this split problematically cut him off from humanity, isolated him in a personal world.

However, in either the fall of 1953 or spring of 1954 events occurred that over the next decade would offer him a way out of the dream. Near to his school he fell into a ditch — one he believed he could have drowned in. After he was extricated by the fire department, he came home so cold and dripping wet that he was severely ill for a week or more after. He may have partly hidden the cause of his coming home soaked; Deanna remembers only hearing of him have gone "into a ditch, getting stuck there." Trying to analyze a dream he had just had on March 18, 1975,

Barrie described the incident in a notebook ("Notebook Begun February 21, 1974"), writing that he had been 10 years old and had stumbled into a ditch, that he had known how close to disaster he was and didn't care one way or the other. But after being rescued he had started writing — which, he pointed out sardonically, was one way of dealing with things.

His recollection that he hadn't cared about his plight echoes his thoughts about being tempted not to live when he was an infant. At the time of the ditch incident he was more likely nine years of age rather than ten, for Deanna associates the incident specifically with his being in Grade 4. "He got a bad chill, he was at home sick after that, recovering, and that was when he started writing his stories, lying in bed and printing them into scribblers. And his teacher apparently read them out, like a serial . . . that you'd see in the newspaper. And he always kind of thinks that might be where he got his idea to be writer."

Of the newly written stories the first and most important to Barrie was called "The Sailor from Mars." At the end of the school year he brought the manuscript home, inadvertently triggering the second crucial event of his Port Arthur period — in a year or two his mother absent-mindedly gathered it up with other items she thought disposable and threw it out with the weekly trash. Although he did not complain, Barrie was devastated, and began to imagine the story's destruction as a kind of death and rebirth — the death of a singular "Barrie" and a strategic rebirth as multiple — multiple stories, multiple copies, multiple versions of the same stories, multiple Barries all embedded in the stories and actions of others. On May 1, 1972, he recorded the moment in a notebook section of "An Autobiography" as part of an impossible autobiography, writing that the moment his mother had thrown out the story was also the moment that autobiography had died, and that "i" had died and "we" had come into being as both a replacement and a completion of the dying "i." While his writing had marked a return to participation in collective humanity, the loss of the manuscript also showed how only the social could have provided for its survival — his mother, the family, the bookstore, the library. Independence is an illusion, he wrote. And thus so too is autobiography. This is likely why he soon renamed "An Autobiography" "The Autobiography of Phillip Workman by bpNichol" — because bpNichol

aka{ barrie phillip }Nichol

understood the impossibility of autobiography while the earlier version of bp, "Phillip Workman," had not. Paradoxically, it now required a "we" to create an *auto*biography.

On May 15, 1972, he marked this passage, and possibly all of the "An Autobiography" writings, as "Part III of Book III of The Martyrology," a plan that he did not carry out in the published book. The only hint of it in *Book 3* occurs in Part V, in lines that echo the illusionality of "i" which the above passage had asserted.

> i am afraid of writing something which does not end
> as we does not
>   only the link which is i
> to be replaced
>   other i's to see it thru
> 'in the true time & space called meaning'

This passage forecast the relief he would feel each time he believed *The Martyrology* had ended. However, *The Martyrology* was to be a text in which Barrie Nichol's personal stories were indeed embedded in the stories of others, from those of Gilgamesh to those of his ancestors and Toronto friends, and in which Barrie himself appears in different versions of "we" as his contexts and relationships change.[2]

Overall, the incidents inscribed in this draft of "An Autobiography" created yet another mythic scene of origin — the start of Barrie Nichol transferring his unrewarded passions for his mother to writing, to the "we" of those collective creations the alphabet and language, thus linking his passions to ones that he would later associate with another ambiguous and linguistically rooted autobiographer, Gertrude Stein.[3] He would come to call Stein, in her own words, "the mother of us all," his emphasis being at least partly on the "us" — as well as on finding a substitute mother who did not throw away manuscripts. This mothering "Gertrude Stein" would be as much a metaphor as a person — a metaphor for the materiality of language Barrie had embraced and which Stein's writings had foregrounded. In 1969 he would tell his new-mother story in yet another metaphor in his six-part CBC "Ideas" radio serial "Little Boy Lost Meets Mother Tongue."

In the 1980s he wrote a third version of the ditch incident as part of the prose poem "The Hips" for *Selected Organs: Parts of an Autobiography*.

> It was because of my hips I started writing. I was in Grade 4. It was late fall or early spring. I can't remember which, but I remember the ditch, the one near the school, and it was full of icy slush and a friend dared me to jump across it and so I did. [. . .] I landed like some bad imitation of a ballet dancer, struck, my left leg burying itself in that slush right up to my hip, stuck, my right leg floating on the top. My hips kept me afloat. Or at least that's what the firemen said to my Maw when they brought me home after rescuing me. [. . .] [T]he firemen said that that ditch was so deep and the sludge so like quicksand I would've drowned if it hadn't been for the strange position of my legs and hips. And the cold I caught from being stuck in the ditch turned into bronchitis and they kept me home from school for over two weeks and during that time I wrote my first novel, *The Sailor From Mars*, all 26 chapters written by hand in a school copy book. (39–40)

He went on to recount that "my Maw threw it away by mistake three years later" and that when he returned to school "I showed it to my teacher and she read the whole thing to the class, a bit every morning for a week or two, just like a real serial. [. . .] I was alive and now I was a writer too" (40).

Although Barrie wrote here about his mother's discarding of the manuscript as if it had no impact on him, this was not necessarily the case. He would later come to believe that while his subconscious motivation to write had been to create worlds and mythologies more satisfying than those he was obliged to live among, his motivation to become a publisher and self-publisher, and to write the same story in several different "forms" or genres, had been to increase the odds of being listened to or read, to give his writings greater social materiality, greater "we"-ness. No one, not even his mother or sister, seemed to want to hear what he had to say, he would write in his "Autographs Mickey 4th Short N(te)book" in April 1975.

Barrie's preoccupying fantasies would gradually expand past Dick Tracy, Junior, Sam Catchem, Sparkle Plenty, and sailors from Mars to include the imaginary and actual heroes he was seeing with his sister at the movie theatres. "Rex Allen, Lash LaRue, Roy Rogers, The Lone

aka{ barrie phillip }Nichol

Ranger, Cisco Kid, & Ghost Rider" are the ones he listed in his draft essay "Comics as Myth: Notes on Method in *The Martyrology*" as the ones that had also fascinated him in 1954 (untitled September 1968 notebook, and Peters 78). Moreover, certain graphic real-life events would occasionally — but very selectively — lodge in his memory, such as ones from a train journey he took in 1954 with his father and Deanna. However, her 2011 recollection of that trip makes a revealing contrast with Barrie's 1969 narrative about it, which he drafted to be part of "The Plunkett Papers." Deanna recalls:

> One time my dad was taking Barrie and I to Calgary — I can't remember why Mom wasn't going — but it was Barrie and I and my dad on the train from Port Arthur. And it was a branch line, and then you had to transfer to the main line once you got to Winnipeg. And so we stopped in Atikokin because there'd been a derailment ahead on the track. We ended up having to stay overnight in Atikokin. Mom had given us some candy, and we'd spilled the candy all over the floor, and my dad was embarrassed, and my dad [had us] in the smoker. You know there used to be this smoker on the trains, because he was a smoker back then, and he was snoring, and we were embarrassed. There was all this stuff went on, and then we pulled out of Atikokin in the morning and there were men still working on the tracks, and our train hit a couple of these men, and killed them, and I had blocked that completely out of my mind until years later when Barrie said to me "Remember that time when our train hit those men on the track and killed them and their bodies were lying there beside the track," and it came back to me in a flash. [. . .] Then we got to Winnipeg and my dad put us up in the McLaren Hotel or something, near the train station, it was a pretty seedy area, and I remember Barrie and I sitting up in the window of the hotel watching for my dad to come back — we were scared stiff. We thought that everybody that walked past looked suspicious. How old were we? — maybe 14 and 10 I suppose. I guess my dad had gone to meet his buddies. And then we got back on the train and went to Calgary. (Interview, February 5, 2011)

Barrie's passage of poetry reads:

> we rode the train back west in 54
> my dad sister & me
> outside of red rock had to stop 12 hours
> coz of a slide
>   ran over 2 workers
> just after getting under way again
>
> . . . .
>
>
> heading out to plunkett from port arthur
> the summer before i turned ten
> meeting uncle bill in saskatoon
> drove down to my uncle mike's farm
> running over this prairie chicken on the way
>
> . . . .
>
> & later
>   my sister & me
> walked down the road from hun & mike's farm
>
> just the two of us
>
> death all around us
>
> determined to make it
> on that last mile to plunkett

("The Plunkett Papers," *An H in the Heart* 39)

In Deanna's narrative it is the accidents and the deaths she has forgotten. In Barrie's the most surprising absence in his notebook draft is his father, whom Deanna constructs as the major character. In fact in Barrie's poem it's almost only the deaths of the men and the prairie chickens that are recalled. His father's presence, the overnight wait in Atikokin in the smoking car, their father's embarrassment, the puzzling fact that their

aka{ barrie phillip }Nichol

mother is not with them, the need to transfer in Winnipeg, the frighteningly seedy McLaren hotel — he has apparently experienced without closely noting. Plunkett — the town he may be already in 1954 creating family mythology around — is for him the destination, while for Deanna it is a forgettable stop along the way to Calgary.

Barrie's unrequited infatuation with his mother also appears to have continued in Port Arthur and to contribute not only perhaps to his "forgetting" of his father in the train accident poem but also to the dance and dress scenes on the final pages of *Journal*. Barrie drafted those scenes originally in an undated notebook, seemingly from the early 1970s, as parts of that "An Autobiography of Phillip Workman by bpNichol." Whether these drafts were themselves fantasies or descriptions of innocent scenes that actually occurred at 441 Marks Street is not clear, although Deanna remembers her mother being avid about dancing and recalls that she and Glen went regularly to dances at the Port Arthur Country Club where they were members — much as they had gone to dances Friday and Saturday nights at the Charleswood and Wildwood clubs in south Winnipeg. Whatever their factual ground, the emotions of these passages were what Barrie was carrying with him — in the 1950s as in the early 1970s — in his relations with his mother and father and with his female and male friends.

It was you you taught me everything do you remember youd dress up in your long gown with the purple sash your hair tied back with a ribbon & youd take my hand telling me to dance & we'd dance mommy the two of us would dance all around the room and i was no higher than your waist my arms held up to where youd take my hands & lead me you would never hold me close you held your arms out holding me away holding me still in the dancing leading in the careful three step three step you were lovely mommy i wanted to hold you close to me like i'd seen it done the way men held women & we'd dance you smiling at me repeating one two three one two three & never held me oh i get sick of blaming im not blaming you mommy its all over now isn't it that time is gone forever the music stopped that was never playing we made it up the tunes i mean as we danced me humming the songs i'd learned from the radio you marking the time i am still dancing mother. . . .

[. . .]

you would let me help you when you dressed you would ask me saying please zip me up & I felt the skin on your back moist and pale white . . . my fingers tugged the zipper up closing you in in your whiteness my fingers seeming ugly i would stare at them for hours wishing them longer imagining them travelling over the surface of your skin . . .

(*Journal* 69–71)

Read with minor alterations in a novel titled *Journal,* these passages read much differently from how they do in a draft manuscript titled "An Autobiography of Phillip Workman by bpNichol." The more lurid and hallucinatory passages of Oedipal desire in *Journal* also had their origin in these notebook drafts of "autobiography" and offer even stronger hints of why Barrie's teenage years would be so tumultuous, and of why — despite outward cheerfulness — he would come to be struggling against thoughts of suicide in 1965. When he later wrote in *The Martyrology, Books 3 & 4* that without the help of his Toronto psychotherapist Lea "quite literally / none of it would have been written," the "quite literally" likely carried much more information than most readers — including myself — could recognize.[4]

4. Winnipeg, 1957–60

Barrie needs to try harder in language.

— Miss Neitherent,
second-term report card, February 1958

The Nichols' time in Port Arthur came to an end in the spring of 1957 when Glen was promoted and sent back to Winnipeg. Don had already left the family in 1955 for Toronto where he had begun studying to be an architect. In Winnipeg Glen found there were very few houses for rent, and settled for a small one at 43 Morley Avenue. Avis disliked the house immediately and intensely. Barrie, relegated to a crudely constructed room in the basement, was also unhappy, despite his mother's attempts to brighten the walls with yellow paint. In less than a year, Glen moved them to the upper two floors of a large old house at 235 Oakwood Avenue where Barrie and Deanna had the entire top floor.

Barrie enrolled in Grade 8 at Churchill Junior High, a school paired with a similarly named senior high school. He completed the year with an 80.4% average and ranked second in his class. His best grades were 92% in social studies and spelling, 88% in literature, and 83% in science. After receiving the first-term comment from his teacher "Barrie is a splendid student," in the second term he was told "Barrie needs to try harder in language." His grade had been 57%, which he raised to 74% in the third and final term.

For Grade 9 he moved to the Churchill Senior High where he developed a powerful interest in long distance running and joined the school track team. To his fascination with comic strips and musical comedies, he added a new curiosity about jazz. A letter from one of his classmates shows them by 1960 having developed a mutual interest in the music of Charlie Christian, Dizzy Gillespie, Charlie Parker, Fats Navarro, Wardell Gray, Stan Getz, Lester Young, Charlie Ventura, Sonny Rollins, and numerous lesser known players.

In his various "autobiographies" Barrie makes little mention of this Winnipeg period. One allusion to it occurs in *Selected Organs* in which he depicts his time of puberty discovery. "On the edge of thirteen when Carol Wisdom's chest started to develop you couldn't take your eyes off it" (21).

> You didn't think of the chest as sensitive until you danced with her. You were thirteen & the dance floor was crowded & tho the moving bodies of your friends pressed you together you would only allow your chests to touch & there was heat & pressure & movement between you & your chest was ten times more sensitive than your hands, felt more than your eyes could see, & your trapped heart pounded as if you would die, explode, right there before her eyes. . . . (22)

But it is only by calculating where Barrie would be at this age that one can identify the city.

By and large Winnipeg 1957–60 seems to have been for him an amnesiac period, in which, as he would later write in a May 1972 notebook draft of "An Autobiography," he had been so deeply enmeshed in his fantasy worlds that everyday life could pass virtually unnoticed. He wrote here of visiting his parents and looking through his childhood photos. He was already gripped by sadness, he noted, that seemed always to arise whenever he was with his family, and was finding himself struggling to choose whether or not to succumb to it. Among the photos was one of his high school's soccer team. It was a newspaper photo from when the team had won a city championship. In the middle, among former friends that he could recognize, was himself. But he had no memory of being on the team or even of playing soccer or of the excitement of winning a championship. He reflected that it was not as though he had merely forgotten these events; it was as if he had never participated in them at a conscious level. He wrote that he must have moved through the motions of the game like an automaton, smiling and laughing as his mind had played another game elsewhere.

Smiling and laughing and playing everyday life-games on automatic pilot is what he would still be doing when he arrived in Toronto in 1964. "My defence structure . . . was this ho, ho, ho thing, so much so that no one would believe that anything was bothering me, I was such a happy kid," he would tell interviewer Loren Lind in December 1968. It was a defence structure that made it difficult for him to get help, or for his parents to see or ever fully accept the psychological difficulties he would soon be having to deal with. In 1971, Barrie would ironically insert the soccer photo near the end of his book of visual poems *ABC: The Aleph Beth Book.*

High school appears to have been Barrie's most athletic period — possibly because athletics allowed him a veneer of normality beneath which he could indulge the fantasies that he preferred to his actual surroundings. He slowly improved at running middle-distance races, in 1959 placing third in his high school's 880-yard event and winning its intermediate-level one-mile race in a time of 5 minutes 30 seconds. At the 1959 Pan-American Games trials he set an under-16 Manitoba record for the two-mile race; he also helped carry the torch into the stadium. In his notebooks he mentions only the Pan-American Games trials events, in a 1971 draft of the poem "Plains." His track activities were however linked to book-creating. He assembled at least six large scrapbooks of photos and news stories concerning world-class track and field athletes, from Canada's Harry Jerome to international stars such as Gordon Pirie, Chris Chataway, Vladimir Kuts, Roger Bannister, Emil Zátopek, Derek Ibbotson, Herb Elliott, and Chris Brasher. He hand-drew the covers. Barrie's fascination with these runners came toward the end of a period in which distance running had enjoyed an unusual prominence in world culture. At the 1952 Olympics in Helsinki the Czech runner Zátopek had been celebrated for winning an unprecedented three gold medals; 1954 had seen Bannister, with the help of Chataway and Brasher, run the first four-minute mile, and the Australian Landy break that record just

46 days after; the British Empire Games in Vancouver later that summer saw Bannister out-duel Landy to win the much hyped "Miracle Mile" with both runners finishing in under four-minute times. A larger-than-life bronze statue at the entrance to the games site, Exhibition Park, still commemorates the event. Ibbotson would lower the record in 1957 and Elliott in 1958. At the 1956 Melbourne Olympics, Pirie — arguably the best middle-distance runner of his time — twice lost gold medals to Kuts in sensationally unusual circumstances.

At the same time as creating these scrapbooks — themselves very likely the grounds of fantasy — Barrie was also working on his first comic strip, called "Bob de Cat." He wrote, "age 15 i begin the comic strip adventures of Bob de Cat, his sidekick Yaboo, and the evil Dr. Nasty influenced heavily at that point by Chester Gould . . . " ("Comics as Myth: Notes on Method in *The Martyrology*," Peters 75). Barrie argued in this "Comics as Myth" essay that his youthful attempt at a comic strip, with its serial structure and seemingly unending narrative possibilities ("entirely open-ended"), was the "original origin" of *The Martyrology*. With the "hard-boiled" beatnik detective Bob de Cat he had begun establishing "my own mythologic base" from which he could later move to an attempted historical novel "(age 18) THE JOURNAL OF COLONEL BOB DE CAT" that a few years later he "incorporated into ANDY." Whether he showed these creations to anyone, or merely let them accumulate as parts of his private world, is unclear. The two letters he received from Winnipeg friends after he moved to Vancouver made no mention of his writing, nor did his high school's yearbooks, which indeed do give prominence to literature, over the three-year period featuring, with poems and photographs, a young woman as Churchill Senior High's outstanding writer.

In "Comics as Myth" he also wrote that when he took up the comic strip form itself again in 1965 — stimulated, he recalled, by the 1962 arrival of Spider-Man and the resurgence of both Marvel and DC Comics — he caused Bob de Cat, Dr. Nasty, and Yaboo to evolve into "Captain Poetry, nemesis of Madame X, lover of Blossom Tight." In this understanding of his own history, his main body of writing has both its formal beginnings — its open-endedness — and much of its mythology in Winnipeg in a daydreaming 15-year-old's apparently private writings. "C.P. [Captain Poetry]," he wrote, "was a simple extension of Bob de Cat, an amalgam of disparate intent who also flourished briefly under the pseudonym John Cannyside in a couple of unpublished prose takes" (Peters 79). With the words "flourished briefly" Barrie very modestly represented his Cannyside project — it was in fact one that obsessed him more than any other except *The Martyrology*, one that he worked on recurrently over a similar number of years despite never deeming any of the several versions of it he produced worthy of publication.

In the fall of 1960 when his father got word that another promotion and move was likely, Barrie appears to have been leading two very different lives. In one he was a cheerful A-student and promising athlete; in the other he was a confused, withdrawn, sexually troubled, and secretly productive creator of various fantasies, both unwritten and written. Such a condition is perhaps not all that unusual for an adolescent, but Barrie was also putting much more than usual energy into both his selves.

5. Vancouver, 1960–64

"I wanted to be an archaeologist . . ."

— bpNichol, quoted by Niechoda in *A Sourcery*, 95

Unlike Glen Nichol's earlier promotions and transfers, the one that ended the family's second period in Winnipeg did not occur in late spring-time. Glen was transferred in the fall of 1960 to Vancouver to look after Canadian National's international freight operations there. Barrie and his mother left Winnipeg in December once he had completed the fall term of Grade 11; they settled with Glen into an apartment on West Seventieth Avenue in south-central Vancouver. Deanna, who was now in the second year of nursing school, remained in Winnipeg. On enrolling at Sir Winston Churchill High School — a name coincidentally echoing that of the Winnipeg school he had just left — Barrie encountered the same confused perception of Manitoba's 11-grade-plus-senior-matric school system that Don had encountered on moving from Manitoba to Ontario in 1953. In British Columbia, as in Ontario, the senior matriculation year followed Grade 12, not Grade 11. Thus the Vancouver school board reasoned that if Barrie had been six months from entering senior matric in Manitoba, he should be placed into Grade 12 at Sir Winston Churchill. He was enrolled in ongoing Grade 12 versions of the Grade 11 courses he had been taking in Winnipeg. Lacking much of the background that had been taught in the first term, he struggled, particularly in physics, and his marks plunged from an 81% average during his half-year in Winnipeg to a C average in Vancouver.

His one new friend at Sir Winston Churchill was Andy Phillips, who would later become the title character of Barrie's novella *Andy*, and whose

"THE POSTMAN," A 1955 SCULPTURE BY PAUL HUBA COMMISSIONED FOR THE VANCOUVER POST OFFICE.

brother David, a year younger, was an aspiring poet. Like Barrie, Andy was a track athlete. Both of them ran for the school's track team and also joined the Vancouver Olympic Club. On graduation they enrolled in the fall of 1961 for Grade 13 — senior matriculation, and equivalent of first year university — at King Edward College in Vancouver's Kitsilano district. Here Barrie encountered and made friends with a number of students — most of them graduates of Lord Byng High School — who like him were seriously interested in poetry and the other arts. Among these were James Alexander, who would soon launch the poetry magazine *Adder*, Neild Holloway, and Dezso Huba, whose recently widowed mother Sybil had returned to university to complete an arts degree. Dezso's late father Paul had been a sculptor, and his various works in stone filled the Huba apartment.[1] Andy Phillips recalls Sybil Huba as both spiritual and artistic, and their apartment on Yew Street as a place not only of art but of incense, art magazines, and spirited discussions of aesthetics and inspiration — a much different home from the functionally furnished one Barrie was sharing with his parents. At this apartment Barrie met another member of the ex–Lord Byng circle of students, Arnold Shives, who was beginning his first year at the University of British Columbia, but would have preferred to be studying drawing and painting. Barrie also met poet Judith Copithorne, who lived in the same building and was a regular visitor at the Hubas' — as Barrie himself quickly became.

In a 1976 interview Barrie told Caroline Bayard and Jack David that his favourite poets when a teenager were "Walt Kelly's *Pogo*, Dr. Seuss, Wilfred Owen. I loved Keats."

> Up to seventeen, those were the people — and D.H. Lawrence. Dave Phillips and I used to read Lawrence and Patchen. It was about then that I started to get into Creeley and Ginsberg. The person who particularly impressed me at that time was Lew Welch and some of Philip Whalen's things. I was into the visual thing from Patchen — through his poem-drawings — and around that time, a friend of mine, James Alexander, introduced me to some of the Dada people and Apollinaire. (Bayard 17)

Barrie was telescoping his Vancouver period somewhat here. The first part of his list of poets — from Pogo to Lawrence — reflects mainly his Port Arthur and Winnipeg years. The second part — from Lawrence to Patchen — are most likely the writers who came to Barrie's attention through Andy and David Phillips and James Alexander in his half-year at Sir Winston Churchill and Grade 13 year at King Edward, January 1961 to June 1962. Creeley, Ginsberg, Welch, and Whalen were poets that he was much more likely to encounter in Vancouver, particularly at UBC at this time more than anywhere else in Canada. Creeley had already made two well-received visits to Vancouver and by the spring of 1962 had been appointed to teach Creative Writing there. All four were in Donald Allen's *The New American Poetry Anthology, 1945–60* which, because of UBC professor Warren Tallman's classes and the activities of the *Tish* writers during 1961–63, had become known throughout the city's arts communities. Barrie noted in a 1979 interview with Ken Norris that he had learned of the last writers on his list — the Dadaists and Apollinaire — from Alexander in 1963. In the case of the Dadaists he truly had learned only "of them" — "I wasn't quite sure what exactly they'd done. . . . I didn't really have examples because you couldn't lay your hands on examples. I wasn't going to a university" (Miki 2002 238–39). Barrie did attend university in 1962–63, and spent the summer of 1963 with his brother Don in Toronto, so his learning "of" Dada probably occurred late that year.

His year at King Edward seems to have been mainly one of making important friendships and updating his knowledge of literature. For the first time he was discovering young people with interests and ambitions similar to his own. On enrolling he had on a "sheer whim" selected teaching as his academic objective. He told Irene Niechoda:

BARRIE'S 1962 KING EDWARD HIGH SCHOOL GRADUATION PHOTOGRAPH.

I had gotten into teaching through sheer whim, there was no real desire. There was just a teacher standing in front of the room, so I ticked off the role "teacher" — there was no real thinking at all. I wanted to be an archaeologist, but couldn't figure out how to do it from university calendars. It never occurred to me that you could get counselling. I got a scholarship [$500] to go to King Edward College that paid my costs. (Niechoda 1992 95)

He was writing, but privately — showing his work mainly to his new friend David Phillips. "I was a very secretive writer for the first six or seven years of my writing," Barrie recounted to Caroline Bayard. "Dave Phillips and I used to show each other our stuff in Vancouver" (Bayard 24).

Both he and Phillips enrolled at UBC in the fall of 1962, Phillips in first year arts, and Barrie in second-year education. Barrie also got permission to audit UBC's introductory creative writing course, English 202, taught by Jake Zilber, and began attending the meetings of the student club the "Writers Workshop." In both Zilber's course and at the workshop he encountered the already publishing student-poets Robert Hogg, David Cull, and Jamie Reid. At the time Reid was a co-editor with myself, George Bowering, Fred Wah, and David Dawson of *Tish*. Barrie's insecurity and secretiveness, however, were such that none of these writers took much note of him, or would later be able to recall his presence.

He began keeping a journal or notebook. He made one of the earliest entries on January 15, 1963, after attending a Bob Hogg reading and talking with Neild Holloway, writing that the problem with his own poetry was that it was too melodramatic and vague — and that he, Holloway, and James Alexander all agreed about this. He then added quotations or misquotations from Arnold Shives; Holloway (advice that he should keep a notebook); his Grade 13 teacher, Mary Fallis (that "concrete better than abstract in a poem"); Creeley ("FORM is merely AN EXTENSION OF CONTENT"[2]); James Alexander ("It's the baldness of the Black Mountain style that troubles me"); and Jake Zilber ("The system of notation now coming into use may one day become a convention"). The entry reflected many of the commonplace arguments occurring that year in the Vancouver poetry communities.

Toward the end of the 1962–63 academic year there was excitement among the writing students at UBC over the impending summer-session poetry writing workshop and associated events — later to be mythologized as the "1963 Vancouver Poetry Conference" — at which Robert Creeley, Charles Olson, Allen Ginsberg, Robert Duncan, Denise Levertov, and Margaret Avison would be lecturing and advising. Hogg, Cull, Reid, Dawson, and Wah all enrolled, and Bowering audited. Possibly because he felt unqualified, or more likely because of increasing psychological distress, Barrie instead accepted his brother Don's invitation to spend the summer with him in Toronto, where he could meet Don's lay psychoanalyst Lea Hindley-Smith. It was also the last year Barrie would be young enough to travel on one of his father's CN Rail passes. Once arrived, he got a casual job at Frontier College from which, he wrote in his notebook, he could take hours off at any time to visit Mrs. Hindley-Smith. In a 1968 interview Barrie gave this explanation for how he was spending that summer:

> So I came to Toronto to visit my brother and in those days I would say I was pretty freaked. To put it mildly. I sort of went into six month

aka{ barrie phillip }Nichol

> long depressions and stuff, pretty out of it most of the time. And my
> brother knew of this group that was just forming. He recommended
> that I should come and see Mrs. Smith. (Lind interview, December
> 11, 1968)

In his new notebook Barrie recorded only a few hints about the causes of
his distress and depressions. Most of these centred on women, and were
quite possibly occasioned by his increasing interactions in Vancouver with
young woman friends. Among entries that begin on July 13, 1963, there is
a poem "For Laura" that describes him and her as "one-way" lovers who
are travelling toward hell. Then there's an outline for a short story that
would take place in a theatre and beside a nunnery. A guy who had been
watching a movie would see an attractive nun and want to know her and
love her despite being afraid of sex, but then think of her as unattainable
and his love as pointless and useless. Quite possibly Barrie had encoun-
tered a young nun through therapist Lea Hindley-Smith who, with the
permission of St. Michael's College at the University of Toronto, had
begun counselling one or two. And then he wrote a disturbing entry
about material in his recent dreams: there had been landscapes like the
Everglades swamps, enormous naked bodies, mountains that resembled
vegetables, and in one dream three naked Brobdingnagian women. Barrie
would have encountered Jonathan Swift's Brobdingnag and its women
while reading *Gulliver's Travels* in his English 200 course that spring at
UBC. At roughly 10 times human size, the young Brobdingnagian "maids
of honour" and their playful sexuality overwhelm and disgust Gulliver.
When they place him "directly before their naked Bodies," he writes, it
is to him "very far from being a tempting sight, or from giving me any
emotion other than horror and disgust."

> Their skins appeared so coarse and uneven, so variously coloured
> when I saw them near, with a mole here and there as broad as a
> trencher, and hairs hanging from it thicker than pack-threads. . . .
> Neither did they scruple while I was by to discharge what they had
> drunk, to the quantity of at least two hogsheads, in a vessel that held
> above three tuns. The handsomest among these maids of honour, a
> pleasant frolicsome girl of about sixteen, would sometimes set me

astride upon one of her nipples, with many other tricks, wherein the reader will excuse me for not being over particular. But I was so much displeased, that I entreated Glumdalclitch [his assigned teenage "nurse"] to contrive some excuse for not seeing that young lady any more. (95–96)

It seems likely that these passages in Swift had reminded Barrie, at least unconsciously, of his childhood baths with his mother and his anxieties about having offended his father.

Despite Don's misgivings about Barrie's well-being, and Barrie's own about having received only a pass in practice teaching (the UBC course, according to transcripts from that year, offered grades of First class, Second class, Pass, and Fail), Barrie left Toronto by train on August 15, planning to visit Deanna in Winnipeg for four or five days before arriving back in Vancouver on August 24 or 25 to take up a teaching position at Viscount Alexander Elementary in surburban Port Coquitlam. He had written to ask the Port Coquitlam school board what kind of class he would be teaching, but would not receive the news that he had been assigned a Grade 4 class of "slow learners" until mere days before school began.

In mid-September he arranged to rent a room in a house at 1335 Comox Avenue in Vancouver's then-bohemian west end where his friend David Phillips was also renting a room and where David's long-term girlfriend Barbara "Barb" Shore lived nearby. Both David and Barbara were continuing their studies at UBC. Sometime that fall Barrie became involved with a young woman named Louise, who appears to have also rented at 1335 Comox, variously referred to in letters from Barrie's friends as "Lou" or "Lulu." It is clear from letters she would write to him the next year that she took their relationship seriously, and wished they might have married, even if somewhat unhappily. However, although Barrie will frequently refer to "Dave" and "Barb" in poems about "1335 Comox," he will never mention Lou by name, and may in fact have not answered many of her letters. Virtually living with a couple such as David Phillips and Barbara Shore had quickly awoken old Oedipal emotions in Barrie; his attraction to Barb and its consequences will result in numerous references in his poetry to Comox Avenue being a scene of pain, confusion, and disaster — and possibly also to "Lou" slipping out of his memories. The line in *The*

Martyrology, Book II in the "Auguries" passages about Comox Avenue, "she is a ghost who walks among my feelings" (identified by Irene Niechoda as referring to a later lover, Dace Puce), probably refers to Barrie's mother, and to his increasing Freudian insights into his unhealthy relationship with her, rather than to Puce or one of the Vancouver young women. That is, the line appears to quietly signal his realization that he had been unconsciously transferring his much earlier (thus "ghostly") sexual feelings toward his mother into the feelings he experienced when with young women his own age.

In his notebooks he appears to mention Louise only three relatively brief times. In the most extensive of these she appears as a "chick" that he breaks up with early in 1964. He wrote that he had had to break up with her before his emotions had become too involved, but that he was also recognizing that for some reason he tended to break off quickly with each woman he had a relationship with, and was wondering what it was he feared with them. Then he answered himself, saying that the explanation was obvious, and painful, but that he couldn't deal with it until he was back in Toronto and seeing Lea. Was he already recognizing the Oedipal trap he was in? — his reflections were pointing that way, but were in no way explicit.

By name he mentions Lou only twice. On one April 1964 page there is a blank space that once held a photo, and beneath it her name, that she had inspired most of the poems he had written in the past four months, and that the photo had been taken in the yard of a house in New Westminster. On the page before he had written a summary of a dream he had had on April 28. In it he was visiting Viscount Alexander Elementary, and some children who were playing a game had asked if "Mr. Nichol" would join them. Their woman teacher, who he wrote he thought was Lou, told him he was supposed to touch one of the girls, so he touched one of the taller ones. He was not sure what she did then, but he found himself on the ground and had worried that he was sinking into it. It's one of several dreams he would record in these years of being overwhelmed or enveloped by a woman. He was being haunted here by the "ghosts" of two aspects of the Oedipal drama — his forbidden desire for the mother, and his fear of being sexually overwhelmed anyway by the forbidden woman, as in his traumatic childhood baths. The tall girl is a plausible description of his young mother. If he touches her, he falls into her.

Barrie would later recall 1963–64 as an uncomfortably divided year in which he spent half of his time wearing a tie and attempting to be the respectable schoolteaching "Mr. Nichol," and the other half at Comox Avenue believing he was trying to be a hard-drinking, peyote-eating, and carousing young poet.

> I was still very much involved with all the old crowd I had been involved with before, running around doing freaky things on weekends, all of that, so there was this real sort of dichotomy, sort of the mad bohemian and the straight school teacher — your choice of exciting roles. That's really what they were then, each one was just [a] kind of a role, where I was I don't know, I was just somewhere in between all sort of this mania. (Lind interview)

In literary terms, however, 1962–63 was not a particularly bad year. It began with his declaration in his notebook that he intended to purchase and read all of Malcolm Lowry, Irving Layton's *Balls for a One-Armed Juggler* and *A Red Carpet for the Sun*, and F.R. Scott and A.J.M. Smith's anthology *The Blasted Pine*, as well as most of the *Paris Review* interviews, and subscribe to the *Paris Review*, *Evergreen Review*, *Tamarack Review*, *Evidence*, and *Tish*. In November he read Lionel Kearns's essay "Stacked Verse," and listened to Jamie Reid read Charles Olson poems. In December he recorded that he was halfway through reading Pound's *ABC of Reading* and had become unhappy with everything he had been writing. In January he wrote that he was reading one of Robert Duncan's "The Structure of Rime" poems and reflected that his most important influences were probably Allen Ginsberg, Kenneth Patchen, and William Morris. He recorded reading numerous books by Kerouac, Burroughs, and Trocchi, as well as Sheila Watson's *The Double Hook* — although his response to these was that there was nothing left for one to do in prose and that all he could hope to do was write poetry.

He went to writers' meetings and listened to the arguments of Jamie Reid, David Cull, and Bob Hogg, whom he somewhat scornfully called Black Mountain "devotees" and declared himself at least partially unconvinced that their way was the only way. On November 13, 1963, he reconsidered his own ideas about poetry, having had a long talk with Reid

aka{ barrie phillip }Nichol

and Shives. He wrote that he thought his style was due for a change. He argued with himself about whether poetry was an act of communication, and if so with whom did it communicate — with one's intellectual peers or only with oneself? Was it ethical to want to communicate only with oneself? By January 1964 his arguments brought him to a frantic despair in which he printed a line of expletives in capital letters across the page, and in further capital letters wrote that he could see no sense in the notebook he had created, that it was useless and stupid. Then in smaller letters he wrote that everything he had done before and most likely everything he would do in the future would be pointless, no matter how hard he worked. And then he jokingly wrote a title for this text that declared it the work of a masochist, but followed that with more capital letters in which he seemed to shout at himself for never being serious about anything. It was a clumsy text, but oddly foreshadowing the playful and graphically adventurous work he would create later. From it he segued into another unsuccessful but highly innovative text — a mock dramatic script about a Vancouver poetry gathering at UBC's Brock Hall at which Hogg, Cull, Shives, Alexander, Nichol, Roy Kiyooka, Kurt Lang, Fred Douglas, and Judith Copithorne were all characters and uttered amusingly predictable non-profound lines.

But while his literary education that year was broad and stimulating, his teaching year was not going well. He explained to Irene Niechoda:

> I was just eighteen when I started teaching, just a babe — and a crazy one at that! I was teaching grade four, thirty-nine of them, the "slow learners" class. And I was terrible, probably more disturbed than them. And most of them *were* disturbed, it wasn't that they were slow. [. . .] I had no sense of discipline, so I'd be grabbing kids by their hair, and then I'd start feeling total guilt and mortification about it. I'd sworn I'd never have a kid strapped — I was death on strapping. Mind you, I'm pulling their hair! In fact, when I finally did have a kid strapped, that's when I finally quit. (1992 95)

It was March 13, 1964. Although Barrie went on to tell Niechoda that he had then decided to move immediately to Toronto and re-enter therapy — a move he said that he had previously hoped to make in September in the company of David Phillips and Barbara Shore — there were other factors in this decision. One was a stern letter from his brother Don, who had heard through their parents of Barrie's resignation from teaching and surmised the crisis Barrie now was in. He told Barrie that he had written to them, telling them that their youngest was passing through some "natural" changes, things that most young men encounter. He hoped that he had prevented their mother from feeling too concerned or guilty. The word "guilty" perhaps suggested Don's own interpretation of Barrie's past. He indicated also that he had been talking to Lea about him, and that she was surprised that he had lasted in Vancouver as long as he had. Ordering Barrie to leave Vancouver at once, he wrote that the current crisis at least showed that his neurosis was ripe for treatment. He added that jobs in Toronto were plentiful, and would be until the university term ended in late April.

A second and possibly more likely reason Barrie left for Toronto so suddenly was the abruptly burgeoning Oedipal tension in his growing relationship with Barbara Shore — at least one of Barrie's friends at the time believed that this was the only reason. James Alexander, David Phillips, Barb Shore, Dezso Huba, and Arnold Shives were among those who accompanied Barrie to the CN train station. It was April 11. Alexander and Phillips were somewhat angry; they did not believe in psychiatry or — as they put it — in "getting adjusted," and feared that it would be the end of Barrie's creativity. Shives, however, recognized the desperateness of his situation and was glad that his friend would at least be receiving some kind of help. Barrie himself felt as negatively about his situation as any of them. In his notebook he wrote that even though he was heading to Toronto he was sure that he had no future and certainly no idea of what the coming years might bring. He again wrote about pointlessness — that the struggle inside him, the struggles around him, and his struggles to write were all without point. There was no one who might understand.

6. Lea or Dace

why does it always come back to this, to the sea

— bpNichol, *Two Novels*,
"For Jesus Lunatick," 34

The last things Barrie created in Vancouver, on April 7, 1964, were two visual poems, "Mind-Trap #1" and "Mind-Trap #2" — which he drew in his notebook. He signed the first "bpn," and the second "bp." The latter — seemingly an alteration of the previous "bpn" — may be the first time he had used this signature. The next entry indicated he had been reading Jack Spicer, and the third was a poem in which he wrote that he had left his room and city to travel to a strange land — possibly a reference both to Exodus 2:22 and to Robert A. Heinlein's recent novel *Stranger in a Strange Land*. Barrie lamented having left his friends and being unlikely to see them again for a couple of springs, and described how his train was moving through a landscape of frail trees and melting snow. Despite Barrie's evident despair here at a move that was recapitulating all his other railroad journeys away from vanishing homes, the small trees would prove to be merely trees, and the snow merely snow, and his friends would soon begin to increase, exponentially.

In the first dream that he recorded in his notebook after reaching Toronto, April 28, 1964, he was a brakeman on a train that was almost demolished by a longer train. The symbolic son–father encounter left

Barrie on foot trying to find his way along the tracks. Coming to a ravine, he saw a chubby naked slightly older woman running like a deer between the trees. She reminded him of the character Sarandell from Fellini's movie *8½*. Her skin looked like baked brown clay. She called up to him, asking him colloquially if he would like to have sex with her. The idea repulsed him, a response that his face betrayed. He tried to run away, hoping to reach the forest before she could get out of the ravine. He took a shortcut across a sharp embankment that led to the ocean, but it was muddy and he slipped, and fell down into deeper mud at the ocean's edge, becoming stuck. Suddenly he heard Sarandell's animal-like voice approaching and announcing her delight at finding him there. He felt panicked, nauseated, but could make no effort to get away.

The dream brilliantly merged his recent dream about the three Brobdingnagian women, his falling into and getting stuck in the muddy Port Arthur ditch in 1953–54, and his childhood baths with his mother — a stunning dream, and undoubtedly terrifying. But it was not one that would lead Barrie to keep distant from women. His having perceived himself as having "won" the Oedipal struggle to "possess" his mother had left him not only filled with guilt and fear — of being sideswiped by that longer train — but also viewing all women as eagerly available.

On arrival Barrie went to live with his brother Don, and resumed therapy sessions with Lea Hindley-Smith. Through one of her other clients who worked in the Circulation Department of the University of Toronto's Sigmund Samuel Library, Barrie learned of a job opening there and was quickly hired. Already working in the section was the young poet David Aylward and a young Australian woman of Latvian descent, Dace Puce, who was somewhat older than Barrie and whose name her Toronto friends would often spell as it was pronounced — "Datsi," or "Datsi Puttsi." Also working there was Grant Goodbrand, who would become a lifelong friend and colleague. Barrie's integration into this group was rapid. On May 7 he recorded a dream that appears to be an extension of his Sarandell and Brobdingnag dreams: he had been caught on a muddy bank by a large and unpleasantly pink fish, and as he struggled away his trousers had become smeared with blood and mud. On May 13 he had a dream in which David Aylward appeared. By June he was in a sexual relationship with Dace Puce and had persuaded her to begin seeing Lea.

Also in June Grant Goodbrand began seeing Lea, again at Barrie's recommendation. For Grant, like for Barrie, this would be a life-altering move.

Lea Hindley-Smith — known as "Mrs. Smith" in this period — was a largely self-trained psychoanalyst whose skills and insight surprised nearly everyone who worked with her. Born in Wales to impoverished Jewish immigrant parents, she had worked in London in the early 1930s and early 1940s as an artist's model while — concealing her Jewishness — independently studying the psychoanalytic theories of Freud, Melanie Klein, and Edmund Bergler. She acquired enough expertise to be hired as a counsellor by the Leeds Board of Education in the 1940s. She had brought her husband and children to Toronto in 1948, at first supporting them by operating boarding houses, later by selling real estate, and in 1953 by beginning to accept a small number of therapy clients. Her success with them led to a rapidly expanding practice. She had recently been reconfirmed in her view of psychoanalysis as potentially liberating by her reading of Robert Lindner, who in *Rebel Without a Cause* and *The Fifty Minute Hour* had opposed "adjustment" psychotherapy — such as that feared by Barrie's Vancouver friends — and urged psychoanalyses that would lead to more open and progressive cultures.

Goodbrand, who in his 2010 book *Therafields* offers a much fuller version of her early life, recalls Lea as having six impressive qualities:

> She had an unswerving commitment to tell it as it is to her clients and to relentlessly delve into the secret places that were interfering with their lives. Secondly, Lea had remarkable intuitive gifts that allowed her to see within her clients. She also arrived at a technique to induce abreaction. She was committed to go as far as any client needed in therapy and sometimes unconventionally outside her sessions. She developed her voice forcefully in order to reach the nervous systems of her clients. And lastly she had a heroic energy that broke boundaries in the practice of psychotherapy, upset social norms and envisioned revolutionary social change. (Goodbrand 25)

He also suggests that "Lea idealized artists and the importance that artistic talent could have in psychological healing." Such a view of the arts, plus her intellectual curiosity about psychoanalysis, and the various periods of enterprising self-employment that poverty had led her to undertake, made her a considerably different person from Barrie's mother.

When Barrie began regular therapy sessions with Mrs. Smith in the summer of 1964 she had 64 individual-therapy clients who also met in "deep" groups, 36 of whom lived in "house groups" she had invented and established, plus a dozen or more who came to her only for individual therapies. She was also meeting with a "Catholic Group" of monks, priests, and nuns, which had been brought to her through her friendship with Gregory Baum, a senior professor at St. Michael's College and a theological advisor to the Vatican II Council. Barrie would very quickly decide to live in one of her house groups — large houses in which Hindley-Smith clients would live together as a "family" and meet approximately twice a week with her to analyze, examine, and attempt to understand whatever disagreements and conflicts had occurred among them.

But there was another forceful woman now in Barrie's life — Dace. Barrie and Dace's relationship was torrid, tempestuous, mutually obsessive, reckless, and at times as disastrous as his dream on May 7 possibly foretold. Both lovers were almost suicidally insecure and yet also would-be free spirits. For a short time Barrie and Dace lived in the same Hindley-Smith house group at 152 Howland Avenue, and later in neighbouring house groups. From the numerous scribbled notes that Dace wrote and shoved under the door of Barrie's room — and which he preserved — their interaction would appear to have been a long series of breakups, desperate pleas, threats of suicide, passionate reunions, drunken remorse, heartfelt apologies, and more passionate reunions — much like the young woman he later portrays in "For Jesus Lunatick."

fucking bastard pawing at her god no but hold me please for christ's sake hold me it gets so lonely who was he shit she just didn't know what she was doing here please hold me where are you going i can't even find you sometimes lying on top of her and looking up into his eyes wondering don't go i mean do you have to it's early still why did i do those things i mean why did i hold me please phil hold me i love you you know do you love me phil do you you seem so far away phil you fucking bastard think you can come in here and use me for your little thrill and go well piss on you don't go please phil don't go i'm sorry i must have been drunk you know stay awhile longer and just talk to me why don't you you're always going to sleep on me just talk to me why don't you do something for christ's sake don't just lie there i feel so fucking frustrated please phil make love to me phil please you bastard. . . . (25)[1]

Barrie's entrenched fear of being engulfed by women contributed to the frequent breakups as much as did Dace's history of pain at being seemingly thought unworthy by those she loved. Barrie appears to have often retreated into solitude, to which Dace would respond with melodrama, excessive drinking, and threats of recklessness and self-damage — threats that would often, as she hoped, draw Barrie back to "save" her. In his book, Goodbrand gives a glimpse of the two of them, in which he assigns Dace the pseudonym of "Sheila":

> Sheila, a young and lovely Australian girl doing her walkabout through the rest of the world, worked with us at the library and had also temporarily moved into the house. Sheila and Barrie became romantically involved. [. . .]
>
> When I arrived, Barrie came down . . . from an upstairs room and asked me to wait for him . . . because he was involved in trying to calm down an upset house member. [. . .] Within minutes, Sheila, clearly drunk or on drugs, flew down the steps from the third floor, taking them two at a time, pursued by Barrie. She screamed that she would go to Yonge Street and find herself a man. I heard the screech of a car, and as I bolted for the door I saw her pick herself up and run off. Barrie apologized to me and said he was going to go to Yonge Street to try and stop her. (13–14)

Their extreme romance — Goodbrand would come to see it as an "infatuation" while others who worked with them in the library would view it as the throes of "first love" — would continue throughout 1964 and most of 1965. It was not a therapeutic relationship for either. Dace would have a long and painful induced miscarriage from mid-January to late February of 1965 — in his notebook Barrie recorded numerous days of comforting her and himself before she was rushed to hospital. He recorded the room number where he visited her — and recorded also his various feelings of selfishness, love, depression, and self-disgust. In March he wrote that he felt like destroying her mentally. In May he wrote that he felt very warm and affectionate with her, and that their relationship was improving. By the end of the year, however, they again tumultuously separated. Goodbrand's recollection is that Barrie still wished to get back together with her but that Lea told him that if he did, he should find another therapist — essentially telling him that he would have to choose between them.

At the beginning of his notebook entries about Dace, Barrie usually called her *D*, then changed to referring to her as *A*. In late February 1965 when visiting her in hospital he referred to her by her name and continued then to do so. In his entry of May 10 he noted explicitly that he had called Dace *A* in many of his earlier entries — as if foreseeing that someone might someday read the notebook and perhaps think he had been deeply involved with two women concurrently. My guess is that someone as alphabet-conscious as Barrie — who had once lived in Wildwood Park's *H* section and had used the alphabet to find his way home — considered Dace to be *A* because she was indeed his first love, his first. She was not the first woman he had not run from, but the first he had come back to after running from. He was running and coming back over and over. In a way this was progress — but, as Lea was observing, not a progress one could easily progress from. Dace was often unwittingly like the two people he had once perceived his mother to be — one holding him away from her tempting beauty as they danced, the other engulfing him in her Sarandell-like sexuality in the bath.

In the "Clouds" section of *Book II* of *The Martyrology*, written 1969, Barrie intermittently found himself remembering Dace. Like many of the sections of the early books of the poem, it is one in which he addresses saints who are, as he wrote in a marginal note on the manuscript of this section, "real figures ripped from the mind of my own voices . . . finally then it is myself that I address everything to." The lives of his saints, including their sexual lives, "weren't in fact allegorical," they were Barrie's own lives (quoted in Niechoda 1992 121). Irene Niechoda in her *Sourcery for Books I and II of bpNichol's The Martyrology* reports that Barrie told her that, four years after his "compulsive attachment" to his relationship with Dace had ended, confused recollections of her puzzlingly returned while he was writing the "Clouds" section. Writing of the amorous relationships of his saints had, to his surprise, somehow invited Dace and his relationship with her into his writing. In a second marginal note he had written, "always there is this dual rhythm of opposites since it is true some things are over   dead and gone these past four years   why is it now I find myself returning to her face as in the image of a poem that is not forgotten tho it should be." (Niechoda 1992 121–22)

Numerous of the lines of this section have double meanings, as when Barrie writes:

> yeah & when you looked in there
> into those clouds they called her eyes
> was it a surprise to see your own death mirrored

and the "you" can be either "saint and" or Barrie himself, or the bpNichol poet speaking to Barrie. Or again,

> i enter the softer world of women
> seeing your face saint and
> I remember the tales they tell
> how you fell from the cloud world to the earth
> from the earth into her eyes
> who was not a woman but simply the disguises trouble wears
> braiding up its hair
> so you would touch her

Or yet again,

> you pissed it away in suffering
> looked [sic] up with a chick the village fool could see thru
> & avoided

> that lady almost destroyed the muse
> & you let her use you

> willingly for your own destruction

aka{ barrie phillip }Nichol

these are the times I could curse your name
were it not so pointless blaming you

In later parts of the section, Barrie's writing and memories become less
ambiguously personal:

faces cloud in on me

lost as i am mostly dreaming
streets filled with memory brush against me

library daze
the dust & centuries pile up within the mind's
gestures

as if she were a part of history
history being in me is my story
my vision of the world's end &
beginning

Dace is a part of his history, he recognizes, as the library books that he has
read directly or indirectly are also a part of his history. "Who did I love
having said I loved you / holding your body in the narrow bed" he asks.
"Fear," is the answer, as the following stanza, written by Dace herself,
should have told him.

"now that spring is here
winter anguishes that froze upon the air
reinstate their agony"

Moreover his own part in their recurring difficulties — that fear, the fear
of giving up the solitude he embraced while watching the clouds over
Wildwood Park, or imaginarily walking the streets of Port Arthur with
Dick Tracy — is still with him; and interfering with his more recent
relationships.

who is it in this other room I've found
holds out her hand I cannot take it
[. . .]
i am i because i fear the we
deeper mystery without solitude

Dace's letters and Barrie's notebook entries firmly suggest that this fear of "the we" wasn't just a fear of being close to another human but specifically of being close to a female partner. The similar textual records of his interactions with Vancouver friends such as David and Andy Phillips or with new friends such as Goodbrand and David Aylward show no signs of such desperation, tumult, or fear of "we." Moreover, the fear of women shows much more severe extremes than *The Martyrology* passage suggests, ranging from the anxious pursuit portrayed by Goodbrand to the callous disregard implied by Dace when she wrote to her "Dearest Barry" that he had "closed" on her completely. On one remarkable 1966 occasion she wrote accusing him of sounding unemotional and detached whenever he declared his love for her, and announcing that she was again breaking off with him, and he turned the page over and sketched on the back one of his most successful verbal-visual poems of that year, "Historical Implications of Turnips" (also published as "Turnips Are"), and its evocative ending of the fleshy "punstir" turnips "spurtin."

7. Becoming bp

You & I were "other" to ourselves, our minds.

— Jerome Rothenberg, "Je est un autre"
(http://poemsandpoetics.blogspot.com/2010/
09/je-est-un-autre-ethnopoetics-poet-as.html)

The fiction makes us real.

— Robert Kroetsch, *Creation,* 63

On May 8, 1964, while familiarizing himself with his new job and work-mates, Barrie paused to sketch a plan in his notebook for a series of five or more poetry books that he hoped to present to his Vancouver friend Sybil Huba. Volume I was to be *Tedious Ways* by fourth-century poet Pao Chao, volume II to be *Fire and Water* "by bp (me)," volume III to be called *Jazz* and contain seven poems by Jack Kerouac, volume IV to be *Over a Plea* by James Alexander, and volume V to be *The Singing Head* by Jamie Reid. The Kerouac and Chao volumes were to be typed, and the others to be written by hand. The small "b" of the "bp" of "bp (me)" was written over top of the capital "B" that Barrie had instinctively written rather than the low-ercase "b" that he had intended. The overall title was "Paper Press Poets Series." His note "for Mrs. Huba" left it ambiguous whether this was to be a series dedicated to her or perhaps one created — at her request? — for her to distribute. The two-page plan also included a sketch of the title page of the "bp (me)" book on which the monogram/motif "bp" occurs nine times, and one of its contents pages on which it occurs 12 times. There was no mention of such a series in the several letters Barrie received this year from Sybil Huba, nor any evidence that he did more work on the series than these two pages — although he did, according to her son Dezso, in the next few months send her numerous single-copy hand-drawn or typed pamphlet editions of what he/"bp" was writing.[1]

The notebook pages do, however, show him working, as he was the previous month when signing the two drafts of his "Mind-Trap" visual poems "bpn" and "bp," toward this new signature identity — toward creating a new writing self out of letter-forms. Perhaps because of his growing preoccupation with Dace, most of the remaining notebook entries for 1964–65 concern dreams he has remembered or his current thoughts about her. But he was sending out visual poems for possible publication, and requesting subscriptions to magazines, and doing both of these over his new name. bill bissett replied to his April 1964 subscription request to *blew ointment* by addressing him as "b. p. nichol." George Bowering replied to a similar request Barrie had sent to his magazine *Imago* by writing to "B. P. Nichol," as did Margaret Randall when he requested a subscription to *El Corno Emplumado*. In August Victor Coleman rejected some poems Barrie had offered to his magazine *Island,* writing to "bp Nichol," and in September, after Barrie had ordered from Victor a copy of my book *City of the Gulls and Sea,* replied to "Mr. Nichol." Barrie would also receive "Dear B. P. Nichol" replies when he began contacting international visual poetry magazines and their poet-publishers in 1965.[2]

On the notebook pages immediately following his sketches for the "Paper Press" series of poetry books, Barrie announced to himself in two-inch high letters his "TASK" now that he had come to Toronto, and then listed its parts. The task included both writing and psychotherapy as interlocking projects. His first goal was surprisingly mimetic — to record in words the things he saw, including things of "nature" and of the "real" world — instead of what his brother Don was calling his dreamworld. His second was to jettison that dreamworld by entering deep therapy. Another was to "become" by transcending the barriers that were containing him.

And the last was to become a proficient writer of poetry. He signed this list "bp." Somewhat ironically, the signature suggested that the distinction between real world and the dreamworld might be much more complex than either Don or the signifying capabilities of a list were suggesting. Was "bp" "real" or a new "dream"? Was it possible to dwell in both worlds? Or could dreams and other inventions be a part of a "real" world?

But his pen name, or perhaps his dream identity-name, was not the only aspect of his writing that Barrie wanted to change now that he had left his Vancouver friends and arrived in Toronto. The new name was part of a larger project to change how he wrote poetry. For some time he had been struggling to perceive a way to make his poetry less artificial in its rhythms and apparent emotions. In a November 27, 1963, notebook entry he had asked himself — again in theatrically large capital letters — whether the complexity of one's emotional responses to an increasingly complex world meant that a poet should utterly abandon old ideas of poetic patterns of rhythm and possibly the concept of pattern itself. He added, foreshadowing some of his later pronouncements, that he was not trying to imply the destructiveness associated with Dada but merely one that was needed for starting anew or for finding earlier or better foundations on which to work. Despite his apparent misunderstanding of Dada as "destructive," a simple dichotomy — destruction/construction — was again being at least unconsciously questioned.

Barrie had also been looking for ways to make his poetry less self-serving, but despite having encountered in debates among Vancouver poets ideas such as Olson's "against wisdom as such" and Duncan's understanding that poets serve the language rather than themselves,[3] or that content can result from the poet's following of the music of a poem through "tone-leading," he had experienced difficulty overcoming older notions that a poem is an expression of one's ongoing experiences or makes important statements about life (notebook, November 13, 1963), or that it should honestly express one's feelings (notebook, November 27, 1963). His discussions with himself on these pages had tended often to be as confused and agonized as his thoughts about his relationships with women. However, on April 8, 1964, scant days before leaving for Toronto, he had written after a discussion with his friend Neild Holloway — again employing theatrical capital letters — that a poet should be "directed" by his poem rather than

aka{ barrie phillip }Nichol

by the words he is using. His distinction between the poem and its words is somewhat obscure — but by "words" he seems to have meant a poet's conscious intentions. And in Toronto in a notebook entry of May 8 he was able to foresee being a poet who does not merely fulminate and lament but can offer invented experiences of which he is only part. He added that the poet should forget playing at being a poet as if it were a role, and give up any preoccupation with self-celebration. In a few months these were to be the goals of an "ideopome"-writing bpNichol.

Barrie was much clearer about this period in his poetry and in his thinking about poetics when interviewed about them in the next decade. In 1978 he told Ken Norris that in 1965

> I just became aware that it didn't matter what I set down, what mood I was in. I was essentially churning out the same poem, and that I could become very proficient at that poem cause that's what it was, it was a poem and had this minor variation. . . . There was a type of arrogance, I thought; that is to say I was coming to the occasion of the poem to force myself upon it. I was being arrogant rather than learning. (Miki 2002 237)

He used the same word, "arrogant," when replying to Dwight Gardiner in a 1976 interview:

> . . . I thought I was being too arrogant, that . . . I was coming to the situation obsessed that I had something to say per se: a very didactic purpose as opposed to simply giving myself up to the process of writing. And as a result, I was not learning anything from the language. . . . (154)

He told Jack David in an interview later that year that he had been automatically "imposing some sort of preconceived notion of wisdom on the occasion of writing." His way out of this impasse was to stop writing any poetry except visual poetry.

> So my focus shifted onto form and I stopped writing lyric poems and began writing what I at that time called "ideopomes," which were

just these little ideogram type things. [. . .] So that I, in essence, abandoned "straight" poetry for a period of about a year and a half . . . . (Bayard 19)

Barrie's concerns about "arrogance" and about imposing a "preconceived notion of wisdom" were expressing a common concern among poets at this time about intentionality. In Charles Olson's "projective" poetics this concern had been reflected in an environmental poetics: the poet wrote out of the field of events in which he or she was situated, and those events contributed to the linguistic events of the writing. In Duncan's poetics the poet followed the sounds proposed by the phonemes of the poem. In Jack Spicer's poetics one imagined one's poems being "dictated" by minds from another place and time. In the "serial" poetics that both Duncan and Spicer practised, the sections of the poem were to emerge from a series of "riming" events that the poet encountered. In the visual poems or "ideopoems" that Barrie was now proposing to restrict himself to, the content was generated by the shape of the letters, or by the words concealed within words and the contrasting meanings those words might have. Later Barrie would realize that he could avoid intentional expression of meaning through dialogue — by talking to the saint characters of his poems, and to their persona-character bpNichol, and creating dialogical meanings.

However, there was something more to these interrelated decisions to give up "straight poetry" and invent an arrogance- and intention-avoiding bpNichol. In his notebooks as early as 1963 he had begun linking the problem of "honesty" and honest communication in poetry with the problem of honest communication between human beings that Lea Hindley-Smith had begun helping him resolve. As in his notes on his "Task," he had begun to see the blocks he was experiencing in his writing as inseparable from the blocks he was encountering in his emotional life. In April 1964 he copied long quotations from Wilhelm Reich's *The Murder of Christ* into his notebook, beginning with "It IS possible to get out of a trap. However, in order to break out of a prison, one must first confess to being in a prison. The trap is man's emotional structure, his character structure. There is little use in devising systems of thought about the nature of the trap if the only thing to do to get out of the trap is to know the trap and to find the exit."

aka{ barrie phillip }Nichol

In a notebook entry in mid-May 1965, which Barrie titled "Thots on the Creative Process," he reflected on the fact that his old 1335 Comox Avenue friends Dave Phillips and Barb Shore were now unable to write. He commented that not being able to write anything that you can perceive as "good," or feeling that you have nothing to say, was a problem that he thought he had found an answer to in psychotherapy. He added that anything that blocked one's ability to write or express was also a hindrance to one's personal development and thus properly a problem of health, and then repeated that any barrier that prevented personal growth, particularly in one's creativity, was not only unhealthy but unnatural. Once one had recognized such a block or barrier, he wrote, any further action was useless — except that of breaking through the barrier. He again quoted Reich, this time printing most of the quotation in capital letters: "All that is necessary to get out of a trap is to recognize that it exists and to find the exit, knowing anything further is useless, except where it has a bearing on your escape."

THE COVER OF *DADA LAMA*, 1968, PUBLISHED IN BRITAIN BY TLALOC.

The concepts of traps, barriers, blocks, dead-ends, and finding exits were ones that Barrie would repeat in various poetics statements over the next few years, as in the "statement" he would write in 1966 for inclusion in his boxed Coach House Press book *bp*: ". . . we have come up against the problem . . . of finding as many exits as possible from the self (language/communication exits) in order to form as many entrances as possible for the other." In the concluding paragraph of this "statement" he would make the soon to be well-known pronouncement that "there is a new humanism afoot that will one day touch the world to its core: traditional poetry is only one of the means by which to reach out and touch the other." One of the other means, although Barrie would only hint about it here, was of course psychotherapy: "dialogues," he writes, "with the self that clarify the soul & heart and deepen the ability to love" (Miki 2002 18).

In September 1968 in an extended entry on "time" in his notebook he would describe the psychotherapy offered by Lea Hindley-Smith's recently christened therapy institution Therafields as a "communication therapy," repeating a word he had been using in his thoughts about poetics since 1963. What role Barrie was playing in the creation and general use at Therafields of this phrase is unclear. However the next year when he was editor of the new Therafields in-house newsletter *Axis*, and launching its first issue, he would emphasize this phrase while writing a lead editorial with a striking rhetorical resemblance to his "statement" in *bp*.

> Now we are beginning the move outward, outside of ourselves moving to take over the inward feelings and realizations to present them here first in a form accessible to all of us to be shared. This is the very real necessity. The very real necessity is that the insights that our working is now generating be shared as a common source of energy to further us all in our searches in these areas of human communication. What *Axis* is is first of all a living dialogue, a living continual communication to be shared among us, an ever growing work and source book for the work which we call communications therapy. (December 24, 1969)[4]

He would sign the editorial "bpNichol," just as he had signed all his literary writing after April 1964 and all of his writing for Therafields. By this point he had firmly established two trademark signatures — one the actual signature of bp/bpNichol and the other a signature style, a liberation rhetoric of barriers surmounted, freedom to live achieved, communications established, exits discovered, lives renewed, poetry resurrected. As he would write three times in his 1971 *ABC: the Aleph Beth Book*, "the poem will live again." So too, he believed, would the Therafields client.

aka{ barrie phillip }Nichol

The undeclared keyword of the above passage was translation — concealed there within the word "communication." "Inner feelings" were to be presented "in a form." "Insights" were to be shared as an "energy," and from there become part of a "dialogue," and from there become a "book." Like poets, and like the subjects of Freud's "talking therapy," the Therafields clients were to outer themselves — "communicate" — in words, and find their insights in words. They were to create meanings through "dialogues" with their selves, and with their internalizations of their analysts. Barrie had also translated himself into a word, "bpNichol," not only finding within it an "exit" from his self, but also creating an alternative Nichol who was a position in language as well as a rhetoric and a deployer/product-in-process of an expanding number of genres. Translation of course sallies out from but does not eliminate the item translated. Barrie, another position in both linguistic and biological systems of signs, was still here keeping his notebooks, having feelings and insights, making and changing plans, attempting to "communicate," engaging in dialogue, and both translating and blurring himself into that increasingly imaginative communications device, "bpNichol."

8. Ideopoet

how's the living experiment going? sounds like a good idea, but 3 sister-type nuns, are you for real?

the mag [Ganglia] is the BEST I8ve [sic] seen in Canada and is better than most American mags — keep it up, baby, we need people like you.

"u & Bissett & levy doing the most exciting things in N. American Konkretian"

— D.r. Wagner to "bp!" 1966

Barrie's decision on arriving in Toronto to concentrate on visual poetry, or "ideopomes," as he then was calling these works, was probably the most fortuitous artistic decision he could have made — not necessarily because it would allow him to be less "arrogant," predictable, and intention-serving in his writing, but because visual poetry had been, unbeknownst to him, enjoying since the early 1950s an international surge of interest as "concrete poetry." In his notebooks Barrie had been creating since 1963 various visual effects through drawings, such as "Mind-Trap #1," and through arrangements of letters, but it was only the latter that he was now thinking of as "ideopomes" — most likely because they were constructed out of words, syllables, and letters — though not necessarily out of sentences. Because these "pomes" focussed mainly on words and their component letters and syllables, and not on sentences, they steered him away from the predictability and melodrama of the narcissistic "i-fall-upon-the-thorns-of-life" kinds of poetry he had become increasingly wary of writing. He was referring to these cryptic word poems when he wrote to his old Vancouver friend Arnold Shives on June 12, 1965, that until recently he had been dubious about the literary value of his new ideopomes, but had decided — after reading William Carlos Williams's endorsement of Joyce's "maiming" of words in *Finnegans Wake*[1] — that they were every bit as valid as literature as those he thought of as his "regular" poems. He wrote that in his ideopomes he had been going even further than Joyce and other writers — by dismantling real words, by ripping into the roots of language, its syllables and its phonemes, by tearing words apart and regrouping the fragments, by doing things to words that you just wouldn't do in ordinary poems. As if to illustrate, he signed the letter with a column of variations of the word "barrie" beginning with "beerie."

Arnold Shives was probably Barrie's most important correspondent during much of 1964 and 1965. He was the only one of Barrie's Vancouver circle to continue to attempt to think through aesthetic problems and to respond to Barrie's evolving ideas — although not always positively. Others such as Dave Phillips, Barb Shore, Jim Alexander, and Neild Holloway continued to write to him but had little to relate except events in their personal lives, and very little to say in response to what Barrie was writing to them. Phillips and Holloway would merely urge him to come back to Vancouver and terminate his — in their view — dangerous dalliance with psychotherapy. Barrie characterized them to Loren Lind as "artists who were fantastically suspicious of any form of . . . 'therapy' because they equate their art with their illness and figure if you take away their illness you will take away their art." Barrie had also contacted bill bissett in April 1964 to request a subscription to his magazine *blew oint-ment*, and later that year had a poem — "yur Appolainaire poem" bissett called it — published in one of its issues, Barrie's first publication. But their correspondence would not flourish until the middle of the next year.

In the fall of 1964 Arnold Shives had enrolled at the San Francisco Art Institute. In a statement he deposited in 1990 at the Simon Fraser

University Library he recalled his first year there as a lonely time during which Barrie's letters "encouraged me in my work and inspired me to continue writing poetry. I don't think I'd be exaggerating to say that I found my correspondence with bp as creatively stimulating as my art classes at SFIA." On Barrie's side, his letters to Shives seemed to have been opportunities to explore or expand ideas and theories. In one late-1965 letter he told Shives that each thing that a writer writes is a creative experiment, including the letters that they were exchanging.

In one of his letters to Shives he drafted a manifesto, again using a rhetoric of walls and barriers, and typed in emphatic-looking capitals. Here he announced that when one writes a poem one is only creating an environment for words to interact within. The poet's responsibility is to create the environment that is most suitable to the words. Because self cannot be kept out of the arts, Barrie argued, the artist must more vigorously throw himself into its processes. Barriers and other impediments to the development and growth of the poem — which he seems to think of as occuring at the poem's own instigation — must be smashed and removed. Necessarily ignorant of how inspiration happens, the poet can be merely a medium through which the poem creates itself — despite the attempts of many artists to take credit for that creation. His or her main role is not construction but simply to remove any barrier that might prevent the poem from freely constructing itself into being. The manifesto appears to combine Reich's discourse of barriers with Blake's, Spicer's, and Duncan's understandings that the authors of poetry are elsewhere, in language, or "in eternity," and to move sharply toward creating a kind of psychoanalytical poetics.

In a January 1965 letter he complained to Shives about the "coterie of poets" — he named American poet Robert Kelly as one member — who have gathered around North American magazines such as *Matter, Sum, El Corno Emplumado, Wild Dog, Tish, Jogglars, Fubbalo,* and Victor Coleman's *Island,* and told him that he knew personally that such coteries or groups always tend to stifle one's own convictions. He added that he was not at all one who believed in the "myth" that to be successful artists should seek to live in artists' colonies or collectives. More than likely he was thinking of his recent little 1335 Comox Street "group" and its stifling interactions. He was also of course scorning the "regular" poems that his list of "coterie"

aka{ barrie phillip }Nichol

magazines was publishing — "regular" poems that he now believed he had left behind for his "ideopomes." He concluded the brief diatribe by telling Shives — who in his own letters had suggested that Barrie's drawn poems seemed to lack complexity — that he was willingly following his own path, that there was no value in getting distracted by someone else's.

In a May letter he offered an expanded definition of the "ideopome," writing that the distinction between "poem" and "pome" was meaningful because the "pome" could be numerous things — a piece of typography, an optical trick, a small burst of sound. A "pome" can tear words apart as well as link them together. Through them a reader can learn to fill gaps, anticipate the unexpected, to see things that aren't openly visible, he argued. He adapted Philip Whalen's definition of a poem as a "graph of a mind moving" — which he'd probably encountered in Donald Allen's *The New American Poetry* anthology (420) — to call a pome a graph of a mind moving through space into various elements of language. But he also told Shives that the pome has no author because any person could have created it. It identifies a framework of meaning and shows what else could dwell there.

Meanwhile, he had been sending some of his new "pomes" to various Canadian magazines, including Coleman's *Island*, as well as *The Canadian Forum*, George Bowering's *Imago*, and James Reaney's *Alphabet*. Some were accepted by *The Canadian Forum* and *Alphabet* — Reaney commented in an April 29, 1965, letter that his wife Colleen Thibaudeau had been writing similar texts for children, which she had called "lozenge poems." Bowering, in a letter dated July 29, 1965, informed Barrie that his "ideopomes" elsewhere in the world would be called "concrete poems," or "Kon," and that he hasn't seen any Kon that makes him "excited or very interested." He recommended that Barrie contact Cavan McCarthy whose British magazine *Tlaloc* did publish such poetry. Barrie would later mark Bowering's letter as one of the turning points in his publishing career, telling Caroline Bayard and Jack David that through this letter and "through Bowering I found the European underground of concrete" (Bayard 24).

There are some complications to this story, however. In a letter to Shives dated March 10, 1965, Barrie had used the term "concrete poetry," telling his friend that he had wanted to send him some poems but, having

realized that he hated everything he had written (he was evidently refer-
ring to his "regular" poems), he had been seeing what he could pro-
duce in "concrete poetry" and similar forms, and was enclosing four
of these results. He had got news of the term two months before from
his friend Andy Phillips who had been travelling in Europe and sent
him a *Times Literary Supplement* article about concrete. Also, in Barrie's
archives is a letter from Cavan McCarthy dated July 19, 1965, two days
before Bowering's letter, which began "dear bp, Thanks for poems, which
are receiving the most serious consideration." The poems were some of
Barrie's "bpNichol" ideopomes, one of which McCarthy would publish
in the December 1965 *Tlaloc*. The remainder of this McCarthy letter was
definitely door-opening, giving Barrie postal addresses for such concrete
poetry stalwarts as Dom Sylvester Houédard and Pierre Garnier, and the
names of magazines that would publish concrete. It could not have been
occasioned by Bowering's subsequent letter. Possibly Barrie had reasons
for wanting literary history to record that he had gone his "own path" in
ignorance of international concrete until pointed toward it by Bowering.
Or possibly he had believed his "ideopomes" would not be thought of as
concrete. He said this in fact to Nicette Jukelevics in a 1974 interview,
that in 1964–65 "I never thought about my poetry as concrete, I thought
about it using the fact that the page is a visual field to do visual things"
(Miki 2002 135). Or possibly the spring 1965 was so busy and stressful for
Barrie that he simply forgot what he had been learning from whom when.

Barrie's personal path to seeing "the page as a visual field" and con-
ceiving of "ideopomes" is obscure. One clue, however, is that many of his
early visual poems explore the effects of making minimal changes to words
— "barrie" to "beerie" for example alters one phoneme, creating what
linguists call a minimal pair, as would the change from "rain" to "pain" in
one of the untitled visual poems he would publish in 1967 in his first Coach
House Press book, *bp*.[2] Others, by merely substituting a space for a letter,
change the meaning of the remaining letters, as when "rumbled" becomes
"rum led" in "Cycle #37," a poem in his earlier book that year, the British-
published *Konfessions of an Elizabethan Fan Dancer*. Still others explore a
minimal change of accent, as when he changes "warbled" to "warBLED"
— in the poem "Popular Song," also in *Konfessions*. In email conversations
Goodbrand, who shared a room with Barrie in 1965–66, as well as working

aka{ barrie / phillip }Nichol

with him at the Sigmund Samuel, recalls him voraciously reading books on both linguistics and psychoanalysis throughout this period, including Ferdinand de Saussure's *Course in General Linguistics* and possibly Edward Sapir's *Language: An Introduction to the Study of Speech,* and Benjamin Lee Whorf's *Language, Thought and Reality,* and discussing eagerly linguistics' fundamental principle that language is a system of differential signs — a system that creates meanings not by reference to objects outside itself but by minimal differences within. Why would Barrie be reading these? Most likely it was because linguistics' usefulness for poetry, including the work of Saussure, Sapir, and Whorf, had been widely discussed in the Vancouver poetry scene of 1961–64 — forming part of the basis, for example, of Lionel Kearns's manifesto "Stacked Verse," which Barrie had read in the Vancouver issue of Louis Dudek's magazine *Delta* in November 1963.

As well as informing the word changes of the poems above, this understanding of minimal difference would appear to have been the ground of Barrie's "Vowelgrrgyrations" and "The Evening's Ritual" in *Konfessions,* in which the words of each line move one position to the right, and later for his "developer" poems in which each letter of every line would shift one space to the right until the first line was restored. Moreover, in the course of beginning the serial poem *Scraptures,* 1965–66, and along with it unknowingly beginning his lifelong poem *The Martyrology,* Barrie would discover, in the company of his friend and library colleague David Aylward, *The Martyrology*'s founding saint, "St Ranglehold" — and would discover him because of how phonemes are altered by the introduction of a single space between two letters. Visually, "St ranglehold" and "stranglehold" are a "minimal pair." All of *The Martyrology*'s saints would thus be Saussurean — broken not in religious conflict but in language. Like "bp" himself they had emerged from written language.

Goodbrand also remembers Barrie at this time reading and discussing writing by Jacques Lacan — possibly articles that had been published in English (Lacan's first book publication in English was not until 1968). Goodbrand's recollection raises the intriguing possibility that as well as encountering Saussure's understandings that meanings are created within language Barrie was encountering Lacan's account of the Oedipal period as one in which the infant surrenders the illusion of being one with one's mother, and thus with the world, for access to the second-order world of language — a world in which all events, objects, and emotions can exist only through the mediation of words. Such theories would have resounded for Barrie of his childhood substitution of writing stories, like "The Sailor from Mars," for his Oedipal yearnings for union with his mother, and illuminated as well his new resolve both to substitute letters, phonemes, and syllables for embarrassingly "arrogant" desires and intentions, and to write and publish as that secondary signifier, "bpNichol."[3]

The second fortuitous move that Barrie made in this period was to found a magazine. He and Aylward decided in the fall of 1964 to begin publishing a magazine to be called *Ganglia*, which would be open to various kinds of new poetry including concrete. One of the earliest records of it is a March 1965 letter from Barrie to bissett in Mexico, which mentions that Barrie and a friend are thinking about starting a magazine. The letter is signed "love barrie" with the added explanation that "barrie" is also "bp." The magazine was mostly his own idea, he would tell interviewer Geoff Hancock in 1985, but the title was Aylward's. It was to be a site of communication, much like a ganglion is in physiology — or Therafields was for its members. "*Ganglia* was more like a newspaper in my thinking about it. A lot of my editing was news edited. 'I like this line — the rest of it is just okay' and 'what's happening in this line is goddamn exciting, let's develop it and get it out right away!' [. . .] I was not looking to preserve immortal works in magazine form," he would explain to Hancock (34). Barrie was also feeling far from "immortal" himself. He told Hancock that much of his impatience to publish whatever he partly liked in *Ganglia,* and to get something of his own into print, was that he expected to have a short life. "The model for me was Keats, dead at 26. All that bullshit about 'make it wait, make it a considered thing,' was not for me. I could be dead. I thought I would die at 18" (35-6).

Barrie and Aylward had otherwise set up *Ganglia* as a conventional eclectic poetry magazine. It would consider all types of poetry, and would sell subscriptions to interested readers. Barrie recalled to Jack David and Caroline Bayard that Aylward himself was initially uninterested in visual poetry, thinking "it was all bullshit at the time" (Bayard 24). Barrie's main goal was to make young British Columbia writers that he knew — bissett, Phillips, Judy Copithorne — better known in Ontario by giving them an Ontario outlet. The two editors printed and distributed the first issue in

October 1965. It contained artwork by Shives, poetry by British Columbia writers Alexander, bissett, Bowering, Copithorne, Holloway, and Phillips, and poems by bpNichol, Aylward, and Barrie's recent friend Margaret Avison, who also worked at the Sigmund Samuel. Barrie had solicited the Copithorne poems through bissett. In that summer 1965 letter he had told him that they already had four issues planned, and for the second issue had a Red Lane manuscript that he'd obtained from Bowering, and would like to make the fourth issue a bissett book, and later alternate between doing issues devoted to one person and anthology-type ones. He also wanted to do a Jamie Reid issue, telling bissett that Reid was the poet in the first period of the *Tish* group that he admired the most, and that for a considerable time he had been hoping to publish a large collection of his poems. He asked bissett to speak to Reid about such a project.

Phillips, who had four poems in the first issue, wrote in early November that he had received Barrie's "neat mag" but didn't like bissett's poems, and his drawings even less, and also disliked Barrie's visual poems, saying that they did "nothing" for him and asking Barrie to please explain. On November 9, Barrie, Aylward, and the local contributors arranged a *Ganglia* benefit reading at the Bohemian Embassy coffee house but, as he wrote to bissett, the reading had coincided with a power failure that affected most of eastern North America, and attendance, and receipts, were low. In this letter Barrie complained about his difficulty in writing letters, saying that he had a "teerrrrrrrrrrrrbell" block about letters and indicating that he worried that his prose in them would seem stilted to the recipient. He also worried about his ideopomes, telling bissett that he was aesthetically torn between continuing to call these works ideopomes and succumbing to popular convenience and calling them concrete or op-art — and that for some reason he couldn't find enough mental space to think that problem through. Then despair evidently overwhelmed him, and in an extraordinary outburst he exclaimed that this entire letter was shit, and then cursed all poetry, poetry mags, and their idiot-editors and wished them condemned to hell. He vulgarly and somewhat incoherently cursed the goddess of poetry for having seduced, captured, and enslaved him. Whether he'd been drinking, was overtired, or merely determined not to seem stilted is unclear. In his reply bissett — perhaps pondering the same possibilities — assured him that everything would be all right if he could "find yur place in the wheel."

The second *Ganglia, The 1962 Poems of R.S. (Red) Lane*, with an introduction by Bowering, was published shortly after the unfortunate Bohemian Embassy benefit. Barrie's attempts to obtain a Jamie Reid manuscript, however, were in vain. bissett's letters suggest that either Reid didn't have sufficient poems for a collection or that he was worried about the political implications of having his poems associated with Barrie, with Toronto, or possibly with bissett. Barrie told bissett in an early 1966 letter that he might write to Reid himself, and then exclaimed again that he was exasperated, "pissed" at poetry. This time it wasn't the goddess who had angered him, but the poetry scene. Too many of the current poets, he complained, kowtow to established contemporary taste and opinion. He hadn't written any poems for weeks, he boasted, and if this killed the bitch of poetry he

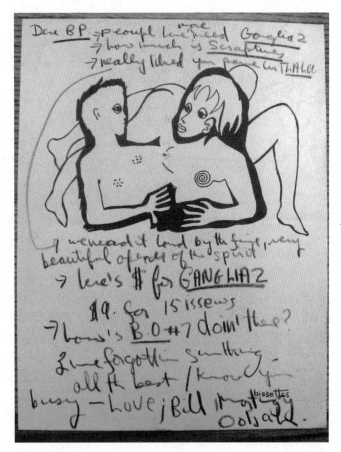

A PAGE FROM A 1966 LETTER TO BARRIE FROM BILL BISSETT.

(bill bissett)

didn't care. This condemnation of his contemporaries was similar to the one he had made to Shives the year before, and may have reflected his frustration at getting magazines to accept his visual poems. However, he had actually been having some success at this. In the past year 31 of his visual poems had appeared in various magazines, in addition to those in his own *Ganglia*. But

aka{ barrie phillip }Nichol

this success was evidently not enough, and his anxieties about "coteries," and about getting wider Canadian acceptance for his "ideopomes," were continuing to fester.

In May 1966 Barrie and Aylward published *Ganglia* 3, with poems by Alexander, Aylward, Bowering, Martina Clinton, Victor Coleman, Judy Copithorne, Pat Lane, Pat Lowther, d.a. levy, and Ian Hamilton Finlay, as well as by Barrie and his brother Don. For issue 4, they published bissett's collection, *We Sleep Inside Each Other All*, with a preface by Sam Perry and an afterword by Barrie. The issue came out in early July in time for Barrie's first visit to Vancouver since his 1964 departure. Victor Coleman and his wife Sarah had done most of the final typing.

For both editors *Ganglia* was a learning experience. It moved Aylward toward becoming a writer of visual and conceptual poetry. It caused both Barrie and him to lose interest in publishing an eclectic poetry magazine for paid subscribers. "Gradually our interest waned," Barrie wrote in his introduction to his *Ganglia Press Index* (1972), "there seemed so many mags publishing more or less straight ["regular"] poems & really as far as publishing went we were less & less interested in that." He continued, "We were discouraged with the whole business of subscribers . . . demanding where their paid for copies were . . . of poems & the endless stream of self-addressed stamped envelopes." Their declining interest meant that it is difficult to know when the fifth and seventh issues were "published" — sometime in 1966 and 1967, receiving, in Barrie's words, "truly pitiful distribution."

But Barrie had enjoyed publishing the small bissett and Lane collections, and printing the occasional pamphlet to give away to friends. With Aylward's financial help, and the co-editing of Rob Hindley-Smith, Lea's son, and the young *Ganglia* fan David W. Harris, recently arrived from up north in Collingwood, Barrie launched in January 1967 the irregular pamphet series *grOnk*. All of its issues were to be mischievously numbered as parts of *Ganglia* 6. All were to be given away to whomever the editors thought would be interested in receiving them. The first issue would include work by the French spatialiste poets j.f. bory and Pierre Garnier, as well as levy, Wagner, bissett, Nichol, Smith, Harris, and Coleman; the second would include the British concrete poets Kenelm Cox, John Furnival, and Cavan McCarthy, as well as Nichol, Harris, and David Phillips. For Barrie this change from selling the magazine to subscribers to giving it away "for free as a news-sheet" (Hancock 32) was both personally liberating and useful in terms of poetic theory.

> *Ganglia* was becoming burdensome. I wanted something that was quicker, and I wanted something that involved no accounting. Since you lose money anyway with a small press, why not do it for free? Do it for free as a news-sheet. Part of the reason for this was *Tish* which I read in Vancouver.
>
> *Tish* was an inspiration for one notion — you didn't have to have subscribers. It could be just something you sent out if you thought the writing was interesting to people. (Hancock 32, 34)

THE COVER OF *PORTRAIT OF DAVID*, GANGLIA PRESS, 1966.

Publishing for Barrie was becoming an act of both communication and friendship — "The results were fantastic. We were able to send news from Canada to other writers we admired" (33). The press's various chapbooks and pamphlets were no longer products but gifts — a concept that would eventually inform not only Barrie's private printing of the personal pamphlets and booklets, such as *Familiar* (1980), that he created as gifts to family and close friends, but also the poetics and overall conception of the seventh book of his *The Martyrology*. It would also inform his later refusal of publication with large commercial publishers.

aka{ barrie phillip }Nichol

At a 1964–65 New Year's Eve party Barrie had been introduced by Lea Hindley-Smith's daughter Josephine, at that time a young folksinger, to Stan Bevington who had gone into business that year as a printer and would soon found Coach House Press. Only slightly older than Barrie, Bevington welcomed young artists into his shop, which quickly became a place for Barrie and others to hang out, learn how to set type, print single pages on Bevington's Vandercook proof press, and meet other Toronto-area writers. The shop was also a source for Barrie of random pieces of paper left over from commercial printing work, and suitable for irregular pamphlets. Much of *Ganglia* was printed on a hand-cranked mimeograph machine, but some of Barrie's first self-published ephemera, and some *grOnk* releases, would be hand-set by Barrie on Bevington's proof press and then xeroxed at the Sigmund Samuel Library. He recalled in 1987 that these early 1965 experiences at Bevington's shop

> had a fundamental effect on my view of literature. i was already heading this way anyhow, which is to say toward an increasing awareness of how visual literature was, because of my interest in visual poetry, etc., but there's no doubt about it, the effect of setting my own texts, letter by letter, word by word, line by line, was to create in me a whole new awareness of all the components that go into any literature.

He also recalled that Stan and early Coach House editor Wayne Clifford invited him to start work "on what became known as my purple package, a slipcase that included a long poem, a flip poem, a record of sound poems, and an envelope full of visual poems and poem sculptures" (Miki 2002 425). This was to be the box book *bp*, whose contents and shape evolved over the two years it took to produce it. In a sense, Barrie had been invited to compile a book.

With *Ganglia* Barrie had quickly plugged into an international network of visual poet-publishers: bill bissett and his *blew ointment* magazine and press in Vancouver; d.a. levy and his Renegade Press and Seven Flowers Press in Cleveland; D.r. Wagner with his press : today : niagara in Niagara Falls, New York, and later magazine *runcible spoon* in Wisconsin and then California; and in Europe Ian Hamilton Finlay and his magazine *Poor.Old.*

Tired.Horse; Bob Cobbing and his Writers Forum Press; Cavan McCarthy and *Tlaloc*; Nicholas Zurbrugg and his magazine *Stereo Headphones*; and Dom Sylvester Houédard who on first receiving Barrie's "packet of truly surprising concrete" in October 1965 was able to quickly forward and recommend them to Jasia Reichardt. She was curating a show of international concrete work, "Between Poetry and Painting," for spring 1966 at the Institute of Contemporary Art in Arlington Mill, Gloucestershire. That show and its catalogue introduced Barrie's work to more European visual poets such as John Furnival and Pierre Garnier, who exclaimed in his first letter to Barrie "vos poèmes . . . sont une révélation."

Each time Barrie wrote for a subscription or publication list from such poet-publishers he would offer to send some of his own work, which, in such a small circle of visual poetry practitioners, was quickly becoming known. Needing interesting work for *Ganglia*, he would also invite them to send work to him. *Ganglia* would publish the book by bissett, and individual poems by bissett, levy, and Finlay, and in its 70-plus-issue successor *grOnk* would publish poems by bissett, levy, McCarthy, Wagner, Garnier, Furnival, and Zurbrugg, and a book by Wagner. bissett would become the *Ganglia* and *grOnk* distributor in Vancouver, levy in Cleveland, and Cobbing in England.

Poems by Barrie would be published as pamphlets by levy's Seven Flowers Press in Cleveland in 1965 and by Wagner's press : today : niagara in Niagara Falls, New York, in 1966 and by his press Runcible Spoon in Sacramento in 1968. Barrie's poems would also be published in England by Finlay's *Poor.Old.Tired.Horse*, as well as by McCarthy's *Tlaloc*, during 1966. Tlaloc Press would publish his *Dada Lama* as a pamphlet in 1968. His first book, a collection of visual poetry called *Konfessions of an Elizabethan Fan Dancer*, would be published in England in January 1967 by Bob Cobbing's Writers Forum Press — a month before his first Canadian book, Coach House Press's *bp*. His visual poetry would be exhibited not only at Jasia Reichardt's Gloucestershire show in 1966, but also at shows later that year in Paris and in San Sebastián, Spain. In 1967 his work would be included in shows in Paris and Madrid, in 1970 in a show in Indianapolis; in 1971 in shows in Holland, Germany, and England; and in 1972 in shows in Uruguay, Chile, and Spain. When Emmett Williams began editing his international *Anthology of Concrete Poetry* for New York's Something Else

Press in 1966, Barrie was among the first writers he invited to send work. In less than two years Barrie had gone from being a confused young man who could see "no future" to being — in the small but intense world of visual poetry — an internationally respected literary figure. His brother Don would be astonished by his sudden shift from timidity to the self-confidence required to perform the strange noises of sound poetry — Barrie's newest genre — in public.

Lea Hindley-Smith had a large role in this — Goodbrand writes that she could "almost magically reveal to individuals what was hidden within them" (27). It seems in fact likely that much of the work Lea did with Barrie was to make him see himself as worthy of speaking, writing, publishing, of releasing his voice. Lea herself, according to Goodbrand, had in the late 1950s been strongly influenced by Edmund Bergler's theories of psychic masochism in his book *The Basic Neurosis*. That book and its insights, she had told Goodbrand, had been the key to her own renewed confidence in Toronto in 1955 — confidence that had freed her to resume work as a therapist. "Lea [had] now realized it wasn't others who were holding her back; it was her own self-hatred." She had been moved by Bergler's book to "change her own destiny rather than blame others."

> Bergler believed that the internal, frequently vicious voice of self-criticism is interested in inflicting pain, not in remedying our deficiencies. We are controlled by our guilt because we listen to and accept its cruel judgments. More sinister still, we take unconscious pleasure in being punished because we hate the helplessness that persists in us from our infancy. (23)

Barrie — convinced that he had been ignored by a depressed mother when a "helpless" infant, and that he had been given little parental encouragement when he had become a budding writer — may have had ample reason for the lack of self-confidence his brother had noted in him on his arrival in Toronto, or to blame circumstances or the non-understanding of others for his unhappiness.[4] It is very likely that psychic masochism was a part of Lea's diagnosis of him. Paul Dutton recalls Barrie telling him once that, early in his therapy, Lea and another woman had praised him repeatedly while he was under relaxation, and that he had wept and writhed at having to endure their words.

The various letters in Barrie's correspondence files also show that the poets he was contacting in Europe — Finlay, born 1925, Houédard, born 1924, Cobbing, born 1920, Garnier, born 1928, McCarthy, born 1943 — recognized him as a talented peer from the outset.[5] That alone, to be judged by his work rather than by his history, appearance, or ability to amuse and entertain, must have given Barrie an enormous boost of confidence. The European poets also routinely mentioned their sound poetry performances as extensions of their visual poetry, and inquired whether he was also doing sound performances. The question made a certain sense, because unlike writers of "regular" poetry, visual poets had nothing to read in public unless they could find a way to perceive their visual poems as scripts for sound poems — as Barrie would do in 1966 with "Dada Lama" and the "Turnips Are" poem he had written on the back of Dace's despairing letter. Both of these works would be included on Barrie's amusingly titled 1968 sound poetry LP *Mother Love*, and the jacket would feature photos of some of those who had presumably, in various ways, helped make it possible — his mother and father, his brother DJ, his sister Deanna and husband Barrie, bill bissett, Andy Phillips, David Phillips, Rob Hindley-Smith, and David Aylward.

Certainly Barrie's reception by European visual and sound poets was different from the one his parents were giving to his new life. Being told in 1965 that some of Barrie's new poems were being published, his father declared that some people might like them, but they would never be included in a school textbook. His mother responded to a new photograph Barrie had sent her that year by telling him that the picture hadn't been a big hit with his brother Bob, and that it didn't look like her son. She urged him to take better care of his appearance and advised that he could be quite handsome when his hair was much shorter.

And in 1971 she would write a poem in couplets for him, saying that she had never believed that the day would come when she wouldn't understand her youngest son — possibly hoping to gently remind him how different his poems were from her understanding of poetry. She and Bob were not alone, however, in lamenting Barrie's ever-lengthening hair. His future wife Ellie recalls that one of his Sigmund Samuel supervisors had offered him five dollars to get it cut.

His reception in Canada in this period was similar to that in Europe. When accepting one of his poems for *Alphabet* in April 1965, James Reaney respectfully asked him how he would like his author-name to appear. In February 1966 Louis Dudek asked him if he could publish six of his poems in the final issue of *Delta*, and concluded his note, "I'm definitely with you." Also warmly receiving him as a writer was Margaret Avison, whom Barrie seems to have met in late 1964 or early 1965 at the Sigmund Samuel, where, as a doctoral student, she had a study carrel for which he was responsible. His playful letters to her in the summer of 1965, when working toward including a poem of hers in the first issue of *Ganglia*, together with her similarly playful replies in some of the margins, reflected an easy and comfortable relationship.[6] He told Bayard and David that as well as being a good friend, Avison "was a tremendous influence. When I got into *Winter Sun* and read those poems — once again it was an education to the ear. The same sort of education Sheila Watson was to me. I heard better after reading those books. It extended my sensibility of how language could move."

In late 1965 Avison would also be the one who inadvertently pointed him back toward "straight" or "regular" poetry — poetry constructed primarily out of sequences of sentences. She had heard of Raymond Souster's project to edit and publish a Contact Press anthology of "new" poetry by young writers, tentatively titled "Poetry 67" after the now defunct Ryerson Press "series" of *Poetry 62* (ed. Mandel and Pilon) and *Poetry 64* (ed. Colombo and Godbout). Part of Souster's plan was rumoured to be to include all the *Tish* poets whom Colombo's anthology had been too early to include — Marlatt, Wah, Reid, Hogg, and Cull in particular. These were poets who would not be able to have full Contact Press collections now that the press was about to cease operation. Souster had already solicited submissions from numerous poets with whose "regular" poetry he was familiar through *Tish*, *Island*, *Evidence*, *Imago*, *The Canadian Forum*, and similar magazines. In the 1976 Bayard/David interview, Barrie related that on hearing about the project from Avison,

> I roared home and literally sat down with everything I'd learned in a year and a half of focussing on form and on the page as a

field of play, and rewrote those [earlier "regular"] poems. My ear was better. I could hear better after that year. I had a much better sense of rhythm, of music. I was better able to listen to the words and less concerned with imposing some sort of preconceived notion of wisdom. . . . (Bayard 19)

He was attempting to transform old Barrie Nichol poems into new bpNichol ones. He sent a package of 29 poems to Souster, 14 of which appeared in the anthology, now titled *New Wave Canada*. It was published very late in 1966. Some of these poems would reappear the next year in the booklet "Journeying and the Returns," as part of the Coach House box-book *bp* that Barrie was still assembling. In *bp* Barrie would thus be a "regular" poet as well as an ideopome poet and sound poet.

THE COVER OF *GRONK*, VOLUME 1, ISSUE 6/7, SHOWING DAVID AYLWARD, DAVID W. HARRIS, BARRIE NICHOL, AND ROB HINDLEY-SMITH.

aka{ barrie phillip }Nichol

9. Captain Poetry

at certain points his idiocies became my own. particularly
the Captain Poetry sonnet which is pure autobiography

— bpNichol, *Captain Poetry Poems Complete*, 2010

Ceci n'est pas une pipe.

— Magritte, 1928

I didn't feel M's film unjust to you. I just found you
more confident and articulate than I remembered you.
You seem so far beyond me. M says he feels that's a
fault in the film — cutting made you seem more confi-
dent, more aggressive perhaps?

— Sharon Barbour to Barrie Nichol, March 1970

Barrie had spent much of 1964–65 trying to distinguish his bpNichol
ideopomes from his "regular" poems although paradoxically by the end
of this period he believed that it was by creating ideopomes that he had

learned to write more interesting regular ones. In late 1965 bissett argued strongly against this segregating of ways of writing.

> . . . does it help to name yur pomes at all, bp, theyre there grown, the name is possibly for the filers, th staff cards, like "sweet william" or hollyhock, whether they're ideopomes or whatever, they are still being there, an it doesn't become an ideopome rather than an cap pomes just because they're calld one or th other, they surely always become what they are, an' by ideopome, yu mean they're not as poem as untyped pome, sure they are, yu maybe suggest that th form is in sum ones a caprice by calling them anything, peopul are so slow to see a pome at all i know tho th name may encourage them, to see it as the sumthing else it is-like, what's in a name, th ideopome is as much yu as th more "conventional" one 'bout andrew

bissett could have pointed to parts of Barrie's "Captain Poetry" poems, which he was currently writing and beginning to publish parts of in *Ganglia*, as being as visual at times as the ideopomes. He knew and admired this new work, calling it in one letter a "work of genius," and would eventually publish it as a joint grOnk/blew ointment press book — in March of 1971. However, in terms of Barrie's intentions — to satirize and ridicule "the kind of *courier du bois* [sic] image of the [Canadian] poet; you go into a bar, slam your poems on the table and order a few rounds of brews for all the guys, which was an image I was never too attracted to" (Norris interview, Miki 2002 241) — the sequence pretty well failed, which possibly was why bissett liked it. A more mature Barrie speaking to Norris in 1978 was able to articulate his intention much more clearly and interestingly than the novice poet of 1965.[1] Much of the text's humour was both juvenile and ambiguous, which left it easy for someone to mis-read the text as being in praise of "the poet as super-hero" (241). But in its numerous stanzas that physically deconstructed words and phrases, and its inclusion of cartoonish drawings, it combined Barrie's ideopome techniques with sequential narrative in ways that foreshadowed how he would write in the later books of *The Martyrology*.

Exactly which macho Canadian poets Barrie believed had cultivated a "super-hero" "courier du bois" image was not clear in the poems nor in the interview. Was it Archibald Lampman, Bliss Carman, and Charles G.D. Roberts, and their poems about canoes and photographs of themselves with Native Canadians? Was it Al Purdy brawling over poetry at the Quinte Hotel, Irving Layton celebrating his sunburned back, or bissett in his fringed deerskin jacket? Certainly Barrie himself was not attempting to develop a macho image — "an image I was never too attracted to." Even the book's self-parodying "autobiographical" sonnet, most likely addressed to Dace, is more black romantic than macho. While many of his male contemporaries were tasting their blood, organizing poet baseball teams, bragging about their long peashooters, or meeting regularly and "creatively" at Vancouver's Cecil Hotel beer parlour or Toronto's Grossman's Tavern, Barrie was meeting with therapy groups and earnestly seeking to develop "honest" communications and, with women, long-term and trustingly monogamous relationships.

But the superhero idea of a "Captain Poetry" was attractive at a time when poetry magazines were beginning to proliferate, public poetry readings increase, and Canadian nationalism surge. bissett in a slightly later letter would jestingly refer to Barrie as "capn poetry" — because "chef" Barrie was beginning to solicit visual poems for his Oberon Press anthology *The Cosmic Chef.* And Michael Ondaatje would later use the title *Sons of Captain Poetry* for the film he shot of Barrie and other poets in 1970. Who Captain Poetry is in this film, or whether the sons are prodigal, Oedipally troubled, or chips off the old block, Ondaatje would leave largely to the film's viewers.

Meanwhile various changes had been occurring in other parts of Barrie's life. In the summer of 1965 he had joined an evening group of Lea Hindley-Smith's clients, mostly Catholic priests and nuns, whom she had agreed to train as psychotherapists who would eventually leave their orders and help her deal with her expanding practice. Then in the spring of 1966 Barrie took a course in diagnostic testing, after which he was hired by Lea to administer such texts — the Rorschach, the Thematic Apperception Test, the House-Tree-Person Test — to incoming Therafields clients. The new job enabled him to leave his position at the library and to spend more hours on his writing. In September he and the other trainee therapists took on their first clients, while also continuing their own therapies, most of them with Lea. Barrie would record in his 1984 resumé that he worked as a Therafields psychotherapist from 1966 to 1982. Both the resumé and his surviving appointment books show that he often had as many as 15 clients, seeing them once or twice a week for one-hour sessions — a similar caseload to that of the other therapists. He moved that fall of 1966 from the house group in which he had lived since 1964 into a large main floor room, which he shared with Rob Hindley-Smith. The house was located at 59 Admiral Road, and the front rooms were Lea's office. She and Harry Hindley-Smith shared the coach house behind. Next door, at 55 Admiral, was a house group in which one of the new members was

Eleanor Hiebert, a member of the Sisters of Our Lady of Sion whose order was — like those of the earlier priests, monks, and nuns — allowing her to consider psychotherapy.

Another event during this busy September was Barrie's meeting Ondaatje, possibly when Ondaatje was visiting Coach House Press to discuss the publication of *The Dainty Monsters*. He wrote to "dear bp" later that month from Kingston, where he was completing his M.A. at Queen's University, saying it was good to see

THE JACKET OF BARRIE'S FIRST SOUND POEM RECORDING, "BORDERS," COACH HOUSE PRESS, 1967.

him and that he was enclosing four poems for *Ganglia*, and then signed his full name. The poems would appear in Barrie's irregular *Ganglia* offshoots *grOnk* and *Synapsis*.

The next year began with Barrie's first two book publications. Bob Cobbing's small January 1967 edition of Barrie's *Konfessions of an Elizabethan Fan Dancer* sold out in England, and would be reprinted in 1969, but it would have little distribution in Canada. The February release of *bp*, Coach House's unusual box or "slip case" of bpNichol items, however, attracted national attention if only for its uniqueness — one of a "mind-blowing succession of whatsits" Dennis Lee would recall during a 2010 Coach House celebration.[2] The box contained literary constructions in four media: a "conventional" book of "regular" poems; perfect bound and titled "Journeying and the Returns"; the small vinyl recording of sound poetry "Borders"; an envelope of single-sheet poems, many of them visual poems, titled "Letters Home"; and a "flip book" of bound pages that created a moving image when riffed with a thumb, titled — with a bow to the Troggs's Billboard number one recording of the previous year — "Wild Thing." The box presented a quadruple-threat writer, one who could, as the accompanying manifesto "Statement" declared, "reach . . . thru the poem by as many exits and entrances as are possible" — who could deliver regular poems, sound poems, visual poems, or poem-constructions. That many people believed its title to be "Journeying and the Returns" amusingly revealed their preference for the "regular." It would have been equally reasonable to have believed the box's title to have been "Borders," "Letters Home," or "Wild Thing." Some of these titles reflected the ambiguity of Barrie's personal understandings of his situation. Was he a Vancouver writer temporarily in Toronto? Where was the "home" that his letters were written to? To what places were the "returns" of his journeys? What did it mean that bill bissett was now his most trusted border-testing writer friend — as he had declared in a 1966 letter, his "brother" as a writer?

The box's *bp* title was also a covert "othering" of Barrie's "bpNichol" persona, a signal — largely undetected at the time — that this persona was the name of a text and a process of writing that Barrie Nichol oversaw as much as it was an alternative name for his person. The two alphabetic signs of "bp" pointed to additional alphabetic and visual signs. "Ceci n'est pas une pipe." This divide between the mortal Barrie Nichol and his creation, the potentially immortal bpNichol, would become both more striking and more poignant as the former aged and the latter matured with the spectacular later books of *The Martyrology*. The mortal Barrie had in fact already gone into one of his still not infrequent depressions. He wrote to bissett that he had become depressed once his book had been published and was now sitting around and wondering what he was going to do next. He was confident that he would be continuing his work in psychoanalyis, he wrote, had some idea of what he soon would be reading, but had no idea about what he might next be writing.

A little later that spring he wrote bissett to apologize for a "misunderstanding" that had caused him not to tell bissett that there had been still time to send poems to Souster for consideration for *New Wave Canada*. He blamed it partly on his own continuing difficulty in writing letters, and then adopted a Steinian style as if it could help himself write this one. He told bissett that he was currently almost the only one he could bring himself to write to, that something collapsed within him whenever he attempted a letter, and that he couldn't communicate in them like he could

BARRIE IN 1967.

when he talked. He asked bissett to not only write often but also to write from his heart — that writing from his heart might cause him to be able to do the same thing. Then he told bissett that he not only doubted his current writing but was no longer sure even about what he believed, that he was nauseated by

the poetry he had written since the *bp* book, and that he was experiencing an utter collapse of faith. He asked bissett what he believed. He worried that too many people lie to themselves and others; he asked bissett to write to him about ordinary things, not just about poetry. As in some of his earlier letters to bissett, desperation smouldered in every sentence. bill seems to have been the one correspondent that Barrie trusted with such feelings, and unfortunately in this instance his reply does not appear to have survived.

Despite his various confusions, 1967 saw Captain Barrie — already the leader of the small group who were publishing *Ganglia* and *grOnk*, and clearly a leader through *bp* in the range to which new poetry might aspire — offered more leadership roles. In the spring he was invited by Ray Souster, the first president and primary organizer of the new League of Canadian Poets, to be its founding secretary. Barrie was the only writer under 50 years of age on the executive. In the summer he was invited by the Canada Council to be a member of the Soundings Committee that was to be tasked with reorganizing its system of grants. In the late fall he was named by Lea Hindley-Smith to be vice president of the now formally organized Therafields corporation. The appointment, together with that of her 20-year-old son Rob as president, baffled and enraged many of the older newly trained therapists, but Barrie would hold the position until 1982. Moreover she also named Barrie to co-chair with Rob the weekly therapists seminar — the seminar that oversaw their work and dealt with counter-tranferences — during her absences.

In his history of Therafields,[3] Goodbrand explains the circumstances that brought about these eyebrow-raising appointments. The 1966 expansion of Lea Hindley-Smith's work from a single practice into an institution in which eventually more than 40 therapists would serve the needs of upwards of 600 clients, and operate approximately 25 house groups and therapy centres in downtown Toronto and at a farm in Mono township north of Toronto, had occurred at a time when the symptoms of Hindley-Smith's largely untreated type 2 diabetes had begun to grow. The newly practising therapists, most of them in their upper thirties, holding university degrees, and backgrounds in Catholic religious orders, were eager to take initiative and responsibility in shaping the new institution, and had collectively raised the money to purchase a farm suitable for retreats and weekend-long group therapies. They had named two of themselves to liaise with the ailing Hindley-Smith as her "advisers and assistants in the administration of the nascent organization." She, however, expected the two to "take charge" during her illnesses and absences, and when this did not happen at a crucial moment at the end of the summer, requested their replacement. She wanted people she could trust to "replace her . . . while she was away," Goodbrand writes, "and convey her input and directions to the [therapist] group" (91). This group — called by Hindley-Smith "Hypno I" because of its training in hypnosis therapy — was one that

aka{ barrie phillip }Nichol

Barrie was both within and without. He trained within it, but also lived with Hindley-Smith and her son and daughter, and was now virtually a member of her family.

Quite possibly Hindley-Smith was wary of losing control of her new organization to people who were still neophytes as therapists but overshadowed her in academic knowledge. Several of them were close to completing doctoral degrees. Goodbrand suggests also that she was aware that Barrie and Rob would have much more understanding for the new generation of clients Therafields was attracting: no longer mostly ex-priests and nuns influenced by the new freedoms of Vatican II but now predominantly young people of the 1960s who were seeking the self-understanding and group friendships that the "age of Aquarius" was promising. A typical therapist response to their appointments, Goodbrand indicates, was that of Dan Macdonald: "I thought Robbie was far, far too young with no experience. Barrie was a poet. That [administration] wasn't his forte, and besides, he couldn't stand up to Lea. At that point I felt we lost the dream of Therafields."

Goodbrand suggests that such a response was understandable given the ages and backgrounds of those involved:

> Rob was twenty years old, had not formally attended school since early high school and had no administrative experience. Barrie, a few years older, had been part of the learning experience in Therafields from the beginning, and had administered psychological tests and interviewed clients seeking therapy. bp, as he now preferred to be called, was thought to be astute, because he recommended the pairing of clients and therapists, and he was trusted. Rob and Barrie were best friends with a giddy bonhommie, joking around in a way completely foreign to thirty-five-year-old priests accustomed to more dignified behavior. They were still thought of as boys. Neither was interested in an intellectual or academic career. (92)

Toronto psychologist Brenda Doyle, then a young member of a Therafields learning group, who has written a lengthy blog "Thoughts on Therafields" in response to Goodbrand's book, writes that these Hypno I reactions to their appointments were largely covert — that "[m]ost simply accepted the decision without a struggle." She quotes therapist Philip McKenna:

> When Lea went away to North Carolina she left Rob and Barr[ie] in charge which was absolutely crazy. She would bring up that kind of idea: "Wouldn't it be great for them to lead things? They work so well together." Then it would happen. There wasn't much talk about it but it wasn't much of a surprise. By then they were chairing the group when she wasn't there. But they were "puer" in the Jungian sense — the boys. We allowed them to take over by not intervening. ("Thoughts," October 31, 2010)

In this Therafields/Hypno I company, Barrie's task of proving himself worthy was more difficult than it had been in the world of "letters" and alphabets. Here he was being judged not necessarily by what he wrote or produced, but also by how he looked and how he sometimes acted. He was also being judged by a different understanding of what was "intellectual," and by people who suspected that he was being exploited by Lea for her own purposes.[4] But Barrie accepted the new position willingly, perhaps because it had been offered by Lea, who was at this point was already for him the person that *The Martyrology, Book II* would declare was the one "without whose act of friendship quite literally none of this would have been written." She had "literally stopped me from killing myself" he told Irene Niechoda in June 1984 (1992 67).

In his resumé Barrie described his new assignment as involvement in budgets and in various levels of decision-making, values decisions, supervision of all Therafields buildings, liaison and arbitration between therapists and managers, publisher, editor, and originator of various staff and general community newsletters, and public relations. Particularly important for him was his role in the various newsletters. Here he was on the firmest ground, and could use his command of language to define himself to the therapists and the larger client community while also writing "ex cathedra" from Lea's implicit authority. The manifesto-like tone that he employed that spring in the *Axis* editorial quoted in Chapter 7 was one that had already succeeded in his "statement"-preface to his book *bp*.

aka{ barrie phillip }Nichol

10. Psychotherapy Poetics

*. . . after psychoanalysis, opera, at least in its traditional
form, is no longer possible.*

— Slavoj Žižek, *Lacan: The Silent Partners*, 261

*Most people repress their richness and their fullness,
and this group was disturbed because so many people
were living only half lives because they were not free
enough to live whole lives. We were disturbed by people
becoming old before their time because they've lost the
joy of laughter and the sense of humour.*

*We have come to recognize such a thing as pathological
independence and have seen that the overly-indepen-
dent individual is very frightened and has to deny his
dependencies by denying them altogether.*

— Lea Hindley-Smith, *Axis*, May 15, 1974

This chapter could have been titled "Psychotherapy and Poetics" or
"Psychotherapy and Poetry" — it is indeed about those interactive pairings,
but also about a closer pairing than even those phrases suggest. Beginning

in 1966 Barrie in his "regular" poetry developed a poetics directly out of psychoanalytic procedures and understandings. This is something Nichol critics have for the most part overlooked, or perhaps even tried to overlook, often dutifully misled by Barrie's occasional declarations that his writing and therapy work were only distantly related. In general they have treated Barrie's 15-year work as a lay psychological therapist as if it were similar to Wallace Stevens's employment as a surety claims specialist for the Hartford Livestock Insurance Company — as something that the poet *also* did, alongside his writing, but rarely as part of it. In Barrie's case this was simply not so.[1]

The evidence in Barrie's notebooks suggests that his therapy was relatively conventional for the early Therafields period. It was a therapy built on Freudian concepts through Lea's readings of Melanie Klein, Edmund Bergler, Wilhelm Reich, Jacob Moreno, Robert Lindner, and others. An individual session would likely have begun with Lea leading Barrie into an at least moderate state of relaxation, during which a dream could be recalled and analyzed or childhood events or fantasies remembered and reconsidered. The relaxation — intended to exclude immediate daily concerns and increase one's focus on pervasive memories and associations — would have been especially relevant for Barrie who suffered from frequent anxiety or panic attacks. Lea's relaxation mantra, directing the client to focus on body parts successively and cumulatively from the toes to the top of the head, would — with minor changes of vocabulary and phrase — become internalized and used by Barrie himself for personal stress relief, or later as a therapist on his own clients. Lea may also have employed abreactive therapy, using the relaxed state to direct the client to relive an intensely traumatic moment — such as that moment of utter psychological abandonment by his mother that Barrie writes of believing he was experiencing when an infant.

Barrie also participated in two kinds of group therapy. He was a member of one of Lea's first "deep" groups (later to be known as "standard" groups), in which members witnessed and contributed to each other's undergoing of relaxation therapies and dream analysis work in the group setting. In 1967 this group would become the training group "Hypno I"— so named because Lea perceived relaxation, during which the therapist typically made suggestions such as "every nerve and every muscle relaxes and rests" or "you are going back now to when you are very young," as a mild form of hypnosis.[2] And Barrie was a member of a house group in which he experienced what Lea thought of as "horizontal" therapy in contrast to "deep" — a therapy that focussed not on clients' inner lives but on their social interactions. The group-house residents, who paid rent as part of their therapy fees, would meet once a week or more with Lea as a group to analyze the difficulties and impasses that their living together had occasioned. At this time in Therafields practice "deep" individual material that these meetings revealed would be worked with mainly in individual therapy sessions — a policy that was changed once newly trained therapists began taking over much of Lea's work.

Therafields therapy was based partly on the assumption that its clients would bring their most profound and troubling anxieties to their group or individual session. They were at the very least confronted and told to come back later if they attended either occasion visibly inebriated or on drugs. They were also strongly discouraged from chattering or joking when gathering for groups — in the belief that such chatter could prematurely release anxious energies that were essential to the group's work. The group would sometimes begin with a long period of silence as the therapists waited to see which members' anxieties were so strong that they would find the silence unbearable. It is this understanding of therapy work that Barrie was referring to when he told Niechoda in her July 1983 interview with him that *The Martyrology* was not, or should not have been, a "therapeutic text" because he was already "doing my therapy over *here* — in my therapy [with Lea]." He had similar thoughts about the lyrics he had published in "Journeying and the Returns" (written 1963–66), *The Other Side of the Room* (written 1966–69), and *Monotones* (written 1968–70). He told Niechoda that one "problem he had with those poems is that to a degree I'm doing that. I'm using them."

> In a way I'm taking material to those [poems] I should be taking to my session, to use the language we would use in therapy. I'm not dealing with it over *here*. Instead I'm shoving it in [the poems] as a place to *not* deal with it. Literally for me "dealing with something" meant sitting still long enough to actually look at the thing, see how I felt about it, understand what the source of that feeling was, in a very immediate way. (1992, 135)

aka{ barrie phillip }Nichol

He told Niechoda that if he subsequently used material from his sessions in a poem, that material was no longer an interesting mystery, it was "part of the world of fact. 'This was an emotion I had.'"

> It wasn't something to be treasured, raised above, something that made me a better person because I had this emotion, or superior because I wrote a poem and look how sensitive I am. In those early poems I was kind of making a case over here and saying "look how I'm suffering and look how I'm sensitive." That's what I mean by the sentimentalization. And I find it repugnant. I find it in a lot of contemporary poetry, and it really bothers me.

"Repugnant" — it's a strong word from someone most often thought of as eclectic, generous, and tolerant — especially as an editor. He of course meant more that such poems are repugnant than that their writers may be, although clearly he also found the ambition to write such poems repugnant, as well as what such poems do to popular understanding of poetry — that it is a place to implicitly brag about one's sensitivity, pain, and self-invited misfortunes — again the "I fall upon the thorns of life, I bleed" poem that historically has made numerous writers appear impressively "sensitive."

Elsewhere in this Niechoda interview Barrie said that he had once made more "than needed to be" of the "interpersonal difficulties I might have had with [future wife] Ellie or my mother, or whatever."

> The use therapy had for me — this is thinking about it now from a poetic angle as opposed to a personal angle — was that I could go beyond getting hung up on the level of false mystery — sentimentalization. I read those poems and I think, I'm not confronting the material here. I'm just saying "wow! Is this pain I feel ever mysterious. Does it ever come from a mysterious source!" Well, it didn't spring from a mysterious source. It's because we moved a whole bunch when I was a kid, and I felt alienated from my ma, and my ma was depressed all the time because we were moving etc. etc. etc. It was a no-win situation. But then to say that and say "well hey — I'm in touch with the Eternal Mystery of the universe [. . .]!"

> Through therapy I could get beyond those false mysteries and start to deal with the real mysteries of the world. (1992, 134)[3]

There are echos here of his unrealized intention in the *Captain Poetry Poems* — to ridicule writers who "use" poetry as a means of self-celebration, or assertions, or heroic independence. As well, as elsewhere in Nichol's thinking about poetry, the influence of Robert Duncan is evident. In his various lectures that had resonated throughout Vancouver's poetry scene in the early 1960s, Duncan had deplored what he called "crisis poets" who unconsciously trigger crises in their personal lives so that they can have exquisite sufferings to write about. A poet in his relationship with language was like a priest in his relationship to the Church, Duncan had argued. A poet should not seek self-aggrandizement but rather the flourishing of language and poetry. A poem should not be led by the writer's personal ideas, themes, or feelings, or conviction that he can speak authoritatively about any of these, but by the language and its sounds.

In July 1971, virtually while *The Martyrology, Book I* and *Book II* were being printed, Barrie wrote an unsolicited letter to Duncan. He began by declaring that this was a kind of fan letter, an expression of appreciation, of a kind that he had not written since he was a child and sent letters to various stars of the cinema. He told Duncan how much his poetry moved him, and how instructive that was, since he often had no knowledge of the facts or histories of which Duncan wrote. It was instructive because it demonstrated how the sound of poetry was more important than the allusions it made — and he repeated the word "sound" several times as if the sound of the word was illustrating his observation. He then confessed to Duncan that he had often felt insecure about his own poems because they seemed to lack profound or learned references, but that after reading Duncan's recent series of poems "Passages" (in his 1968 book *Bending the Bow*) he had been both amazed by what Duncan had achieved and reassured about his own writing. The complex musicality of those poems, he wrote, confirmed him in the decision he had made long ago to let the sound of his poems direct their content, even if they consequently moved toward meanings that he had not anticipated or wanted.

Barrie wrote this letter during the period in which he was beginning to understand the relationship between his therapy and his poetry, and how that changing understanding had been reflected in *The Martyrology*'s two books — *Book I*, which he tried to revise even as the pages were being printed (Niechoda 1992 48), misusing his life's misadventures for mysterious poetry and celebrations of fantasy, *Book II* achieving an understanding of how insight into the reality of his life could open a way to writing for its own sake. Earlier, this understanding of creation for its own sake had been available to him mostly in his "ideopomes."

In the various interviews he gave in subsequent years Barrie would often hint broadly at the psychoanalytic ground of his poetics. In his *Axis* editorials he was praising honest communication to the Therafields community, and in his journals deploring how he was not able to declare to friends or in therapy sessions his own honest feelings. In response to the question "what is the use of poetry?" he was telling Raôul Duguay:

> I think poetry is language raised to its highest power & its joy — & language is the expression of the total body [. . . .] — if everybody's using language raised to its highest power then they take what they say more seriously — they don't play cheap in conversation — they really say what they feel — because language is not a cheap thing anymore — it's a felt thing an important thing. (1973, reprinted Miki 2002 125)

Duguay, of course, had no way of recognizing that "the total body" was a reference to the bioenergetic therapies that some Therafields therapists, including Barrie's brother Don, were practising and writing about in the early 1970s, or that the statement "they really say what they feel" was echoing a fundamental dialogical goal of Therafields group therapy.

In a 1974 interview in which Barrie fielded questions from Daphne Marlatt, Gladys Hindmarch, Pierre Coupey, and Dwight Gardner, the first question, from Marlatt, was about his statement published with *The Martyrology, Book II* in 1972 that "we must return again to the human voice and listen / rip off the mask of words to free the sounds." The statement appears to have had one of its origins in the psychodramatic abreactive therapies that Lea Hindley-Smith had developed in 1955 (see Goodbrand 27–28) and later routinely trained her student therapists to employ.[4] In

Therafields, groups and individuals would be confronted by the thera-
pist, with the assistance of group members (who often called out to the
person "use your voice"), with a dramatic reenactment of a childhood
trauma — a reenactment that could drive that person beyond language,
its rationalizations and excuses, into convulsive wails and cries of despair,
anger, and grief. Honest communication, which Barrie would have wit-
nessed in his therapy work numerous times. Barrie replied first with an
account about his work in sound poetry "to free the emotional content
of speech from ideation or from words, necessarily, and to just be able to
let out the voice," detoured into a more intellectual account of the Hopi
Palongawhoya legend,[5] swerved back to a comment about how he aimed
"to not use words as a masking, which a lot of people do in conversations,"
and then to making a list of evasive or dishonest ways of speaking. The
questioners had no easy way to connect the dots within Barrie's complex
response. The next questioner asked him about characterization in his
fiction. But Barrie was already subsconsciously connecting those dots and
began his answer:

> Yeah. Well you see, in the work I do, which is working for Therafields
> as a theradramist and seeing people and talking with them about
> what's bothering them, what you're doing in the situation is not
> imposing yourself on the person but basically being a catalyst: to
> ask questions they can't formulate, to put them in the situation where
> they're going to have to deal with the material themselves and where
> you help them as much as you can. It negates a certain type of
> writing. (Miki 2002 146–47)

But again none of the interviewers appeared interested in a question that
Barrie here seemed to be virtually inviting them to ask. They wanted
him to talk about how he wrote literature, but didn't recognize that he
was. The writing that being a psychoanalyst "negated" was a writing of
arrogance, authority, mastery.

Barrie's openness to talk about the connection between Therafields
and his writing was also not noticed later that year by Caroline Bayard
and Jack David. In their interview, Bayard asked Barrie about the "new
humanism" which he had declared in 1966, in his box-book *bp*, "will one

day touch the world to its core." Barrie candidly replied, "I was talking about my experience with Therafields at that point and the attempt to deal with emotional disturbances, creating a human context of community for people where they could live, where they could function, and where they could . . ." until Bayard interrupted him with the follow-up "Are you saying that some political revolutions are not really touching the individual at all?" Again, Barrie tried to connect the question to his work as a therapist. "No, I'm not saying that at all [. . . .] All I'm saying is that eventually these things tend to run afoul of a restrictive element in the individual which leads to a type of dehumanizing process" (Bayard 27). Various kinds of "restrictive element" in individuals is of course what Barrie as a therapist worked with every day. Bayard, however, wanted to talk not about language and the individual language user but about whether there is a connection "between world order and word order." "Oh yes," Barrie said, and immediately swerved back to the individual — "because I think syntax equals the body structure" (27). This is an intriguing declaration, again resonant of the Reichian bioenergetics practised by his brother and fellow therapist Don at this time, 1976 (although not by Barrie himself). But it apparently interested neither interviewer.

A page later Bayard asked Barrie to elaborate on statements he had made about how "formal constraints limit your ability to develop exits from the self." Barrie replied that indeed "[s]yntax and the way you structure the sentence limits the content you can put out," and how the only way to produce new content is to enlarge or change the forms of writing one is able to practice. He illustrated from Therafields bioenergetics, using the code word "armour" — first used by Reich, and later by his student Alexander Lowen, who in the 1970s had held bioenergetics seminars in Toronto attended by Therafields therapists. At Therafields, "armour" and "armouring" were often being used to describe how people defensively "armour" themselves verbally or physically against revealing embarrassing or socially complicating feelings. Barrie began telling Bayard about

> [t]he form — and the need to free up form — to unarmour the poem. You know how the muscles can get tight and constricted, and therefore the body. I have this arm — let me demonstrate. My arm floats above the floor, you see. Now that's because of the muscles that are too tight

up in here which depends upon all sorts of tensions because of all sorts of other things. The hand does not actually relax onto the floor. I can force it down, but if I just let it go, it just floats above the floor. Same thing happens in poems. Depending on what structures you put in, you limit what can happen, you limit the flexibility of it, you limit what you can do. (28)

Jack David, perhaps not surprisingly, didn't pick up the "armour" reference — nor why Barrie, who in 1980 would co-author an internal Therafields paper titled "Communication and Armouring," may have been lying on the floor as if at a Therafields session — and continued the discussion not with a question about relaxation poetics but with the statement "The great emphasis of contemporary poetry is on the ideational and not the emotional," and asked Barrie whether he found "it difficult to integrate the two . . . the ideational and the emotional."

"Ideational and emotional" were not a Barrie Nichol dichotomy, nor one common at Therafields. But he tried to reply, employing awkwardly complex syntax to say that how this question "reveals itself in the emotional is through formal things. That's where ideas influence the structures — free up the structures — and I find myself able to say things I'm simply not able to say before, because I did not have the language, I did not have the formal ability" (29). In a 1973 notebook, Barrie had said virtually the same thing about the goal of therapy in daily life as he was saying here about his form-centered poetics in his poetry: that therapy "is a process that strides toward expanding your range of awareness your ability to deal flexibly and openly with situations you encounter in everyday life."

In a 1972 article on Therafields he co-wrote with Lea Hindley-Smith, Philip McKenna, and Stan Kutz — an article published in slightly different versions in the January 1, 1972, issue of *Axis* and the January 1973 issue of *The Canadian Forum* — Barrie and his colleagues had written "Where the adult allows expression to the repressed scream of the child the repressing layers (defenses, armouring) are broken through and energy frozen by unacknowledged terror is delivered to the adult" (*Axis* 2:113). Part of this energy in Barrie's case was for writing less conventional or less "armoured" poetry.

Barrie's "syntax equals body structure" statement became the title of a 1982 "conversation" with Roy Miki, Jack Miller, George Bowering, Daphne Marlatt, and others, but again Barrie's precise understanding of what the statement meant evaded the discussion — on this occasion derailed by a Bowering jest. It was Miller who recalled the statement, in a question that appeared to assume that Barrie might have meant writing about the body, or perhaps have been echoing Hélène Cixous's concept of "writing the body." Addressing Barrie, Miller asked, "Could you explain that statement, and George, could you expand on this by talking about [your book] *Autobiology?*" Barrie's response partly repeated his bioenergetic "arm" demonstration to David and Bayard.

> I discovered — and this is what that statement comes out of — that emotionally and psychologically speaking we learn that we often armour the body, the easiest illustration of which is: if I live in a house with a low doorway, I'm probably going to end up walking like this a lot. (Hunching) I've seen tall people do this when they've lived in situations where the ceiling is low. You get an armouring of the body. I discovered that the order in which I wrote my poems allows certain contents in . . . and excludes others. So what I was trying to find, because that is part of a larger thing I've been working towards, is a way to increase my own formal range (something I'm still trying to do), and therefore not merely be stuck, shall we say, by the physical limitation of my body at that point, i.e. just because I'm walking around with my shoulders up like this, if I can learn to relax I can see the world in a slightly different way and so on. If I can keep moving the structure of the poem around, hopefully I can encompass different realities and different ways of looking at things. In that sense I've always seen a connection between the breathing I do and what comes out of me, the words I do, so syntax/body structure, sequence/body structure, but also the body of the poem. I don't know if that makes it clear or muddy, what I've just said. Muddy, eh? (Miki 2002 276)

When Bowering's reply uncomprehendingly linked this explanation to T.S. Eliot and Imagism, Barrie apologized for his failure to communicate — "In a way, it's an over-condensed statement, it's a conversational statement. I mean, were I to sit down and write that out, I'd probably take about five pages — and here I am, yet again, in conversation trying to explain it!" (276–77). The discussion then ended in jokes about the body and Barrie's first magazine *Ganglia* — without anyone recalling that its title had been a metaphor for communication. In a Therafields context, where some groups began with the therapists asking the members to take several deep slow breaths, or with body-relaxing exercises, Barrie's explanation would have been anything but "muddy."

Two years before, in 1980, Barrie had indeed co-authored with fellow therapist Adam Crabtree a more than five-page article, the one titled "Communication and Armouring," for the Therafields internal journal *Axis*. Here are some of its salient arguments:

> Communication . . . does not just mean language, or at least does not merely mean the narrow definition of language as a verbal medium, but rather the whole spectrum of information that is conveyed by a person's bodily movements, muscle tone, voice pitch and tone, facial expressions etc.

> Th[e] tendency to refine, to objectify, to syphon off the subjective bio-logical-emotional content of language is a contracting and shrinking of language out of fear. Wilhelm Reich has given us a valuable insight into this process in its broadest range in his discussion of "muscular armouring." The armoured individual — and few if any can escape some degree of armouring — is in a state of muscular contraction and tension which he is ordinarily not aware of and cannot alter.

> We have talked·of the armouring the body effects as a defense against feeling. It is no great step to carry this over into the individu-al's speech as well as his body movements, since speech is rooted in physical movements. . . . (324–25)

The period in which Barrie does most of his thinking about poetics — from deciding in 1965 to write only "ideopomes" so as to avoid the "arrogance" that he believed infected his "regular" poems, through in the late 1960s when he was learning to resolve personal material in his therapy before including it in his writing, to learning in the early 1970s to "unarmour" his writing so that its possibilities were not boundaried by habitual defensive writing mannerisms, and so that its language could produce unintended and unexpected content (much like a Freudian analysand during a therapy session) — began with him becoming intensively involved with his personal therapy. His thinking about both therapy and poetics would continue to develop, as Therafields itself developed during Lea's frequent illnesses and absences. In the early 1970s he would learn to read analytically as he wrote — to read each line for hidden meaning as if he were listening to the language of a client or the imagery of a dream. He would be combining the discourse of the client or analysand and that of the analyst. In *Books 3, 4, 5,* and *6* of *The Martyrology* this would often result in a text in which each line was a kind of editing of the line before, extending it or implicitly commenting on it, and in which the first draft would often be identical to the eventually published text. That is, his editing was mostly taking place during initial composition rather than in subsequent drafts. The process of editing would become part of the poem. As for bioenergetics, although not adopting it for his own therapy work, he would see its usefulness as a liberationist metaphor for writing.

11. Beginning *The Martyrology*

> *The 'i' is me and it isn't me. The 'i' is a construct*
> *of autobiographical elements; imagined moments which*
> *have taken on realities as well. There's certainly auto-*
> *biographical detail in The Martyrology, but it's not*
> *there so much to track autobiography as to elucidate the*
> *moment of the writing.*
>
> — bpNichol in Niechoda, *A Sourcery*, 178

Barrie's return in 1966 to writing "regular" poems had been enabled less by psychoanalytic insights — most of which were still to come — than by what he had learned by writing ideopomes — that a poem could be a visual object that interacted with, and in a sense incorporated, the field of its page, rather than a script for the "arrogant" declaration of emotions or ideas. The ideopome's components could be words, syllables, letters, drawings, and blank space; the relationships among these could be investigated and elaborated by the poet. In that investigation, however, there were indeed hints of psychoanalytic activity — as he had written to Shives, his ideopomes could show the mind how to bridge gaps, to not fear the unexpected, and to see beneath the surface appearance of things. Suspicious reading of a text, image, or event — that its "surface" meaning might not be its only meaning — had been one of Freud's earliest discoveries.

This return, however, was largely also to poems that had originally been written in his "arrogant" period. It had been to those poems from 1963 to 1964 that he had hurriedly rewritten in order to have something to offer to Souster's *New Wave Canada*. The poems of "Journeying and the Returns" included in the *bp* box and written from 1963 to 1966 were similar — lyric poems that reported being sensitively "inside" particular situations and experiences, but were linked into six sequences, the longest composed of seven sections. Barrie's expressions of unease to bissett following the publication of *bp* — that he was sick of the poems he was currently writing — suggest that his return to discursive poetry was not always a happy one. His next collection of "regular" poems was *The Other Side of the Room*, written 1966–69 and published in 1971. These were mostly one-page lyrics, many of them untitled. Many of them were plaints, such as the untitled one that begins:

> If there is one I've sought
> who is she
>   who is not
> the ones I've found
>
> never in my life
>   I've known peace
>
> seldom can I hear   see
> clearly (20)

But there were also several dedicated or addressed to various friends — to Phyllis Webb, Victor Coleman and his first wife Sarah Miller, to artist and curator Dennis Reid and his wife Kog, to David Phillips and his first wife Denise. These poems implied dialogue and "communication," a key word in Barrie's early therapy years, and foreshadowed other dedicated poems he would write. However, *The Other Side of the Room* is a book that Barrie would rarely talk about in his interviews, or mention when later classifying his books as "failed," or "dead," or "living" and therefore possibly worthy of revision or reissue.

Barrie had worked or begun work on numerous projects in the 1965–68 period: *The Captain Poetry Poems*; "The Journey"; "Journeying and the Returns"; *The Other Side of the Room*; the novel "For Jesus Lunatick"; the Nichol family poems "The Plunkett Papers"; *Scraptures*; the long poem "Land"; a two-part work titled "Lungwage: a domesday book"; and a *Hamlet*-alluding long poem "The Undiscovered Country." He had also been working on ideopome ideas that eventually became *Still Water* and *ABC: The Aleph Beth Book*. Even at this time, however, he was apparently thinking that most of these might be part of a single work, or that someday he would have the "intelligence" to see how most of them fitted together, much as how in *The Captain Poetry Poems* he had found a way to combine ideopoem, comic strip, prose, and "regular" poetry. He suspected that many of the very early writings that he now regarded as failures might actually belong to a collection he could conceive of as "The Books of the Dead" and the later writing to another collection "The Books of the Living" — which he might be able to combine someday into a single book. In February 1979, while attempting to map a new direction for *The Martyrology*, he wrote in his "The Encounters" notebook that he was thinking back to his late 1960s idea of splitting his writing into "The Books of the Dead" and "The Books of the Living." He remarked that back then he had believed that his work would soon change, that he would soon be reborn, "completely" born this time, with an intelligence he had previously lacked, and that he had hoped to find a structure that could contain both this new work and his earlier failures, such as "The Journey" and "The Undiscovered Country," both of which, he thought, would have benefitted from his later discovery of the *utanikki*, the traditional Japanese poetic travel-diary.

Barrie was recalling here a causal link in the late 1960s between his growing command of poetics and literary structure and his being reborn into the world through his therapy. His psychoanalytic thinking had been giving him the conviction that his current writing would eventually be part of larger things that he was not yet capable of conceiving or creating. The "Books of the Dead" were books attempted while he was suffering from recurrent depressions and in which he sentimentalized and "romanticized my experience to a disgusting degree" (Miki 2002 234) — but he still hoped somehow to save them as early parts of an evolved life's work. The "Books of the Living" were to be ones in which he had become able to see beyond self-preoccupation to rhythms and insights his own writing was proposing.

Irene Niechoda outlines how in 1965 his personal research into various non-Western creation myths had led him to consider creating his own creation story for his Cloudtown and its saints, and to — perhaps playfully — place this Cloudtown slightly west of Wildwood Park in one of the sites of his own creation, the small farming town of Plunkett, Saskatchewan (1992 20–22). This is where members of his mother's Workman and Leigh families had farmed, where the Workmans had operated the Plunkett Hotel, and where her parents were living when his father had encountered her. The majority of "The Plunkett Papers" was written 1967–71, a few pieces of which Barrie printed in 1980 in the chapbook *Familiar* for distribution to friends, and a few more Niechoda herself published in *A Sourcery* as a possible aid to understanding *The Martyrology*. Barrie's mostly unpublished "The Plunkett Papers" presented Plunkett as the realm of the creator "Cloud-hidden" and a "ground where the saints walked." Niechoda writes: "All the major saints, as well as Captain Poetry and Billy the Kid, visited Plunkett. (In one passage St And mourns the death of the latter)" (1992 22). Barrie's controversially award-winning chapbook, *The True Eventual Story of Billy the Kid* (1970) was written in 1967 either as a possible part of "The Plunkett Papers" or in association with them.

The Travellers' Home
Away from Home

Our Aim is to Please
Our Patrons

Phone:
Viscount, No. 38 ring 4

Plunkett Hotel
Mrs. W. Workman
Proprietress

A 1929 ADVERTISEMENT
FOR THE WORKMAN
FAMILY'S PLUNKETT
HOTEL, PLUNKETT,
SASKATCHEWAN.

In the summer of 1969 he and Rob Hindley-Smith drove slowly from Toronto to Vancouver through Port Arthur, Winnipeg, and Plunkett, taking photographs of various Nichol family buildings as they went, including the Plunkett Hotel. Very likely this was at least in a part a research trip for "The Plunkett Papers" — as well as a personal pilgrimage. While they were in Plunkett, Barrie drafted in his notebook that poem's mythologized version of his parents' meeting and his own coming into being. In the poem he translated their names: Avis, he wrote, means "free" in French, and marries

Glen whose name in Scottish is a small forested valley, becoming one who once "was" free, and later bearing as her third son someone who sings songs, who some predict will be a "simpleton." Later that summer Barrie recorded in the same notebook genealogical information about the Leigh, Workman, Fuller, and Nichol families for use in this Plunkett project, on pages adjacent to ones on which he was drafting *The Martyrology I's* "The Sorrows of Saint Orm."

In an obvious revision and expansion of his 1979 notebook entry about having once hoped to write a combined "The Books of the Dead" and "The Books of the Living," Barrie wrote in a 1979 note for Michael Ondaatje's *The Long Poem Anthology* that "somewhere in my 20s" he had begun "to think of this [my poetry] as one long work divided (roughly) into two sections: *The Books of the Dead & The Books of the Living*. [. . . .] The problem was I couldn't make it work."

So in 1967 he had "temporarily abandoned this notion" and "began work on *The Martyrology*" (335), a book-length poem in which he could expand on the saints he had recently discovered in *Scraptures*, and revisit, re-envision, and attempt to understand many of the childhood fantasies that had begun the morning in Wildwood Park when he had seen a "cloud town" floating above him. In a sense, *The Martyrology* began as a recombinant work written as a substitute for the much more combinant and unifying books of dead and living whose construction he was now postponing. At the same time he also began the poem sequence to be published in 1971 as *Monotones* — seeing it, however, as a yet formally unplaceable part of the new *Martyrology* project. That sequence would be the first of his "regular" poetry books to be published as a single book-length work. He was now working on three *Martyrology*-like projects concurrently but without an understanding of their interrelationships — *Book I* of *The Martyrology*, *Monotones*, and "The Plunkett Papers."

Monotones, written mostly 1968–70, can be precisely dated by its title and photographs by Andy Phillips. It was written during the first years of the Therafields farm at Mono Mills. Barrie's new duties as Therafields vice president, which also included being custodian of the farm tool room, saw him spending many days there as the barn and other buildings were renovated to create dormitories, a dining area, and a meeting space. Fields were planted, and the site overall was prepared for the hosting of therapy groups. Phillips's photos — printed by Talonbooks in a sepia "monotone" — show the barn and a lush field on the cover, and on the frontispiece Barrie and Therafields financial officer Renwick ("Rik") Day amid the barn renovation. Most of the sections have little intense personal content; instead they address Barrie's daily life when on the farm, and at times express gratitude for the friends and experiences his farm responsibilities are giving him. It is a work that is close to being a journal — unlike his short lyrics, which are mostly about occasional thoughts and moments — and is quite unlike the other texts Barrie was writing and believing to be part of the new *Martyrology*. Noticing this difference, and being unable to write his way past it, Barrie severed the two works sometime in 1970. Ironically, some of the later books of *The Martyrology* would have a striking resemblance to the journal-like *Monotones*. In fact he would tell Niechoda in her July 1987 interview that he now realized that in 1968 he had unwittingly had something of a single work in his grasp and been unable to see it, that *Scraptures* had taken "two branches, but I didn't have the sophistication as a writer at that time to understand that." He felt that "*Monotones* has to go back and have its place restored." He told her that it was his conviction that *The Martyrology* was to be "processual" (i.e. that it had to follow the sequence of his consciousness while he was composing it) that had caused him to overlook the possibility that he could be writing three concurrent parts of the same text and in each one employing different composition techniques (1992 31).

But Barrie's other limitation at this time was that he saw *The Martyrology* only in terms of saints and superheroes — only as a text in which to think through once again his Wildwood Park and subsequent fantasies, and the years of evolution and elaboration he had given them while experiencing himself as the companion of super detectives, superheroes, and science-fiction adventurers. Moreover, he appears to have viewed these fantasies, at least initially, as not merely *his* creations or personal mythologies, but as products also of contemporary culture and therefore as the potential basis for a culturally relevant processual long poem. Midway through writing the first two books, in April 1969, he wrote in that "Comics as Myth" entry in his notebook "these saints [of the *Martyrology*] grew out of a Sci-Fi comic strip milieu. And that is what *The Martyrology* is or means. The relevance of myth is only as you make it relevant to your own time" (Peters

81). He went on to tell himself that to apply classical mythology in contemporary writing "seems such a useless thing" (84). Barrie's now almost two decades of fantasies — people in clouds, Dick Tracy in Port Arthur, Bob de Cat in Winnipeg who evolved later into Captain Poetry, Yaboo, and Blossom Tight — were of course also, as his preferred childhood escapes from his unhappy family life, material for his therapy work and for a kind of psychic autobiography. By being able to create written stories and comic strips from his Bob de Cat, Sailor from Mars, and other daydreams, Barrie had, from roughly 1954 on, been reaping what Freud called "gain from illness" or "secondary gains" — from persisting in fantasy at the expense of deeper engagement in soccer games, teaching, or social relationships. In a sense these gains were "free," already created, poetic materials initially created not as literature but as the "primary gain" — defence against darker thoughts, including suicide. Was the new poem a sign of resistance to his therapy? His remarks to Niechoda about the temptation to take similar material to his poems rather than to his therapy and how in therapy he learned to ask himself "Was this really happening or was it my imagination?" (1992 135) suggest that he knew such was a possibility.

The most immediate formal starting point for *The Martyrology* and "The Plunkett Papers" was undoubtedly *Scraptures*, that series of visual and text poems Barrie had begun in 1965, during his self-imposed "ideo-pome" focus, and which he had published intermittently over the next few years mainly as *grOnk* pamphlets. Like *The Martyrology,* the title "Scraptures" owed something to the distinctly Catholic milieu in which he was then living — the many priests, monks, and nuns of Lea's first house groups and learning group. "Scraptures" was a resonant and multi-layered word, hinting of rapture, scripture, and the scraps and words and images of which the series was composed — scriptures for experimental poetry. Nichol described *Scraptures* to Ken Norris as the first work in which he "cross-pollinated . . . started working between forms." It began with a visual poem based on the first sentence of the Bible, then "I began to get into prose sections and I got into comic strip oriented sections, two of the sections are done as sound poems, though there are visual versions of those two as well" (Miki 2002 239). It was in the fourth of this series that Barrie and his library co-worker David Aylward discovered the "saints" within language, beginning with "St Ranglehold."

aka{ barrie phillip }Nichol

That was about 1965 or '66, and that's sort of where it ended for David, but I began to see these "st" words as saints. Then I found that I began to address them — and I literally mean that I found, I was not expecting this. I began to address these pretty rabid rhetorical pieces to the saints in *Scraptures*. I realized that these saints had, for me, taken on a meaning and a life. . . . ("Syntax," Miki 2002 273–74)

Their "life" was a new chapter in Barrie's ongoing fantasy, something that Barrie makes abundantly clear when he begins *The Martyrology* with the science fiction preface "The Chronicles of Knarn," or in 1969 when he writes in his "Comics as Myth" notebook entry about contemporary and classical mythology that "lately I find myself attempting to tie them all together — Bob de Cat, St. Reat, Captain Poetry, St. And, Bars Barfleet, St. Ranglehold, Yaboo & Blossom Tight" (Peters 84–85).[1]

Barrie had learned of the concept of a martyrology the year before from Julia Keeler, a former nun, whom he had met while working at the Sigmund Samuel Library, and who would soon also be a member of the Therafields community with a study at 55 Admiral next door to where Barrie was living. Keeler had been working on a doctoral thesis on the minor religious poets of the English 1590s and shared with him some lines from a poem "The Martyrology of the Female Saints." From her Barrie came to understand that a martyrology was "a book in which you wrote out the history of the saints" (Niechoda 1992 63). And Barrie himself indeed had saints, discovered with Aylward while he was writing *Scraptures* — Barrie's "saints were language, or," as he told his interviewers in "Syntax Equals Body Structure," "were my encounter with language." And because of this, he suggested — with rather obscure logic — "the possibility of the journal form or the *utanikki* form also opened up" (Miki 2002 275). Niechoda notes that Barrie did not know about the *utanikki* form while writing *The Martyrology, Book I* and *Book II*, and did not consciously try to use it until writing *The Martyrology, Book 4* in 1975 (1992 169). As well, *Book I* of *The Martyrology* often seems less a journal than a narrative history of Cloudtown interspersed with often painful lyric responses — although it can also be read as a journal of those responses.

Saints are holy figures who are martyred — unjustly killed for their beliefs and commitments. Barrie's writing at this time has been filled with such thoughts of death — from thoughts of wandering into traffic at despair over Dace, to beliefs that most of his poems belong to "The Book of the Dead," to announcements in *ABC: The Aleph-Beth Book* that "the poem is dead," to the anguished lines in *Nights on Prose Mountain* (*Scraptures 8*, 1969):

> NOW THIS IS THE DEATH OF POETRY. i have sat up all night to write you this — the poem is dying is dying — no — i have already said the poem is dead — dead beyond hope beyond recall — dead dead dead

Amidst his own recurring depressions and quick successes with his ideo-pomes, Barrie appears to have begun *The Martyrology* believing precisely this — that poetry as Western civilization has known it is either dead or in danger of imminent dying. Only by exploring how it has died, and by accepting that it is dead, is it possible, as in *ABC*, that "the poem may live again." Later, when *The Martyrology* has both lived and evolved from his preoccupation with language saints, he will think of the title as "downbeat" but still "accurate" (Miki 2002 275) — but most likely "accurate" for different reasons. Metaphorically the looming destruction of Knarn in "The Chronicles of Knarn" at the opening of *The Martyrology, Book I* and the dispersion of the "saints" can stand in for this death of poetry and the exile of its poets. In Barrie's early reading, the archetype for these was Superman's exile from the destroyed planet Krypton. But of course Krypton's story echoed much older stories of loss and origin — the story of Troy's destruction and Aeneas's wanderings before founding Rome, the story of Jerusalem's destruction and its people's subsequent communal wanderings, and the much older story of Adam and Eve's expulsion from Eden. Much of this had been epic literary material. For Barrie personally, Krypton seems to have echoed the loss of his Wildwood, Port Arthur, and Winnipeg homes, and the slow death of both his life-suffocating fantasies of Cloudtown and of his private Jerusalem, Plunkett, Saskatchewan. Plunkett was for him his family's point of origin in Canada, from where his mother had begun as hotel-owner's daughter and become a reluctant wanderer among Canadian cities, none of them Plunkett. Barrie would repeatedly return to both Cloudtown and Plunkett, as both visitor and writer, seeking possible *Martyrology* material, as if they were sainted and originary sites.

12. Friends Much More than Footnotes

> *Now we are beginning the move outward, outside of ourselves moving to take over the inward feelings and realizations to present them here first in a form accessible to all of us to be shared. This is the very real necessity. The very real necessity is that the insights that our working is now generating be shared as a common source of energy to further us all in our searches in these areas of human communication.*

> — bpNichol, "Prelude," *Axis*, December 24, 1969

Nineteen sixty-eight and 1969 were even more eventful years for Barrie than 1967 had been. They began with him learning his new role of Therafields vice president, continuing his *Ganglia/grOnk* publication projects, and continuing various writing projects including the newly begun *Martyrology* and *Monotones*. In his notebooks one can find a proposal for therapists' salaries on the verso of a draft of a poem he will include in *The Other Side of the Room*, and notes about the delegation of Therafields tasks on the same page as reflections on the difficult lives of his Plunkett ancestors. He drafted a possible introduction to *The Cosmic Chef* anthology in which he again linked his psychotherapy life with his poetics, writing that the ability to give was equally important in love and in writing, and that both asked people to draw on "everything" that they had within them.

During these busy years he would also enter into three extremely influential friendships, including one with Ellie Hiebert, his future wife.

The first of these new close friendships was with the Latvian-born architect Visvaldis Upenieks. Upenieks, who usually went both socially and professionally by the single name Visvaldis, had become a client of Lea Hindley-Smith's the previous summer, and by the fall had begun announcing himself in love with her — a love that was not the predictable transference to one's therapist, he declared. Sixteen years older than her suitor, and in an all-but-dead marriage to her unemployed Yorkshire-born labourer husband Harry, Lea found herself attracted to Visvaldis, but rebuffed him for almost a year. To woo her, he had volunteered his labour and professional skills to the farm renovations, designing and helping to build a large and stylish vestibule for the barn. Those already involved in the farm renovations, including Barrie and Rob, found him engagingly energetic and jovial. Most of the therapists not involved in the renovations, however, according to Grant Goodbrand, resented his presence. Goodbrand, who was one of these, saw him as "both shy and an exhibitionist."

> He behaved in a blatantly macho fashion. . . . He was flirtatious with women and uncomfortable and awkwardly aggressive with men. He was prone to smart-ass opening remarks like "How's your love life?" He played with language, using his alleged unfamiliarity with English to construct neologisms or double entendres. (97–98)

In short, he had some verbal habits that would attract Barrie to him — qualities, however, that could cause the older city-dwelling therapists to view both men as immature. Goodbrand notes in retrospect that the "competitiveness, jealousy, hostility, and criticism" that grew among the older therapists toward Visvaldis, "as well as a desire to unseat and exclude" him, amounted "to a classical Oedipus complex." "I don't think Lea was ever forgiven for the relationship, and Visvaldis certainly never was" (97).[1] In her blog response to Goodbrand, Brenda Doyle adds that there were also serious ethical grounds on which to consciously disapprove of Lea and Visvaldis's relationship, remarking that Goodbrand's portrayal of it "is a somewhat expurgated one." Lea had met Visvaldis through his wife who was one of the clients in her therapy group. She had taken him on as an individual client when he "was in a quite broken state." His wife, Doyle writes, "had looked in trust to Lea for help in her marriage but in short order her husband had been taken up in an intensely emotional, later sexual involvement with the therapist to whom she had turned." At least one of Goodbrand's fellow Hypno I therapists declared Lea's behaviour "imprudent, unethical and unprofessional" ("Thoughts on Therafields," October 29, 2010).

If Goodbrand is correct that Therafields leadership then began evolving toward what would be by 1975 two opposing groups, one the "managers [Lea, Visvaldis, Rob Hindley-Smith, and Barrie] . . . alienated intellectually and emotionally from the other therapists" and the other those "other therapists," Barrie's own position was starting to become awkward. In concert with the visions of Lea, Rob, Visvaldis, Renwick Day, and others committed to the farm development, his view of Therafields and its goals would begin to differ from that of the majority of therapists of the Hypno I group, many of them from eccelesiastical backgrounds, who lived and saw clients mostly in the city, and who might visit the farm no more than two or three times a year. When, in part at Visvaldis's suggestion, Lea's vision for Therafields in the fall of 1968 expanded from its being a set of facilities for doing individual, group, house group, and weekend therapies to being a long-term community, an "environment of friends," in which clients could live and use their newly freed energies and abilities creatively — as Barrie and the various therapists were doing — and once the critical stages of their therapies had passed, these differing visions, Goodbrand suggests, became even more defined. Most of the therapists were content to work at helping clients progress in their individual therapies; they were not interested in building communes, communities, or alternate societies.[2] However, financial and leadership control still rested with Lea, who had Visvaldis undertake various architectural tasks, all in his trademark Scandinavian modern style — open spaces, brightly coloured walls, natural wood trims.[3] Spurred by Lea's anti-masochism theory that the new community and its members should learn to be generous to themselves, Visvaldis would design and oversee impressive and expensive renovations of her new farmhouse "The Willow," the downtown "Centre," various group houses, and eventually her new lakefront condominium.

aka{ barrie phillip }Nichol

Barrie would have a room at the Willow, where he sometimes stayed while retaining (and paying for) his space at 59 Admiral.

Goodbrand writes that during that fall of 1968, "A new family of Lea, Visvaldis, Rob and Barrie was formed. They were in constant communication and met every Wednesday night for dinner to discuss things as they were and future plans for the movement. The principal guidance and direction of Therafields continued to come from Lea" (105). While these dinners may have reflected some "family" closeness, it is not clear at all how much they contributed to Therafields administration. According to Doyle and an unnamed informant who worked for Lea at the Willow, these meetings occurred initially in Visvaldis's rooms on the top floor of the Park Plaza hotel, as one of Lea's ways of relieving his feelings of isolation. "Lea sort of forced Barry [sic] and Rob to have dinner with him every Wednesday night," the informant tells Doyle, "so that they could talk. Stella would go down and cook for them at his apartment at the top of the Park Plaza." But beginning June 1969 these meetings may also have occurred on Tuesday evenings at the apartment Lea lived in on Lowther Avenue — near the Therafields group houses — or at her later apartment in Rosedale.

Doyle does, however, also make a "family" characterization of Barrie, Lea, and Rob. She writes of Rob's

> sharing a room in the family suite on the ground floor of 59 Admiral with Barry [sic], Lea's other "son" of trust and closeness.
>
> Barry was profoundly "in debt" with Lea. Like Rob he was his mother's last child and he was very tied to her. He had left home but eventually transferred all of his feelings for his mother to Lea. She encouraged him in his poetry and his personal development but she kept him close. He was as solidly hers as was Rob. For the next decade this special arrangement endured. "The boys" as Lea referred to them in her writing, were tuned into her concerns and needs and they followed her directions and supported her unflinchingly. ("Thoughts" October 31, 2010)

Although certainly as long-term best friends, Barrie and Rob were close both to each other and to Rob's mother and her companion Visvaldis, not all who were present agree with Goodbrand's and Doyle's "family" interpretation. Ellie Nichol recalls that conventional notions of "family" and family mealtimes were contrary to Lea's theories.[4] Nor do all agree with his overall description of a "two-party" (183) Therafields split between a farm-committed management and a resistant group of urban therapists. Ellie's impression is that there were other competing visions for Therafields besides those of farm development and urban therapy. Doyle recalls hearing of no communal goals when the farm was purchased: "We were doing therapy and we had acquired a farm where we could do marathons" (October 31, 2010). She laments Goodbrand's portrayal of an increasingly polarized community, and points out that those who were, like her, in the generation of therapists-in-training following the Hypno I group had their own goals and priorities.

> In the book members of the community are bundled into two groups: the older, Hypno I–based crowd and the newer "counter-culture" group who came after the aforesaid. Both sets are given common attitudes and characteristics, seemingly opposed to one another in their views of Lea and the purposes of the developing community. One has only to speak with people across that divide to brush up against the enormous diversity of locations, understandings, and ambivalences about every aspect of the life of Therafields and of Lea during the periods that Grant is writing about.

Whether Goodbrand's image of a "new family of Lea, Visvaldis, Rob and Barrie" has any basis in reality, or is an image produced in part by his perception of oppositional tensions, it is true that Barrie had more in common at this time with Lea, Visvaldis, and Rob than with his birth family. They respected his career choices, shared many of his beliefs about community and group living, and trusted him to help them work toward their own goals. He could share physical work, word play, and humour with Visvaldis in ways he was never able to with his father, and with Rob share much more of his time than with his actual brother — and previous roommate — Don. In a 1971 passage of *The Martyrology, Book 3* that appears to support Lea's understanding of the "we" of community, and lament the "i" individualism of the nuclear family, Barrie will write about his drifting relationship with Don:

aka{ barrie phillip }Nichol

the second and the third son
dj & me
all of our family that moved east
we do not huddle together
seldom talk anymore
that blindness that does not let you see
start our own families
on our own square feet
no we that can encompass each other

Barrie also, beginning in 1969, became at times a kind of spokesperson for Lea's management group, in December co-founding and co-editing with Visvaldis the Therafields internal publication *Axis*, and in its pages occasionally writing hortatory messages in which he seems to be trying to bridge the growing fissures within the institution, and later to improve Visvaldis's image within the community. Barrie's first editorial reads like both a literary manifesto and an advertisement for Therafields' new direction:

> The need for such a publication was never greater than now. With new urgency the necessity of a constant creative dialogue between working therapists presses upon us and we can no longer afford to wait for that vague magic day we'll get down to it. The need is now and it must be filled now. (*Axis*, December 24, 1969)

His notebook draft of his editorial for *Axis*'s second series, a year later, will portray Visvaldis as one of the institution's major leaders — although he was in fact now neither a client nor a therapist and was plagued by recurrent problems with alcohol. Barrie quotes Visvaldis twice, first as saying that the "duty" of those in Therafields is to make their energies flow, and second as urging the proposing of concrete plans for new ventures rather than talking about "soap operas."

And Barrie would co-write with Lea, for publication in *Axis*, short papers on therapy, including "Milieu Therapy" (December 24, 1969) and the very short "The Paranoiac and the Paranee" (July 9, 1970), a paper that caused controversy among the more conservative therapists because of its attempt to coin a new psychoanalytic term, "paranee." Goodbrand indicates that the paper was also read by the older therapists as a projection by Lea of her relationship with her uneducated and dependent husband Harry; Doyle suggests it was an attempt by Lea to depict Visvaldis's wife as parasitically dependent ("Thoughts" October 29, 2010) — although the pronouns used in the paper suggest otherwise. In it, Lea and Barrie wrote of a paranoid and dependent "he" who controlled and victimized a "paranee" by "awakening the maternal instinct of the paranee" and "relying for strength on the paranee." The writers used masculine pronouns throughout for the paranoid or paranoiac but avoided pronouns altogether for the "paranee" — a usage that presumably encouraged the older therapists' intepretations.[5]

Barrie mentioned Visvaldis at least twice in his literary writing in 1969–70, including in the dedication of the "old years poem" in *The Other Side of the Room*. The poem was not merely one dedicated to him, however. The point of view and voice were poorly indicated, but are probably those of Visvaldis. The poem seems to be an attempt at a dramatic monologue in which a sympathetic Barrie had Visvaldis recount being raised by his mother and being traumatized and enraged by the sacrifices she had had to make to enable him to survive in postwar Europe and gain an education. Its phrase "the unimaginable hell of / my early years" is thus more likely a characterization of Visvaldis's life than of Barrie's. In Barrie's 1970 notebook when he drafted the "Friends as Footnotes" section of *The Martyrology, Book II*, Visvaldis was the second friend Barrie celebrated. He praised him as a friend and helper, with whom discussion could achieve things, rather than merely dispersing otherwise useful energy. He exclaimed how wonderful it was to be able to praise him, and to be able to sing and be heard by him and for them thus to be able to understand each other. The effusiveness of the praise suggests that Barrie's Oedipal history might have been somewhat active in the writing.

> this man
>   this friend
> helps me again
> thus discussions lead somewhere
> create & do not dissipate
>   energy
> . . .

aka{ barrie phillip }Nichol

oh wonderful thing
that i can sing & you can hear me
that i can praise you
praise this man
& thru singing understand
we understand each other

(published in Niechoda 1992 174)

In the published versions of "Friends as Footnotes" in first and second editions of *The Martyrology, Book II*, however, there are only two brief references to Visvaldis, one in which Barrie mentions to him the disappearance of "old lore" and the other in the opening section of which Visvaldis is disconsolately holding the dead body of the dog Terry:

"first friend i've lost in years" visvaldis said
crying he held her body in his arms

This burial scene, with its tender and compassionate Visvaldis, thematically introduces a *Martyrology* section in which the writer recognizes that "'in the midst of life we are in death,'" recalls his fears that he would commit suicide, and disturbedly faces the necessary deaths of his fantasy saints. It's a positive but much less personal portrayal of Visvaldis than Barrie had first considered.[6]

In 1970 in those notebook pages Barrie had divided "Friends as Footnotes" into numbered passages — the numbers presumably intended as indications of footnote numbers. The fifth passage he had titled "sound," the fourth "Visvaldis," the third "Rob," the second "the poem," and the first "Ellie." These were all for Barrie plausible "friends" — Ellie now first among them. Barrie and Ellie had been acquaintances since her arrival in the Therafields house groups as a young nun — although three years older than him — in 1966. They began dating midway through 1968, going together to a Simon and Garfunkel concert; the writers of "Mrs. Robinson" were enjoying enhanced celebrity that year from the runaway success of the film *The Graduate*, released the previous December. Barrie's difficulties in being in close company with a woman had soon recurred

— it would be several years before he would be able to bear living under the same roof as she, and more until he could endure sharing the same floor. In his fear he would often hesitate to say anything that would draw her closer. Still a person who laughingly diminished his difficulties, he would respond jocularly or self-mockingly to friends — such as my wife and I or workers at Coach House — who asked the innocent question, "How's Ellie?" He would make jests about the limited closeness he was managing, or the "panic attacks" he had been suffering.[7] But his private reflections in his notebooks make painful reading. In November 1968 he wrote about a strange fear that he had around Ellie that in some way he was exploiting her. Underneath in two-inch high letters he wrote "WHY?" and in three-inch high letters under that "WHY?" The answer was probably the guilt he had experienced for sexually desiring his mother, and for coming so close to her in their baths, and it may well show the uncanny power of neurosis that he has to print "WHY?"

During his cross-country drive with Rob the next summer he would include himself and Ellie in the Plunkett mythologies he was writing, noting that her name comes from the Greek genitive form of "light" although she has paradoxically dwelled mostly in shadow, and that she was born 30 miles from his mother's birthplace of Plunkett, in the town of Bay Trail. He then wrote that the ruling deity of "The Plunkett Papers," Cloud-hidden (cf. the Plunkett poems Niechoda reproduces in *A Sourcery* 23–29) had once seen them make love, and in a burst of mischief had "cursed" them. Barrie then crossed out the entire passage, as if perhaps retaining it might make its story true. Such crossing out of long passages of poetry, or their later deletion as with the "ellie," "rob," and "visvaldis" passages once parts of "Friends as Footnotes," is extremely rare in Barrrie's notebook-drafted poetry — although he will sometimes delete entire passages while preparing a manuscript for publication. Apart from the frequently revised drafts of *Martyrology Book 1*, the notebook drafts of his post-1970 poems are often the final drafts, or vary only slightly from the published version.

Three years later in March 1972, five days before he was to attend the wedding of Grant Goodbrand and his first wife Linda, Barrie wrote a rather unusual prose narrative in his notebook, "Some Description of Her"; it appears unrelated to other writing in his notebooks or manuscripts, and in its references seems based on his now four years of conflicted

feelings around Ellie. It's possible that these feelings were being stirred
by the imminent wedding. Here he wrote of how he — or a very similar
male poetry-writing character — had once helplessly caused a breakup
with "her" because of feeling confused while they were walking one night
near a cigar store at the Toronto intersection of Dupont and Davenport (an
intersection approximately two blocks from the Therafields Dupont Street
offices). He had told her that he didn't know why he was in a relationship
with her and she had quite reasonably replied that they had better separate
before she became too deeply attached to him. A month later he had sug-
gested they get back together, which they did, until one night with her he
imagined that she was screaming, which precipitated an exchange of angry
words that continued through more nights and more desperate poems.
He wrote that they were throwing each other over for something that he
didn't understand, something that seemed senseless, that seemed not to
have anything to do with her. But, he wrote, he had needed more space,
more distance from her, and she then had said she would try to give him
that, and he had theorized that they were both experiencing old emotions
that had little to do with the present. So they had separated, and then got
back together the next spring — after he had spent time in Nassau and she
had visited Saskatchewan (the home of Ellie's parents) — and then had
encountered the same difficulties. He recounted how they had argued,
how he had said that he couldn't stand the confinement of always being
with another person, how she had accused him of being irrational, and
how they had drifted back together but then he had begun feeling bored
with her again but feared telling her that in case he lost her. And now, he
wrote, he had wondered where things would go with them, how would
they be, and so had sat down to write this "description of her."

Possibly Barrie was considering this short narrative as a potential part
of another semi-autobiographical work of fiction. But the narrative is also
consistent with what Barrie was telling friends in these years about his diffi-
culties in being close to Ellie, and seems without any plausible context in his
known fiction projects. Considering Barrie's psychoanalytical history, this
was also again material that belonged less in his writing than in his therapy
(or his self-therapy, for Lea was now prevented by her type 2 diabetes and
frequent trips to Florida for naturopathic treatment [Goodbrand 158] from
doing much other than occasional work). And presumably he took it there.[8]

The 1970 notebook draft of "Friends as Footnotes" had begun in "Ellie" with Barrie suggesting difficulties that he had not only with his friendship with Ellie but with friends in general. Before the footnotes were deleted, the "Ellie" passage had evolved from one with an unusual proportion of deletions into the manuscript version quoted by Niechoda.

footnotes become your friends in poems

i already said that
yes i did i did say that
once before (earlier today)
i said that very thing
discarded version (earlier) of this poem
friends are the whole of my life saint and i've tried to deny
as this poem is part shall we call it part of a larger thing

(you run in circles from your feelings
as saint and did   try to get away
unable to say you love her
stumble over words you are not clever with)

[. . .]

i love you
that's not simple to say stupid as that may seem
why does honesty seem like a cruel thing when we both know there's
    no other way

(1992 172–73)

But in the published versions in *The Martyrology, Book II*, Barrie presents Ellie as a partner in his life-journey into the unknown.

drove out the 401 the week before
west into the darkness
rain falling all around us

aka{ barrie phillip }Nichol

ellie and i driving into what we did not know
trusting that white line to guide us

She also appears as someone he can make declarations of love to:

lord how i love thee lets love in

words archaic when the feeling is
we walk in shadows
or step out
         free

today words flow

Comparing the various drafts one gets a sense that Barrie's feelings toward both Visvaldis and Ellie may have been evolving almost faster than the revisions.

The other friends prominently mentioned by Barrie in "Friends as Footnotes" are his old Vancouver ones, David and Andy Phillips and Barb Shore, who probably have more prominence in the published drafts than they would have had if the various named sections had been retained. Not mentioned in any of the drafts, however, is poet Steve McCaffery, whose about-to-be life-changing friendship was also new to Barrie in 1968–69. McCaffery had emigrated from northern England in 1968 to begin M.A. study at York University. Born in Sheffield in 1947, he had recently graduated from the University of Hull. He was aware of much of the British visual and sound poetry scenes, particularly the work of Ian Hamilton Finlay, and had written and published some of his own visual poetry. The one Toronto poet whose work he had encountered while still in England was bpNichol, whom he contacted with the help of John Robert Colombo in the summer of 1969. McCaffery recalls:

That first meeting established an instant and lasting friendship between us. Our sympathetic interests and common concern in writing (especially the felt need for an investigative stance and formal risk) helped establish the direction of our conversation. We both realized that we had been starved for critical response and discussion of poetics, theories and forms. (McCaffery 1992 9)

For Barrie his friendship with McCaffery brought him potential answers to questions about the development of radical modernisms and their practices that he had pondered since his teens. It also brought him access to systematically accumulated knowledge about contemporary international intellectual culture, aesthetics, and poetics — much of which he may not have known existed. McCaffery comments about "the scope and content of their readings: Jabes, Derrida, Barthes and Lacan had all been read by 1974" (17). Except for Lacan, these are names that do not appear in Barrie's notebooks or writings or recollections of friends from before his meeting McCaffery. Perhaps even more important, it brought him a view of writing that was much different from his own belief that language had some magical ability to reveal unsuspected meanings. McCaffery valued such events but had only materialist understandings of them, and of culture and language generally. Many of the unexpecteds that Barrie sought and discovered were to McCaffery statistically predictable chance occurrences, or physiologically determined events such as Olson had theorized in his comments about the human breath in his essay "Projective Verse," or various psychoanalytic theorists had discussed as libido or "libidinal excess."[9]

Barrie also found in McCaffery someone especially rare in Ontario at this time — a writer who was, like himself, resolutely international in his understandings of poetics and audience. McCaffery remembers "the late sixties and early seventies in Canada" as, except for the writers associated with *Tish*,

a milieu obsessed with establishing a Canadian identity largely predicated on nationalist narratives and values [. . . and] a "common-sense" aesthetic in writing that nourished a bias to literary realism as an unquestionable norm. . . . Hand in hand with this attitude was a trenchant opposition to American and European ideas. Charles Olson's projective verse, for instance, and the literary legacies of Dada and Surrealism were, in large, considered threatening imports to Canada's anglophone literary community. (18)

aka{ barrie / phillip }Nichol

Among their first ventures together in the fall of 1969 was a joint sound poetry performance at the St. Lawrence Centre in Toronto, whose managers had expected the novelty of such work to draw a large audience. Approximately 20 people attended, most of them other poets. In the audience was the young poet Rafael Barreto-Rivera whose enthusiastic response to the performances annoyed McCaffery but led to the three of them getting together later with another young poet, Paul Dutton, and experimenting with collaborative performance. According to Barrie, Barreto-Rivera soon proposed that they form a sound poetry ensemble (Miki 2002 164). Dutton's recollection, however, in his remembrance of Barrie, "bp: Anecdotingly," is that the idea was primarily Barrie's, commenting that his attributing it to Baretto-Rivera "was typical of beep, whose generous nature it was to spread the credit around." He added that Barrie was "tremendously excited at the prospect of a four-man sound poetry group" and proposed the group name (80). Barrie's own recollection confirms at least his excitement.

THE COVER OF *LAMENT*, GANGLIA PRESS, 1969.

I was very interested in getting into that because I was very bored with the limitations of one voice. What four voices allowed us was more choral, more theatrical possibilities — in short opened up the whole ball game. As a writer this was a tremendously exciting challenge for me. (Miki 2002 164)

In Barrie's fall 1969 notebook he drafted what seems to have been a possible announcement of the new group, listing McCaffery's name first, then

Dutton's and Barreto-Rivera's, and then his own, and under that printing in large letters THE FOUR HORSEMEN OF THE APOCALYPSE, and below that what they would offer, "choral" sound poems, before drawing a spiral with the words "pure sound" at its centre. He had, with even more generosity, printed his own name last, but would have difficulty keeping it from being first in the group's public image. The pronouns "i" and "we" would be as challenging for Barrie in this new context as they had started to become at Therafields.

13. The Meanings of Crocuses

As Gramsci notes, language — and culture, I would add — "cannot be anything but 'comparative,'" always positioned in relation to another temporal moment or geopolitical space and so considered not in terms of identity but of relationality with vectors of power.

— Barbara Godard, *Canadian Literature at the Crossroads of Language and Culture*, 26–7

In May 1964 Barrie had written in his notebook that two of his main tasks were to begin deep therapy and to kick his "dreamworld." By 1970 *Book i* and *Book ii* of *The Martyrology* were emerging as the cryptic story of his carrying out those tasks. The process of extricating himself from his dreamworld was being enacted in those books' slow movement from mythology toward personal history — from fantasy toward autobiography, from timelessness toward time and its correlative death, from imagined "saints" toward "friends." The wail of dread with which the final passages of Book ii were lamenting that the saints were now "dead dead dead" was a wail of resistance to his therapy but also a wail at mortality itself — mortality that Cloudtown and its stories had allowed Barrie to sidestep or ignore. Friends die. "I" dies. The death of Terry the dog — "'first friend i've lost in years' visvaldis said" — was foreshadowing both the deaths of these saints and of Barrie's "dreamworld" and also of the preoccupation with mortality and death that will mark *The Martyrology*'s succeeding books. The "martyrs" of these next books will be not "st and" or "st rike" as much as they will be everyday humanity that must pay the price of unpredictable death in order to have life — as did Barrie's saints when they left Cloudtown, or Barrie when he left his "dreamworld" and entered therapy. [1]

Early in *Book 3*, when he is struggling to identify what he is writing now that his saints are mostly memories, Barrie writes "the saints are so much smaller than / the real worlds this poem is peopled with." Reflecting on "the game of distances" he used to play with people he writes:

> you there in the air before me
> i know your name
> you were saint ranglehold in that old game we played of one to one
> how boring that seems
> we all need so many friends

In the first 30 pages of *Book 3* numerous friends appear: David Phillips, whose letter serves as the first of its two epigraph; Ellie, implied by the second epigraph, a Batak prayer for finding a bride; the brilliant and breathless teenage friend Suzette Rochat; Andy Phillips; Rob; Barrie's sister-in-law Liz; farm staffer Mike Collins; and fellow Hypno I members Nancy Cooper and Julia Keeler.

One of the marks of a successful therapy is the extent to which the patient has internalized the therapist, and begun asking oneself questions similar to those the therapist has posed. As Barrie begins to write *The Martyrology, Book 3* in 1971 seven years after entering therapy and after almost two as a therapist, there are several signs that he was now beginning to take a similarly skeptical and inquisitive approach to his text — asking it awkward questions as he was writing and no longer taking its lines, or its "processual" first-thought-best-thought evolution, at face value. This change is similar to the one he made in 1964 to avoid "arrogant" self-expression when he began writing "ideopomes" in the place of "regular poems." Much of the saint-fantasy narratives of *Book I* and *Book II* had also been a kind of self-expression, one that for the most part was untroubled by questions such as what stories his focus on these fantasies was allowing him to avoid, or what lack of daily friendship his imagined companionship with his saints was concealing. A few pages into *Book 3*, Barrie wrote:

> lay in bed three days dreaming of this poem
> wrote it down the first draft it came out wrong
> the words stilted   awkward
> as if there were no song to sing
> only the flat statement of what i'd seen
> a circle in which saint ranglehold stood
> holding the letter H within his hand
> taunting the man i described inaccurately a poet
>
> the confusion of partial vision
> the agony of half lies
> the endless catalogues
> the exclamations   oh
>
> saint of no-names
> king of fools
> the days are spent in piecing things together
> the night's strewn with pages you do not remember writing
> third person to first person
> am i the fool
> sick of everything i've written
> fascinated by my own distaste
> keep placing one letter in front of another
> pacing my disillusionment

As the evolution of the *Book II* "Friends as Footnotes" implies, these had been years of extraordinary changes and transitions for Barrie — and the speed of change was to continue. From an abject patient of Mrs. Smith he had become vice president of Therafields. From a depressed and possibly failed poet in Vancouver he had become a celebrity of the international concrete poetry movement. From a writer who in his April 1969 notebook essay "Comics as Myth: Notes on Method in *The Martyrology*" had been proud of his fantasy creations and their connections to popular culture, he had become one at least partly convinced that those creations should "die" because they had crippled or even displaced his relationships with actual people. This displacement might have been useful, even life-saving, in his childhood years when his parents had been unable to respond to his emotional needs, but was stultifying now that his acquaintances included many who both understood and cared about him. The speed of these changes was outpacing the speed with which even he could write and publish. His notebooks show that by mid-1971 he was already drafting several sections of *The Martyrology Book 3*, such as the "Book of Oz," that would implicitly criticize and regret his fixation on the saints and other fantasy figures in the still unpublished *The Martyrology, Book 1* and *Book 11*. These sections show him slowly changing his view of the saints as important in themselves to seeing them as parts of his own psychological history, mental states he lived through and came out of — into an everyday world of friends. His saints, and his fascination with them, were becoming parts of his history, his biography, his own myth of origin. When *Book 3* would be published in 1976 as part of *The Martyrology, Books 3 & 4*, this shift would be signalled as well by a change from Roman to seemingly more contemporary Arabic "book" numbers, and by a gradual fading of the purple medieval-manuscript image that had underlain the texts of *Book 1* and *Book 11*. The poem, like Barrie, was emerging from the grip of the past.

The story he tells Irene Niechoda of the 1972 Coach House Press production of *Book 1*, during which, unable to gain any "objectivity over the work," he frantically rewrote passages before the typesetters could render them permanent (Niechoda 1992 48), is thus utterly understandable. There was little that was intrinsically "wrong" — or repairable — about those passages; Barrie had simply outgrown them. From reading them as the story of the saints-companions of language he had begun reading them as the enacted story of his therapy. Or, as he had written in his notebook on December 5, 1971 — again before *Book 1* and *Book 11* were published — it seemed to him on that day that *The Martyrology* was a failure in some important way, that there were large matters of importance to him that it should have addressed.

Most likely recognizing that Freudian psychotherapy is implicitly a process of autobiography — the predicaments of the present are to be

understood as reiterations of traumas and predicaments in one's past —
and that the psychoanalytic process is a journey back in search of origin,
Barrie had begun in 1969 a period of intense interest in family history,
autobiography, and literary ways of disguising, encrypting, or distorting
autobiography. He had already written the two halves of *Two Novels*
(1969), "Andy," and the covertly autobiographical "For Jesus Lunatick,"
and would revise them for 1971 republication. In May 1969 with Rob he
had driven, as a kind of pilgrim to each of his childhood houses and to
his mother's hometown of Plunkett and begun his "Plunkett Papers" in
an attempt to give literary and mythological shape to his family's histo-
ries. In 1971 he would begin several autobiographical projects — a poetry
sequence titled "Plains Poems," most of which would become parts of
The Martyrology, Book 3, the novel "bpNichol by John Cannyside," the
"Autobiography of Phillip Workman," and the novel *Journal*. In April
1971 he had begun a draft of yet another poem sequence, titled "Future
Music," in which he had written, after three deletions, lines that he later
included in *The Martyrology, Book 3*.

> I want to write a history of this present moment
> brings me here pen in hand
> late sun of a spring day
> my own shadow on the dandelion
> "magic words of poof poof piffles
> make me just as small as sniffles"
> the saints are so much smaller than
> the real worlds this poem is peopled with

In the Dell *Looney Tunes* comics, "poof poof piffles" had been a magic
spell by which the little girl Mary Jane could make herself as small as
Sniffles the mouse; Barrie's saints were now that small.[2] He would later
incorporate most of "Future Music" also into *The Martyrology, Book 3*.
Significantly, the phrase "future music" — with different connotations —
had been a part of the opening pages of *The Martyrology, Book 1*. Barrie was
seeing a new future. As well, in the fall of that year he had begun a kind
of autobiography of the present, a "book of hours" — a concept that he
appears to have abandoned and then reconceptualized in 1979.

Thus in many ways the public face of his life in 1970–71 did not match the private face of his current writing and his thoughts about it.

> i am not what I appear
> that straightness or fractioning
>
> nothing like the face that floats above me
> crying always crying (*The Martyrology, Book 3*)

The only area in which the two were congruent were in the sound poems being written and voiced by The Four Horsemen, who gave their first performance in May 1970 in poet George Swede's Toronto studio series, their second in November 1970 at Mount Allison University, and soon began recording compositions for the LP *Nada Canadada* (usually known as *Canadada*), which they would release in 1972. Barrie's 1970 publications reflected mostly his earlier work in "ideopomes" — the boxed and unbound anthology of visual poetry *The Cosmic Chef*, and the similarly boxed unbound collection of visual poems *Still Water*.

It was for these two boxed works and for the pamphlets *Beach Head* and *The True Eventual Story of Billy the Kid*, the latter written in 1967, that in March of 1971 he would be given a surprise Governor General's Award — the most prestigious Canadian award a writer can receive. In this case, it was an odd award in several ways. It was given for four "books" rather than one. One of the books was an anthology that included only a few pages of Barrie's own work. Two of the other three, *Beach Head* and *True Eventual Story*, were slender works with 24 and 11 pages of text. The co-winner, Michael Ondaatje, was cited for the usual one book, coincidentally titled *The Collected Works of Billy the Kid*. It had required four Nichols to equal one Ondaatje. The award would perhaps have been much less peculiar had it been given only for *Still Water*, but presumably the jury members, who included Robert Weaver and Warren Tallman, wished not only to foreground the innovative work of a young writer but also to draw attention to its diversity. (Tallman had written to Barrie in September 1969 that he was interested in "NEW CANADIAN POETRY" and "not innerested [sic] in OLD CANADIAN poetry.") However it was *True Eventual Story* — a short ironic narrative in which poet-analyst Barrie had used Stein-like repetitions and humorous Freudian platitudes to portray Billy the Kid as self-destructively gripped by sexual insecurity — by which the award would become known, and through which Barrie would become — at least briefly — notorious.

The award ceremony on May 18 preceded the notoriety by about three weeks. Most likely playfully mindful of the bardic, visionary, and ritual origins of poetry, and wishing to put a bold and personal face on his win, Barrie had Visvaldis design and Ellie sew a loose-fitting beige velour robe, and his friend John Liguore create a wide gold sash for it with hand-painted alphabet characters. The robe resembled the similarly loose fitting velour shirts, also sewn by Ellie, that he had recently begun preferring for everyday wear, but it also reflected his perception — gained mainly through his numerous sound poetry performances — that every public appearance could be an opportunity for self-production. The robe enacted his emphatic

BARRIE RECEIVING THE GOVERNOR-GENERAL'S AWARD FOR POETRY FROM GOVERNOR-GENERAL ROLAND MICHENER, MAY 1971.

refusal of received forms — the usual uniform of the male award winner being a blue two-piece suit. In that robe he was much more "bp" — the poet he had conceptualized and was still creating — than he was Barrie Nichol.[3] But he would soon be someone else yet again in Canada's House of Commons.

aka{ barrie phillip }Nichol

On June 10, 1971, Mac McCutcheon, Conservative MP for Lambton-Kent, rose in the House to condemn a "questionable piece of literature entitled, 'The True Eventual Story of Billy the Kid,' authored by B.P. Nichol," as "an affront to decency and a discouragement to serious literary efforts" and to move that the House express "its displeasure" at its having received a Governor General's Award, and summon the Secretary of State and members of "the selection board" to appear before the House of Commons Standing Committee on Broadcasting, Films, and Assistance to the Arts (Hansard 6554). Although the motion was denied the unanimous consent required for introduction, Conservative MPs continued to question the government about the award, and the office of the Secretary of State eventually responded by describing Barrie's pamphlet as "bad pornography badly done."

Various newspapers also implied that "the 15-paragraph piece, *The True Eventual Story of Billy the Kid* had won the $2500 from the Canada Council" on its own. In reply, Barrie quipped to *The Toronto Telegram* that the pamphlet must have been "bad pornography" because he was not someone who could write "good pornography" (July 8, 1971, 1). The controversy garnered Barrie nationwide publicity — publicity that was favourably received within most of the arts community, possibly more so than the award itself. He had *"épaté"* numerous Tory politicians, the most stereotypically bourgeois of *"les bourgeois"* — not at all a bad thing for a Canadian writer partly grounded in Dada.

Barrie's public appearance of witty confidence, however, was not necessarily what he was feeling. He had known about the award at least since its public announcement on March 5. On March 13, he had flown to Vancouver to read the next day at the University of British Columbia. He stayed at the home of his juror-friend Warren Tallman, who had arranged the reading. Tallman had been on the Governor General's poetry jury the previous year as well, and been partly responsible for George Bowering also being a co-winner (with Gwendolyn MacEwen) — a win publicly deplored by older poets Irving Layton and Eli Mandel because it had come, they said, at the expense of a more worthy poet, Milton Acorn, and by critic Robin Mathews, who had argued that both Tallman's citizenship and Bowering's writing were treasonously "American." Tallman's presence on the 1971 jury had probably been essential to Barrie's win.

On March 18, 1971, the morning he left Tallman's house to catch a ferry to Victoria to visit his parents, Barrie penned a startlingly poetic two-page rumination about the award in his notebook. During the visit he had been admiring crocus blooms in the Kerrisdale-area gardens. He began the entry by noting that it is enough for crocuses to exist without poems having to be written about their beauty, and without them having to be venerated in bouquets, or awards. The latter idea, he wrote, sickened him. And so, sitting at the Oak and Forty-first Avenue bus stop, he continued, he felt alarmed and frightened, as if on the verge of a perception he would prefer not to have. About the Governor General's Award he could sense a "storm" of complaints about to arise, from the numerous writers and critics who had scorned the things he and bis- sett, Steve McCaffery, David Phillips, and David W. Harris had tried to achieve. Barrie was apprehensive that innuendo and expressions of fear were already circulating; he suspected that the award may have already made the threat that others had felt his work constituted more coherent to them, and that they might attack. He added that it seemed more vital than ever

THE COVER OF *THE TRUE EVENTUAL STORY OF BILLY THE KID*, WEED/FLOWER PRESS, 1970.

that he should have a clear sense of his person, and of the direction of his writing, but that when he looked at the crocuses they seemed reluctant to embrace their own meanings or consider what each passerby might bring. He wrote that he was feeling fearful, unnerved, by what might be about to happen — that it could change, or even "destroy" him.

aka{ barrie phillip }Nichol

That such an attack by literary rivals did not materialize was probably due to Mac McCutcheon and his Conservative Party colleagues — very few writers would have wanted to be associated with that party's widely known contempt for any art not constructable as a "cultural industry." But it remains a fact that Barrie's 1971 Governor General's Award, received mainly because a friend and supporter happened to be on the jury, and given to work that, in the context of Barrie's career, was juvenilia, would be the only prize his writing would receive. Nor would bissett, Steve McCaffery, or David Phillips ever receive a major Canadian award — at least not as of this writing. The year Barrie died he would be refused a Canada Council senior artist's grant. Grants and prizes, awarded by "representative" juries, haphazardly regulate the norms of cultural productions; in all his literary work Barrie would ignore such norms.

Barrie also was aware — and to some extent embarrassed — that the books for which he had won the award were not anywhere as strong, or as important to him, as the unpublished ones still on his desk — *Monotones*, which Talonbooks was about to print, and the two books of *The Martyrology* that Coach House was committed to publishing. In July 1971, he expressed these misgivings to his Talonbooks editor, David Robinson, who was in regular contact with Tallman. Robinson wrote back, enclosing with his letter new proofs of *Monotones*:

> warren wanted you to win the governor-g's thing as soon as he heard you read here in january & i'm sure march only confirmed it more, but looking around at your stuff for last year he had a difficult time. he's told me that *still water* clinched it, the design & all, the fact that it was boxed, & that form & content were so closely allied in it, but without that i'm sure he wouldn't have been able to swing it on the basis of *the real* [sic] *eventual* and *beach head*. just consider that you got the g-g a year early, which is pretty much the way it's going to work out, or better, warren's just that much ahead of everybody. (August 9, 1971)

14. Expository Turns

Continue continuously. Give the text the reality of its existence as an object & let that object be continuously present to you — timeless in that sense.

— bpNichol, "When the Time Came" in Miki,
Meanwhile: The Critical Writings of bpNichol, 319

My note of September 12, 1970, asking Barrie to meet with me currently rests in his fonds at the Simon Fraser University Library's Special Collections. I was puzzled about what to write about Birney's numerous visual poems. I'd written to Barrie four years earlier that visual poetry had never interested me. Now I hoped to talk with him and learn something about visual poetry's theory and history, and perhaps how to read it. I was thinking of him as Mr. Canadian Concrete Poetry, Captain Concrete, the Concrete Chef, Captain Cosmic, or that enigmatic visual poem "bp." He suggested we meet for lunch. What I gathered most from that meeting was a distinction between "clean" and "dirty" concrete — terms that I learned later were probably original with him. Stephen Scobie had implied as much in a June 1968 letter that he'd written after another conversation in which Barrie had used them. He was sending Barrie some of his own visual poems.

You'll note differences between my work and a lot of the stuff you publish in *Gronk* — it is I think what you called the difference between "clean" and "dirty" concrete. I see the interest in dirty concrete but I prefer clean. Actually I've become interested lately in the number of different ways people sub-classify concrete. There does seem to be a definite split in method. Mary Ellen Solt and Mike Weaver use the division "expressionist v constructivist", and you're presumably familiar with Finlay's "fauve & suprematist". [. . .] These 3 divisions — clean, constructivist, suprematist / dirty, expressionist, fauve — don't quite correspond but they come close to it. But the Canadians, especially Bissett, of course, are dirty. You mix the two, but I sense you are more at home in the dirty stuff.

In my book about Birney I wrote — after my chat with Barrie:

In clean concrete, the preferred and dominant type, the visual shape of the work is primary, linguistic signs secondary. In this view the most effective concrete poems are those with an immediate and arresting visual effect which is made more profound by the linguistic elements used in the poem's constituent parts. The weakest are dirty concrete, those with amorphous visual shape and complex and invo-lute arrangements of the linguistic elements. (1971 63)

I evidently would have disagreed with Scobie about Barrie's work and viewed it as mostly "clean."

Also in the Simon Fraser bpNichol fonds are files of 1967–76 letters from the British literary and cultural critic Nicholas Zurbrugg, with whom Barrie in 1968 had been having a lengthy dialogue about increasing conflicts among international concrete poets concerning what can be per-mitted to be called "concrete" poetry. Zurbrugg, who at 21 was about to begin a doctorate at St. John's College at Oxford, favoured what he called "the purist movement," which Barrie had evidently been questioning in his letters as a "great error." Zurbrugg wanted concrete to be only "an extension of poets's work," favouring "a puritanical respect for the 'poetry' in 'concrete poetry,'" and was "hesitant to accept signs by non-poets — letter pictures" — i.e. he didn't seem to want the work of non-writer visual artists to be considered "concrete." He wanted "space and words and type (if possible) all with deliberate care selected to form a new whole a typographic minimal semantic poem . . . word and type should have equal value" (June 4, 1968). Barrie appears to have resisted such rigid definition, and slyly teased Zurbrugg with the question "wots poet tree." The latter's concern that concrete should be something "purely" created by writers only rather than visual artists, seemed to presume that one was unlikely to be both — as Barrie tended to be. His belief that its elements should be "word and type," rather than word and visual design, also suggested that his "pure" had much in common with Barrie's "dirty" in that both assumed a concrete poem was to be read at least as much as viewed. Zurbrugg — who as well as aiming at an academic career was working toward founding the magazine of concrete poetry, *Stereo Headphones* — also seemed concerned by recent remarks by various French concrete poets — "julian blaine   jean francois bory   jochen gers . . . are crying the death and sad obsolete state of concrete" and are "using photos etc integrated (?) in their works" (September 11, 1968). "I've been writing french to surprisingly a lot of french poets who say concrete is obsolete poetry / is sad obsolete there's only the action of reader / and proposal of writer . . ." (November 12, 1968). The near-revolution of the previous May had of course politicized the contexts of much French art.

It is against this background of intense European debate about the nature and possible "death" of concrete poetry that Barrie not only speaks to Scobie and myself in those awkwardly metaphoric terms of "clean" and "dirty" concrete but writes the "poetry being at a dead-end" passages of *ABC: The Aleph Beth Book*, which he would publish in 1971 — and which Zurbrugg would ask to see. Barrie would publish his statement "Concrete" in Zurbrugg's *Stereo Headphones* (reprinted Miki 2002 30) in 1970, with its explicit statement that "some sort of purist movement [in concrete poetry] . . . would be a great error." He wants multiple entrances and exits. He also cites Scobie's September 1968 letter in a way that could be misread as attributing to him the formulation of "clean" and "dirty" — when what Scobie had written was "what you called the difference between 'clean' and 'dirty' concrete." Quite possibly the terms had become so common in Barrie's *Ganglia* conversations with Aylward, Harris, and Rob Hindley-Smith that he no longer thought of how they had developed as important.

Zurbrugg went on to write influential books on Beckett, Proust, Burroughs, and postmodernism, and to professorships in New Zealand

and the UK. Barrie — emphatically more both poet and intellectual than an academic — teamed up with Steve McCaffery in 1971–72 to found "TRG" — the two-person Toronto Research Group — to investigate much the same literary field as Zurbrugg but with activist rather than interpretive intent. Their discussions, McCaffery writes, had included "[t]he possibility of radically altering the textual role of the reader; of extending the creative, idiomatic basis of translation; of a poetry that would jettison the word in favour of more current cognitive codes; and of a material prose that would challenge the spatio-temporal determinates of linearity" (1992 9). A formal print launch of TRG would become possible later that year, McCaffery notes, when "Frank Davey asked Barrie to become involved with the journal *Open Letter*. Davey offered him a section in each issue to 'fill up' in whatever way he wanted" (9).

Barrie's route to *Open Letter* was actually somewhat quicker than McCaffery recalls. Around the time I was lunching with Barrie in September 1970 about Birney's concrete poetry I had been working with editor Victor Coleman on beginning a new series of *Open Letter* in Toronto for which Coach House Press would be the publisher. Our application for Canada Council funding for our non-normal magazine was approved the next August, and we set a deadline of October 15, 1971, for material for the first issue. On October 5, 1971, I handwrote and mailed this note to Barrie:

> I've been trying to reach you on the phone over the past two weeks. The Canada Council has just given me $2700 to restart *Open Letter* as an avant-garde review journal. The mag will be larger, contain mostly articles and reviews of small press publications, will be printed by Coach House, & will pay $3 a printed page. I'm offering a few people guaranteed open space in it for reviews or articles. Would this interest you? Our first deadline is 15 October (we'll be publishing 3 times a year after that).
>
> Do let me know if you're interested.

A few weeks later George Bowering came to Toronto to promote his McClelland & Stewart collection *Touch*, and stayed for almost a week with me and my partner Linda. Various writers dropped in to see him, including Barrie — who tended, I was learning, to visit people rather than receive them where he was living. One night Barrie, George, and David McFadden persuaded Linda to become a writers' agent — and arrange readings for them and try to sell their accumulating manuscripts. Barrie quickly became a regular visitor to our north Toronto house, appearing at the door especially on a Sunday or Monday evening on his way back from events at the Therafields farm. He would read new poems to us, or tip off Linda about hints he'd encountered about what schools or libraries might be open to appearances by her new clients.

His correspondence with Zurbrugg is one of a number of indications that Barrie was now considering adding critical and theoretical writing to his already numerous activities. The larger book projects he had undertaken at *Ganglia* — bissett's *we sleep inside each other all* (1966) and Birney's *Pnomes, Jukollages & other Stunzas* (1969) — had required in his view not only the advocacy implicit in publishing them but an introduction or afterword that explained or defended visual poetry. By the time I met him he had begun trying to write a book on Gertrude Stein, a writer from whom he has learned much but who, he believed, had never received appropriate advocacy or explanation. It was to be "a book on Gertrude Stein's theories of personality as revealed in her early opus *The Making of Americans*" (Miki 2002 318). Barrie offered *Open Letter* one of the first chapters, which he had drafted the previous April (in his notebook the draft accompanies texts dated April 20, 1971), "some beginning writings on GERTRUDE STEIN'S THEORIES OF PERSONALITY." Victor and I had idealistically conceived of this *Open Letter* series as an artist's series in which we would do minimal editing and allow each contributor control of the layout, typography, citation style, and spelling employed; our artist contributors — bill bissett would contribute an essay to the sixth issue — would have thought through their positions on such matters, we believed. Barrie's essay, like his prose in *Two Novels,* and like Birney's later poems, had no conventional punctuation marks; he used space instead. He cited quotations as "(p. 166)" rather than as plain parenthetical numbers. The quotations themselves were unusually long — more of the essay's lines were Stein's than were Barrie's — and undoubtedly offended fair-use copyright laws. Barrie sometimes had little to add to them except that her insights were "amazing," "remarkable" (Miki 2002 77), "precise" (80),

aka{ barrie phillip }Nichol

or "enormous" in their ramifications (74). Victor and I, in our dogmatic respect for artists' wishes, had the typesetters set the essay as received — difficult to do because of the various approximations of typewriter spacing that had to be made. It became the first multi-page article Barrie published in a journal.

A little later Barrie showed me another piece he had written — under the pseudonym bpLichon — "a review of bpNichol's 'some beginning writings on Gertrude Stein's Theories of Personality' as published in *Open Letter* 2/2," and which he was considering also publishing in *Open Letter.* Instead he left the manuscript to be discovered in the sfu fonds; it would be published in Roy Miki's *Meanwhile: The Critical Writings of bpNichol* in 2002. "Lichon" was unhappy with Nichol's punctuation. Barrie had had him write that "Nichol has taken what he was doing in *For Jesus Lunatick* & extended it through the incorporation of hints gleaned from [Hansjörg] Mayer[1] but he has not taken it far enough."

in this i can see his (at this point) failed attempt to express how his perceptual system has been altered by his encounter with Stein's perceptual system [. . .] i know for a fact these first notes of Nichol's were written in the spring of 71 & submitted to *Open Letter* without revision   obviously enough came through to the editors that they saw fit to publish them without insisting that Nichol make his intent clearer   seeing this we can say that Nichol has partially succeeded   but the hesitancy in & tentativeness of these first notes shows through in his lack of mastery over his own structures (he is (for instance) still wrestling with how to handle the differentiation between commas & periods   he has set out to create punctuation anew to serve his own ends & has not succeeded) (Miki 2002 96)

Barrie and Steve McCaffery — an artist whose academic background had led him to be more specific in his arguments than Barrie and arguably more scholarly in his innovations — were now discussing many of Barrie's publications as they occurred. Some of their discussion in this case, Barrie indicated to me, had led to his second thoughts and Mr. Lichon's reflections.

Barrie would soon abandon his Gertrude Stein book project — largely because he was sensing that by extracting his numerous quotations he might be offending her belief in a "continuous present" and her request that her readers "Give the text the reality of its existence as an object & let that object be continuously present to you." He would explain in 1983:

> . . . how could I continue extracting? I was violating Stein's text when I did that, the very spirit of her text, & I was, of course, proving the validity of Heisenberg's Principle of Uncertainty as it applied to litera-ture. By extracting I was bringing the text to a dead halt & we were no longer observing it as it was & therefore our observations ceased to have any validity (Miki 2002 319)

His explanation, with its invocation of Heisenberg, had major implica-tions for the subjectivity of his own writing — for example, could the bpNichol "i" that narrates *The Martyrology* and reads and often disassem-bles and reassembles its words be the same as the "i" that records its text, organizes its sections, or arranges its publication? As literary theorist and critic Terry Eagleton would write in 2003, "The free subject . . . cannot itself be represented in the field which it generates, any more than the eye can capture itself in the field of vision" (214).

But Barrie's April 1971 chapter did illustrate the continued centrality of psychoanalytic theory in his ongoing thoughts about writing. He wrote there of Stein's *The Making of Americans*, its personality theory of "bottom nature," and its subtitle "a history of a family's progress" that the work was

> not so much a novel as an attempt to encompass the shifting forms of human personality in words to create a vocabulary with which to describe them   the subtitle is accurate on more than one level   the family is all of man and the history is everyone   it is in that sense an epic on a scale never attempted before or since [. . .] beyond that it is perhaps the only major work on human person-ality that has never been approached or studied as such   this then is the bottom nature of what i'm trying to do (Miki 2002 72–73)

His curious blending of concern both with "personality" and "epic" operate here to blend psychoanalytic and literary theory. Moreover, his

aka{ barrie phillip }Nichol

description of a text that focuses on family and history and "shifting personality" and that is an "epic" in which "the family is all of man" is one that could also describe the two books of *The Martyrology* which he was about to publish — and that would become increasingly descriptive of the poem as the overall nine books developed. His "epic" would be written on an even larger "scale" than Stein's. As well, in those April pages of his notebook he was also drafting the "Future Music" passages of *The Martyrology, Book II,* and writing to himself the comment "I want to write the history of this present moment" — a line that later became part of the poem and that was most likely inspired by his reflections on Stein's "history" of "everyone." Writing the "history of this present moment" returned Barrie to Heisenberg's paradox — if he were to stop the moment's motion he would be omitting part of its character but if he followed its motion he might never be able to indicate its substantiality.

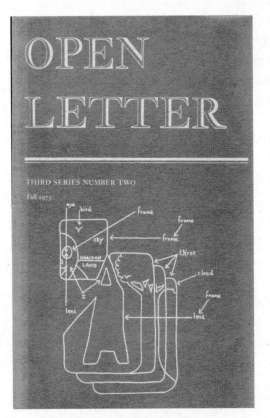

THE COVER OF *OPEN LETTER*, SERIES 3, NUMBER 2, 1975, SUBSTANTIALLY EDITED BY BARRIE AND DISPLAYING ONE OF HIS VISUAL POEMS.

In the following issue of *Open Letter* (Fall 1972) Barrie published a three-page review of Peter Finch's anthology *Typewriter Poems*. Barrie employed a somewhat less ambiguous spatial punctuation, quoted none of the contents, and made cogent summaries of the various difficulties currently being encountered in "typewriter" and other visual poetries. He and McCaffery published the TRG manifesto and first report, on translation, in the Spring 1973 issue of *Open Letter*. The writing in these was anything but tentative. It was factual, confident, self-aware, critically self-referential — probably because of the two consciousnesses composing it — and at times humorous.

This work that Barrie began doing with McCaffery in 1971–72 as "TRG" was in a way one of the last major sites of Barrie's self-training. He had trained himself in visual poetry and in writing "regular" poetry that avoided arrogance and predictability. He had trained himself as a performer of sound poetry and as an editor and small press publisher. He had worked through his therapy to become a psychotherapist, and trained on the job to become an effective administrator of Therafields. In his dialogues and collaborations with McCaffery he was learning about the breadth of research and skepticism necessary to the making of generalizations, and the clarity of presentation necessary to avoid ambiguity and misunderstanding.

15. Me & We

[A]s soon as I see the word I used (or avoided, for even avoiding it is a way of using it) I know that I have a fictional character in front of me.

— Sven Lindquist, *Exterminate All the Brutes*, 104

In early August 1972 something caused Barrie to write to his parents a description of the emotional difficulties that had precipitated his sudden departure for Toronto eight years before. He also appears to have chastised them for their lack of interest in his work at Therafields, and said that in his life choices he had had to be himself. Quite possibly he was moved by an accumulation of developments — his Governor General's Award, his mother's subsequent letter that she and his father were proud of his accomplishment and wished they could have afforded to attend the ceremony, his recent appointment to the Canada Council multimedia jury, the positive reception that was being given *The Martyrology, Book I* and *Book II*, and perhaps the understanding of the limitations of family that he was beginning to envision while writing *The Martyrology, Book 3*, particularly in the parts he originally had drafted in the spring of 1971 as "Plains Poems."

> . . . i need a sense of continuity
> i have no family anymore as you would call it
> no blood kin i can feel close to

only a brother i do not talk to
why?

we is first of all a blood relation
later a station you pay homage
carry your cross of loss thru life
midwife to your own grief
friends are what save you

He had also spent much of 1971 and early 1972 working on his never
to be completed "autobiographies" "bpNichol by John Cannyside" and
"Autobiography of Phillip Workman" — the latter with its numerous pas-
sages based on his confused feelings toward his mother. And in some of the
"Plains Poems"–derived passages of *The Martyrology, Book 3* he was focus-
sing yet again on the troubled 1963–64 Oedipal scene on Comox Street:

listening to the rain
remember a time on comox
andy dave barb & me
                              that form of we
place   vancouver
time   1963
[. . .]
            there is no way to encompass everything
we need to encompass as much as we can

the pain is the recognition the work outlives us
we die before we's completion
                                          whatever that is
these memories of vancouver   an older time
are memories of a we that never worked
existed in a timelessness which is not memory
[. . .]

earlier today
woke up from sleep

a frog in my room
caught it
carried it outside
            it pissed in my hand
terror of me
let it free in the rain and mud

Possibly Barrie hoped by writing frankly to his mother and father that he might end at least the "standing still" between them. Or at the very least that he might be able to let them go free.

On August 15, 1972, his mother replied, in the routine everything-is-normal language that had been characteristic of all her letters. Of course she had always believed that Barrie's childhood was normal, and that his adolescent and adult life decisions had had little to do with anyone except himself. She told him that they had noticed nothing unusual in his emotions when he was leaving for Toronto back in 1964, and joked that perhaps her not noticing had something to do with the "generation gap." The jest implied that Barrie's problem might well have been a culturally systemic one rather than a personal crisis that had arisen from the specifics of his family.

In her next paragraph she seemed to argue that perhaps there had been no problem, that maybe he'd been mistaken about himself. Or perhaps their lack of communication had been his fault for seeming like such a regular lad. She wrote that he had always been a cheerful boy, easy to get along with, seemingly without a care in the world. They had known that he was going through the time of "growing up," a time that is usually tough on the young, but everyone goes through that so they hadn't thought much about it. And because he'd really been a jolly and level-headed boy, she suggested, they hadn't noticed any problems. And he hadn't mentioned any — why didn't he talk to them back then, she wondered, pointing out that his mom and dad hadn't been monsters. But even though that was all long ago, she continued, if somehow they were to blame, they were now sorry. As for rarely mentioning his Therafields work, she told him that he had always been evasive whenever she had asked about it. She wrote that much like he had to be himself, she and his father had to be themselves, and that it was difficult for them to accept the way that he dressed and the way that he lived. Moreover she doubted that these ways were really "him" — that they didn't correspond to the person that she believed him to be. She added that it was even harder for his dad to accept the way he lived — that in his work at the CN offices how one dressed and how neat one appeared had been important. He hoped that Barrie's long hair was at least clean and tidy. Writing these remarks seems to have reminded her how rigidly she and his dad needed to keep to their views. She then wrote that although they still loved him, "we" were "us" — underlining both pronouns. She signed off by telling Barrie that she was confident that her letter had pretty well cleared things up, and that they were "proud" of both his poetry and his work and were sending "lots of love."

Barrie's letter that she is responding to has vanished, but the enormity of what it may have asked of her is evident in the terms by which she tries to dismiss or normalize it — telling him that he had always seemed a good regular boy, that everyone has to face growing up, that his problems, if he had any, happened long ago, and that they still loved him. One could say that Barrie has been unrealistic in asking, but he had most likely been writing at that moment much more as a son than as a novice psychotherapist. His mother's response is probably as warm and understanding as one could expect considering how truly baffled she has been by the life he has chosen, and how "evasive" he may very well have been about this life and the troubles that brought him to it.[1] But Barrie must nevertheless have been at least emotionally disappointed to receive it. He would have to continue to carry his "cross of loss."

However, his letter had somewhat diminished the gap between them, and brought his parents' knowledge of him closer to his own knowledge of himself. He visited them and his sister Deanna the following February, and recorded part of the visit in his notebook. On February 17, 1973, he and Deanna, their parents, and their Aunt Addie (the wife of his father's brother Walter) had talked about the 1950 Red River Flood, and he had learned some details that he considered "important." Earlier that spring, he was told, he had had his tonsils removed, and had felt, with some anger, that in the process he had been lied to. When the flood had begun, both his mother and father had been unable to conceal their fear. When, after evacuation and a brief happy stay with his mother's sister in Saskatoon, his mother had taken Deanna, Don, and him to the home of her brother Bill in Regina, trouble had been almost immediate. Bill had falsely accused Barrie of breaking a window. Bill's wife Ethel had treated Avis as if she were "scum." Barrie had hated both Ethel and Bill because she was aloof and easily angered and he repeatedly defended her. He was also unhappy that his mother had brought them there to be treated like low-class cousins. When his mother had moved them to her mother's home in Calgary he had promptly caught chicken pox and then they had all had to rush back to Winnipeg because of a possible strike by railway workers. While his parents were preoccupied with their Winnipeg lives, he had started his first year of school. In their repaired and redecorated Wildwood Park home he had become so depressed that he had quietly painted the wall beside his crib with black watercolours. Deanna had belatedly noticed and called their mother but by this time he was sleeping and he was awoken by his mother angrily spanking him. In his notebook Barrie recorded all these new recollections in terse abbreviated phrases, as if worried that he might forget something if he didn't hurry on to write them all. He observed that his mother seemed still to feel guilty about the spanking. He wrote also that he suspected that he may have mentally "fused" his mother with her haughty sister-in-law.

This is the only passage in all of Barrie's notebooks and letters that records a moment in which he has been able to talk to his parents frankly about difficult childhood happenings. Whether there had been other such moments in the past, or whether this moment owed something to a change he had managed through his letter, or to the presence of his aunt Addie and the family dynamics her presence released, is probably unknowable. But the brief intense discussion had clearly released vital news from the past for Barrie, and showed him his family not only taking his pain seriously but also able to reveal their own feelings of fear and inadequacy during his childhood years. The family scene sketched is much different from the defensive "all was normal" portrayal of his mother's letter. It may have required all the skills and insights Barrie had learned in house groups, standard groups, and learning groups for him and the others to pass safely through the conversation's various revelations.

Internally dated "late february 73," the penultimate passage of *The Martyrology, Book 3*, titled "last take," followed this scene by only a week or two. Barrie was still in British Columbia, now driving with "dave" — David

aka{ barrie / phillip }Nichol

Phillips — on Vancouver's north shore near the mountains that give their names to the harbour's Lions Gate. Punning on the proverb that has March coming "in like a lion" and going "out like a lamb," Barrie wrote of birth and of time's inexorability — an inexorability that he sees as also the incest prohibition — the door "you are not permitted to open again." The birth image had led him to imagine "the lion's mouth" as a woman's sex:

> time
> the lion's month before us the lamb's born in
> the door
> you are not permitted to open again
> enter thru the lion's mouth the man's root gets planted in
> *not* to be consumed
> as tho the use of lips weren't speech
> a doorway into the woman's soul intelligence comes out of
> SCREAMING
> a complete thot
> born from the dialogue between you

This fast-moving passage in which, as "intelligence," a child is born out of "woman's soul" produces almost immediately in the succeeding lines Barrie's own "birth" out of a series of women, the last of which is Lea Hindley-Smith. The key puns that enable this movement are "lips" and "dialogue," the latter of which begins as sexual dialogue and ends as both the Freudian dialogue of psychotherapy and the words of poetry the multiply-born Barrie can speak. Implicitly his mother's labia are partly uttering the words we are reading.

> or what comes forth from my mouth
> born from the woman in me
> handed down thru my grandma ma and lea
> is what marks me most a man
> that i am finally this we
> this one & simple thing
> my father Leo
> my mother Cancer

                    she births herself
        the twin mouths of women
                    w's omen

It is notable that Barrie here equated his grandma, ma, and Lea in their
roles in helping him toward manhood. He did not compare them.

   Barrie's quest in these first three books of *The Martyrology* to find a
"we" — a quest that is suddenly completed here in "i am finally this
we" — may very well have passed through his frank self-revealing letter
of the previous August and the family "dialogue" that he had recently
experienced. Though focussed mostly on his mother, this process had
not excluded his father — who I surmise has been at least a small part of
the "father" whom *The Martyrology* poet has been recurrently addressing.
Barrie continued the passage:

   our words are spun within the signs our fathers left
   the sibilance of s
                   the cross of t
   there are finally no words for your father
   too many letters multiplying the signs
   you are the one
                   the unifying
   no signifier when we cannot grasp the signified

He had evidently been recalling Lacan's theory of the phallus as the sign
that guarantees symbolic meaning and enables language, but that also
testifies to the "lack" or absence of the signified; he possibly was also
recalling Julia Kristeva's theories of a female "semiotic" and male "sym-
bolic," for he went on to consider that his saints have been conceptually
"in between / the world of men / women."

   The passage — and effectively *Book 3* itself — ended with him real-
izing that visually the word "me" becomes "we" if the 'm' is turned upside
down. He drew an image of this inversion and then wrote:

   the emblems were there when i began
   seven years to understand

                                    aka{ barrie
                                         phillip }Nichol

the first letter / level of
martyrdom

It was seven years since he began writing *Scraptures* and "discovered" the saints. "M" is the first letter of the word "martyrdom" and must itself be "martyred," given up, surrendered, if the "me" is to become "we."

The overall "last take" passage is a graphic example of the non-arrogance Barrie had aspired to achieve nine years before when inventing his poet-persona "bpNichol" and deciding to focus on writing ideopomes so as to reduce the temptation of self-expression and to force himself to look for meanings not within himself but within the words he was working with. Before that time Barrie might have written a poem about driving with "dave" through the North Shore mountains, and found meaning in the scenery they encountered or conversations they had. In "last take" Barrie — through bpNichol — finds meaning instead in the words he has used in the poem, in the alternate meanings they carry and propose. "last take" is visibly a bpNichol poem that speaks to the Barrie who wrote to his mother, visited his parents, went driving with dave, and began a seven-year quest when he had bpNichol start writing and publishing *Scraptures*. The wavering "i" of "last take" is doubly both bp and Barrie — much like the "father" that *The Martyrology* would keep addressing would continue to be simultaneously the Glen Nichol who still wants Barrie to get a haircut, the father-deity who speaks the world into being in the first lines of *Genesis* or in the myth of Palongawhoya, and the Lacanian phallus that allows language's "symbolic order."

It had taken a while for bpNichol — the poet of language and image and reader of their meanings — to become dominant in *The Martyrology* the way he had been in Barrie's visual and conceptual poems. Much of *Book I* and *Book II* seem to have been produced by Barrie Nichol and the various pains and traumas he was taking to Lea. Of course Barrie is still here in *Book 3*, not only travelling through British Columbia but also watching and guiding bpNichol. It was Barrie who decided that he — bpNichol — would write a "Coda" to *Book 3*, the "Mid-Initial Sequence" on the "P" that is much more visible in the word "bpNichol" than it is in "Barrie." The sequence is a tour de force of reading language — starting with reading that "P" for the meanings it may carry, as in the section "bushes":

>dawn
>the r rises
>brushes drawn

>the w hole scene
>into which the world
>disappears

>d is a p
>pear shaped

>dear H
>a p edges
>into the sea

>sun
>the unnenviable s

This section — like all those in the sequence — is a kind of expanded version of the language readings of *Still Water*. It's a bpNichol, ideopoet, cosmic chef passage.

Watching his irrepressible client-persona pun throughout here on how ABCD contains all of human time, the BC before Christ's birth and the AD of the present, with D for death (or the Last Judgement and the re-emergence of the *D*evil) marking its future end, Barrie seems to have realized for the first time in his seven-year poem that bpNichol, and the letters of his initials, would live much longer than him.

>whatever dies
>the secrets do not die with you
>the lore we all seek (l or e)
>choices are not disinterested

aka{ barrie phillip }Nichol

d is in t
it is the old story HE lived thru
HIS death & suffering
33 years into HIS time
22 letters left to pass thru
what birth will herald the change

Christ himself dies 33 years into his time — "AD" — leaving 22 letters more — E to Z, one of which is the P of bpNichol. Barrie, or bp, continues these readings in the next section, with the richly ambiguous thought of "conceiving himself a writer."

11 years since i first conceived myself a writer
took up the task to earn that name
& now i see
i (n) am e

The "name" he has earned is both writer and of course the mid-initial name, "bpNichol, writer." The poem's "i" continues to signify doubly, or perhaps triply as Barrie, bp, and alphabet symbol.

can i speak in the midst of suffering
address the cross we wear too carelessly

t i' m e
part of the movement out of this dark time
we are all trapped in a D we do not recognize

i will never wear the H
never see HIS face

"We" are trapped in the *D* of *AD* and of the death its end signifies. None of us will reach *H*, or *I* and *S*, which all occur after *D* even though the language now goes there and *HE* — *H* and *E* — promises to be.

bp concluded the sequence with a palindrome that Barrie woke up

hearing — the scene appears to argue that the palindrome was not some-
thing Barrie as possible "maker" of poems had made but one that was said
to him.

> 'dogma i am god'
> it is all that's said
> woke up this morning
> these words in my head
> a palindrome
> linked with   an image
> of friends   two poets i knew
> disagreed   were not speaking with each other
>
> d is a greed
> a gluttony of shape
> swallowing the era which it ends

"d is a greed" is of course a reading of "disagreed" — one that returns
Barrie and reader to the "arrogance" that he had hoped to escape in 1964
by taking up visual poetry. This "greed" is inherent in the way in which
the devouring *D* — the end of AD — surrounds the palindrome at both
its beginning and end, effectively containing it; none of the letters in
between can get outside of the two *D*s.

> is it the D of devil then
> the apocalypse the bible prophesied
> ends the age we live in

Barrie/bp asks, and then decides the palindrome must be heresy, a temp-
tation, perhaps, that his sleep had permitted or overheard.

> 'dogma i am god'
> heresy
>   hearsay
> in the worst sense

aka{ barrie phillip }Nichol

> false pride
> who thinks to bestride the world
> because he feels crushed by it.

Barrie has made a surprising return to his thoughts about poetry eight years before when he had realized that he found "repugnant" poetry in which poets appear to seek special status because of pain they have suffered — claiming to be important and "sensitive" because they have been "crushed" by the world. That return, and the apocalyptic concerns that accompany it, mark this "Coda" as an emphatic and seemingly conclusive ending to *Book 3*. Barrie has achieved much of what he has been aiming for in terms of both personal answers and writing solutions. He has brought *The Martyrology* further from the style and poetics of his "regular" poems of the 1960s and extremely close to the poetics of his visual and conceptual ones. The last sections of *Book 3* are as much developments from *Still Water* and sections of *Love: a Book of Remembrances* as they are ones from "Journeying and the Returns" or *Monotones*.

The concerns that emerge from this ending might prompt a reader to ask — as some already have — whether Barrie was religious. He's probably not at this moment in any sectarian or even narrowly Western or Eastern or Aboriginal understandings of that word. But he believes that language, human existence, and our world's existence, have come into being against great odds. He would not object to the word "miracle." He knows that Christ lived for 33 years. And he knows that there are 22 letters that follow *D*.

Barrie would also believe that *The Martyrology* had now come to an end, and not begin work on a fourth book for more than a year and a half. He would intensify his work on his prose autobiographies and on preparing the less personal *Love: a Book of Remembrances* for publication. In June 1973, after an evening session with some house group clients, he would write in his notebook a somewhat confused reflection on about his writing identity — on his self-definition as "bpNichol: writer." To some extent these thoughts appear to have been raised by the Oedipal desires he has encountered once again in trying to write his "autobiographies," and perhaps also by his having recently come, for a brief moment, closer than ever before to his mother. He wrote that his current writing problems

seemed associated with what he had initially wanted from writing —
those Freudian secondary gains — definitions of himself as "bpNichol"
and "writer." But secondary gains, he noted, are not what writing should
be done for. He wrote that he felt suspended between being upset and
not being upset, and also between his work as a psychotherapist and some
out-of-date understanding of himself. But he felt afraid of who he might
discover himself to be, because he knew he was no longer the person he
had once believed himself to be, but could see no new self-understanding
that felt right for him. He noted that he was finding it a struggle even to
think simultaneously about his work in therapy and in writing, and also
experiencing a strong desire to repress his awareness that he was having
such a struggle.

These may seem like strange thoughts to be having after his pow-
erful writing at the end of *The Martyrology, Book 3* — that "Barrie" could
be tempted to belittle or repress the "bpNichol" self-definition that had
unveiled so many openings before him and filled so much of his own
emptiness with sparkling alphabetic activity — but of course poetry was
not therapy, much like the public bpNichol was not merely Barrie. The
poem itself may very well have stirred hopes that were at this moment too
large for him to accept or feel worthy of.

aka{ barrie phillip }Nichol

16. Working Together

the family is all of man and the history is everyone

— bpNichol in Miki,
Meanwhile: The Critical Writings of bpNichol, 73

Although in mid-1973 Barrie — not yet having recognized that *The Martyrology* was itself an ongoing present-tense autobiography — was still in the grip of the unfinished prose "autobiographical" narratives about John Cannyside and Phillip Workman, his new Four Horsemen and TRG associations with Steve McCaffery were leading him in different directions. As early as the spring of 1972, after more than a year of performing with the Horsemen at events in the Toronto area, he had written in his notebook about his dissatisfaction with solo sound — that such poems were now "over" in his work; that he had learned from them all that he had needed. He had begun to see his connection to a collaborating co-performer as more creatively fruitful than his own connection to an audience, telling himself that he had become overly focussed on the responses of the people he was performing for, that he had always "retrogressed" to the material they were most comfortable with rather than moving forward and challenging them with something unfamiliar, that he thus needed to make "drastic" changes in what he aspired to. During 1973–74, the Horsemen, aided by the LP *Nada Canadada*, which they had released in late 1972, would become nationally known, giving performances in Ottawa, Montreal, Saint John, Wolfville,

Hamilton, Edmonton, Winnipeg, and Vancouver. During appearances in
the latter three cities they would record the tracks for their next LP, *Live in
the West*, which would be released in 1977. They also began work on what
they and their publisher believed would be a collaboratively written book,
Horse d'Oeuvres. But the manuscript that resulted, which was published in
the *PaperJacks* mass-market paperback format in 1975, was merely a col-
lection of individual works by the group's members. "When we were first
approached about this manuscript, our impulse was to deliver a unified,
collectively written book — a print parallel to our compositions in sound.
But we have abandoned that idea," they wrote in the collectively written
foreword. Barrie's disappointment at this abandonment (which he seemed

THE FOUR HORSEMEN IN PERFORMANCE, 1973.

at the time to
have experi-
enced as a literal
abandonment
by his fellow
Horsemen) was
partly mitigated,
however, by the
statement in
the concluding
paragraph that
the group con-
sidered the book
"the first com-
positional step in
a process leading to more and more written collaborations."

It was mitigated also by the fact that the group had already begun
work on a collaborative novel to be titled "Slow Dust." But by April 15,
1975, even as *Horse d'Oeuvres* was being published, that effort had been
also, in Barrie's view, failing. He wrote a lengthy passage in his note-
book about it, declaring that real collaboration cannnot happen if the
collaborators work from preset narrative positions, which is what he saw
Barreto-Rivera and Dutton as doing. Each was not responding to any-
thing the others were writing, and thus were taking few risks. For Barrie
collaboration required risk. Why were they even attempting the project?

he wondered.[1] He wrote that he personally had lost "heart" in it when during a discussion Barreto-Rivera had exclaimed that Barrie's contribution was an example of the kind of writing he most detested.

In his usual psychoanalytic way, he connected his disappointment with his childhood traumas. He observed that he now was feeling among the Horsemen much the way he had felt in his family — that not one of them was listening to what he was saying, that not one even wanted to hear him. Maybe he was causing the problem himself by responding to it much as he had in his family — by joking, or compromising, or accepting dubious excuses. He hadn't been asserting his beliefs enough, he concluded. He wrote as well that he now also doubted the value, and possibly the authenticity, of the group's sound poetry collaborations. He wrote to himself that the group had become like a bad marriage. That they were surviving on the memories of the relationship they once had rather than on what they had now. He didn't want to do any more Horsemen performances because such events were no longer where they "were." He doubted that they were anywhere.[2]

In a February 28, 1975, interview with Nick Power and Anne Sherman, Barrie had also mentioned the attempted novel, and said "we aren't doing performances any more," and hinted at the interpersonal difficulties they had encountered. "We've had difficulty ourselves personally, in knowing what we want to do when we finish a reading." The applause ends and "there we are, we're no longer a group and we're just individuals and it's often a very dislocating time. That was something we were never quite able to get a hold of" (Miki 2002 164).

The Horsemen would give only one major performance in 1975, and — despite releasing four more recordings and appearing outwardly "together" at concerts throughout the United States and in Europe — would work together only sporadically over the next 13 years.

Barrie's collaborations with McCaffery as TRG would be equally sporadic, but more because of the formidable preparations that work required and how busy both men were with other tasks than because of any conflict between them. The substantial reading list that eventually appeared in *Rational Geomancy*, "the collected research reports of the Toronto Research Group, 1973–1982," contained more than 180 books, including ones by Barthes, Beckett, Berne, Bory, Brophy, Catullus,

Caws, Chomsky, Cortázar, Derrida, Gins, Graves, Jabès, Joyce, Kafka, Lacan, Lakoff and Johnson, Mallarmé, Marinetti, McLuhan, Nabokov, Proust, Ricoeur, Robbe-Grillet, Sapir, Saussure, Stein, Steiner, Vygotsky, Whitehead, Whorf, and Wittgenstein. While Barrie outlined much of his personal preparations in his notebooks, he made no criticism there of the process, and spoke only enthusiastically about it when bringing texts it had produced to me for publication in *Open Letter*. These "reports" would include "The Book as Machine" in the fall of 1973, "The Book as Machine (II)" in summer 1974, "The Search for Non-Narrative Prose" in fall 1974, "The Search for Non-Narrative Prose Part 2" in fall 1975, and "Narrative Interlude: Heavy Company" in spring 1976. The focus on various aspects of narrative led them to begin jointly assembling an anthology for the Coach House Press "The Story So Far" series. It would be the fourth in the series, cleverly titled *The Story So Four* (1975).

Possibly because of the varieties of writing their preparations were requiring them to read, Barrie's own writing expanded and mutated, moving from visual poetry to collaborative visual poetry with painter Barbara Caruso, to an oratorio version of *The Martyrology* done in 1974 in collaboration with composer Howard Gerhard, as well as to 'pataphysical visual and textual conceptions. There would be little public sign of these changes, however. The four collaborations with Caruso, beginning with *The Adventures of Milt the Morph in Colour* (1972), would be published in expensive limited editions sold mostly to collectors. *The Martyrology: an oratorio* would be privately published in an edition of 40. Parts of the 'pataphysical "Probable Systems" series, based on Wittgenstein's *The Brown Book*, that he began in 1972–73 would not appear until 1985 in the collection *Zygal* and 1990 in the posthumous collections *Art Facts* and *Truth: a Book of Fictions*. The long draft of the serial visual poem *Extreme Positions* that he began writing in a notebook in the summer of 1973 would not become a book until 1981.

Another collaboration that Barrie attempted in these years was with the Quebecois sound poet Raôul Duguay, of whom he became aware through Barbara Godard's efforts in 1972 to translate various Quebecois poets' manifestos for *Open Letter*. Barrie gave a joint reading with Duguay in Montreal in the fall of 1972, and also interviewed him for the Fall 1973 issue of *Open Letter*. In the spring of 1973 he wrote in his notebook a

reminder not only to transcribe the interview but also to write to Michael
Macklem of Oberon Press about creating a joint Nichol/Duguay sound
poetry LP under the Oberon imprint, write to Peter Meilleur about an
article he had written on Duguay, and write Duguay about contributing
some poems to *grOnk*. Except for the interview, nothing seems to have
come from any of these ideas.

Barrie's way of coping with the large number of concurrent projects he
would usually be considering was to work on the ones that were going well
or ones that others were eager to see advanced. He continued to participate
in Four Horsemen rehearsals and performances mostly because he seems to
have believed that the other three members expected him to — for Barreto-
Rivera and Dutton the group's work often had more importance relative
to other projects than it had for Barrie. It was also the most likely means
for them to circulate their work internationally and to be invited to sound
poetry festivals in Europe or the United States. Dutton's recollection, how-
ever, is that it was most often McCaffery and Barreto-Rivera who wished
to dissolve the group. Amusingly, Dutton recalls that the group continued
almost entirely because of Barrie's initiatives.[3] Quite possibly the different
views reflect the chronically poor communication among them. Barrie
worked with McCaffery on TRG because their interests in it were equally
intense, and because timely publication in *Open Letter* was possible. He had
a similar interaction with Barbara Caruso in their visual work, and assured
publication through her own Seripress.

Equally large if not larger editorial responsibilities and opportunities
came abruptly into view in the fall of 1974. Victor Coleman, who had
single-handedly built Coach House Press into the premiere Canadian
leading-edge literary publisher, with books not only by Barrie but by
Robert Fones, David Bromige, David McFadden, Gerry Gilbert, Daphne
Marlatt, Nelson Ball, George Bowering, Christopher Dewdney, Fred Wah,
Robert Hogg, Steve McCaffery, and the Americans David Rosenberg,
Ron Padgett, Robert Creeley, Jack Spicer, and Allen Ginsberg, abruptly
resigned as editor by sending pained and potentially explosive letters of
resignation to Coach House authors, the Canada Council, and the Ontario
Arts Council. In these letters he declared his sharp disagreement with the
ethics of the press's financial policies and announced that he was "in the
process of trying to redirect" approximately half of the arts council funds

that had been allocated to it to a new small press he was hoping to start. He accused the press of "profiteering," of having become "a sweatshop," and of planning to use its latest government grants for "the acquisition of equipment for CHP sole proprietor." He asked all Coach House authors to write to the Ontario Arts Council and the Canada Council in his support. The copy Coleman had sent to Barrie was headed with a handwritten "bp — Help!" Accompanying it and the other author-letters was a copy of the letter he had written to Ron Evans of the Ontario Arts Council, alleging that "for the past two fiscal years the block grants that we [Coach House] received for 'publishing' have gone directly into acquiring equipment for Mr. Bevington's commercial printing business" and that Bevington had "scuttled" any attempt to publicize most Coach House titles. The letter described the recent Canada Council and Ontario Arts Council block grants to Coach House as a "'cultural' grants rip-off."

The "machinery" or "equipment" that Coleman was referring to in these letters was a set of second-hand business computers with which Bevington hoped to digitize Coach House typesetting, thereby both speeding book production and widening the possibilities for typography and visual effects. In 1978 these would enable Coach House to begin publishing on-demand "manuscript editions" of works-in-progress. Whether Coleman had been more than momentarily outraged by what he perceived to be the situation at Coach House, or had thought through all the possible ramifications of his letters is unclear. However, when in 1996 he recalls the events around his resignation, he makes no mention of "sweatshop," business ethics, or diversions of funds. He writes that he resigned from Coach House "to become director of [the artist-run gallery] A Space." He says that he had become less interested in print — had become "increasingly engaged with media other than print as purveyors of the kind of writing I wanted to champion"; and that "[t]he other major reason was my rather naively myopic view of the new technologies of print; namely the dreaded computer/word processor" (*Open Letter* 9:8 33).

For Barrie — much as for the other authors — Coleman's bridge-burning missives had come out of the blue. Many who were regular visitors had been aware of his simmering dissatisfaction with the fact that Bevington's commercial printing necessarily had priority over the production of the Coach House titles, and of his mistrust of Bevington's ongoing work to digitize the press's typesetting. But none had foreseen that it might take such extreme form. In Barrie's case, the situation his letters had created was particularly awkward. Bevington and Coleman were both among his long-term friends. Bevington had befriended him in January 1965, when they had been introduced by Josie Hindley-Smith, and begun almost immediately helping him create his first Canadian book. Coleman had supported him through the stressful publication of the first volume of *The Martyrology, Book 1*.[4] Coach House was the publisher of the work Barrie viewed as his most important, with both a reprint of *Book 1* and *Book 11* of *The Martyrology* and the new *Martyrology, Book 3* scheduled for publication in the next year or two. A book by his old friend David Phillips was also likely to be on the press schedule. At the same time, Coleman's distress was evident in the letters and in his having sent them. But the letters were also potential grenades tossed into Bevington's unusual and long-standing support of new writers and artists.

Barrie's immediate and characteristically generous response was to take charge — although perhaps not even he realized at the time that he was — and attempt to resolve the crisis without harm to anyone. Beginning the day the letters arrived he started telephoning the parties involved, visiting Stan, visiting me and Linda, speaking with Coleman and as many of the Toronto-area Coach House authors as he could. He had a psychotherapist's reading of the extreme rhetoric of Coleman's letters — i.e. that they were probably true to Coleman's experience of the situation but not necessarily true to the situation itself, much like Barrie's memories of his childhood. Coach House had continued to produce the books that its grant applications to the arts councils had promised. Many of the press's employees accepted relatively low wages because they believed in the cultural importance of the press, or because of the flexibility working there allowed, or because they were learning skills or working with equipment unavailable elsewhere. The computerization of typesetting was promising to open up new design possibilities as well as new efficiencies; the opportunity to computerize was in a sense a windfall that had happened because of Bevington's friendship with programmer David Slocum who was at the time working at digitizing typesetting at the *Globe and Mail*. Slocum would later help Fred Wah and myself launch the online magazine *SwiftCurrrent*.

But the immediate task to Barrie and to most of the authors he spoke with seemed to be damage-control — how to replace Coleman with a credible editorial presence and deflect his accusations. Coleman's letters had appeared to leave the authors with only the two choices it had created: writing to the councils in support of his new small press and requesting diverted funding, which might constitute corroboration of his charges against Bevington; assisting Coach House to replace him, which might imply that his charges were groundless and his resignation unnecessary. Coleman himself was reported to have told some authors that not supporting him would constitute a "betrayal." For Barrie, a better course might be to refuse his binary analysis. Coleman's friendship might be possible to rescue in time, but Coach House needed to be helped before it became unsaveable. Although Barrie may have spoken on the phone to the arts councils about Coleman's new plans, there is no evidence that he sent either one a formal letter of support.

Late in November, Barrie convened a meeting with Bevington and others at his Therafields office — a symbolically appropriate site under the circumstances. Here he proposed that the "senior" Coach House authors such as Michael Ondaatje, David Young, and myself join him and others — Art Gallery of Ontario curator Dennis Reid, Barrie's agent Linda Davey — in an unpaid editorial board that would replace Coleman and have regular meetings and minutes, acquire and edit manuscripts, and be able at least to monitor the various issues Coleman had raised. Bevington agreed, and went back to the press to print the postcard, "Coach Announces New Team." The arts councils continued to support the press. Coleman moved to A Space and started a small publishing venture, The Eternal Network. The new Coach House editorial board would publish books by him in 1978 and 1985. Privately, Barrie's "practical" position was that if the press could still produce and distribute the books promised in its grant applications, it mattered little in ethical terms through what channels money had flowed to produce them.

The new board, which began work in January 1975, inevitably brought Barrie new responsibilities and complications. He would soon be editing six or more titles a year for the press. His own future Coach House books would be viewable as "vanity" publications — at least by a few dissident Coach House employees who would prefer to be working on ones with more commercial potential. One of his first editorial decisions was to publish Ian Hamilton Finlay's *A Boy's Alphabet Book* through Coach House — he wrote to Finlay with the news shortly after Christmas. Much to the dismay of Finlay, who at times seemed to imagine that Coach House was a large company, and the embarrassment of Barrie, the book was not to be printed until December 1977. It was not eligible for Canadian arts council support, and had to be financed by Bevington's business.[5]

Throughout this 1973–75 period Barrie had believed that *The Martyrology* had ended. He had been mentioning this to most of his writer-friends, including Phyllis Webb, who in August 1973 had responded that she was happy his *Martyrology* was reaching its end, if that's what he believed, though for herself she would be equally pleased if it were to continue "forever." Then she playfully added that perhaps too much thinking about martyrdom could send one to unexpected places. Her remarks expressed an admirable and ultimately appropriate combination of skepticism, enthusiasm, and good wishes — and probably represented the feelings of most of Barrie's friends. Toward the very end of 1974, however, he began writing what became *The Martyrology, Book 4*. When giving me a copy of the privately printed *A Draft of Book IV of The Martyrology* in 1976 he would inscribe it "for Frank & Linda   the beginning grows out of a conversation back in time re Dudek." And in an acknowledgements page at the rear of *The Martyrology, Book 6 Books* (1987) he would write "Particular thanks too to Frank Davey who has gotten me going again on *The Martyrology* twice now: once in 1974 with a comment on Louis Dudek's work that launched me into *Book 4*, and again in 1978 when i had barely begun *A Book of Hours* and an observation he made put the work back on track."

During 1974–75 I had been writing a book on Louis Dudek and Raymond Souster — a book that because of the publisher's changes in ownership would not be published until 1980. Concurrently, Barrie and I had been editing a collection of Sheila Watson's essays and stories for the spring 1975 issue of *Open Letter*, meeting frequently about it at my house. About Dudek we had discussed mostly his long poems, *En Mexico, Europe, Atlantis* (1967), and his current long poem project *Continuation*, and how in all of these Dudek had begun without any plan or intention other than to write. The first three were travel poems. In the opening of the third of these, he had thematized travel as a poem — unknowingly foreshadowing both the railroad travel poem Barrie would write in the 1980s,

Continental Trance, and Barrie's interest in the Japanese travel-diary-poem, the *utanikki*.

> One could not write a poem waiting for the train to start.
> But once in motion, well in motion,
> how is it possible not to begin?
>
> Travel is the life-voyage in little,
>   a poem, a fiction, structure of illusion!
> . . .
> Travel, to and from (the place does not matter)
>   the Ding an sich in a mirror —
> Let it speak! (*Atlantis* 3)

I had suggested to Barrie that Dudek's challenging himself here to make a poem of his journey echoed both Robert Duncan's accepting the challenge of going "into the open" to write his serial poem *Medieval Scenes* in 1947 and William Cowper's acceptance in 1781 of Lady Austen's challenge to begin his long poem *The Task*, in that in each case the poet had agreed to proceed without plan or purpose. Barrie began *Book 4* with the line "purpose is a porpoise," and proceeded with a passage that was pretty well a riff on the concluding pages of *Atlantis* in which Dudek had proclaimed nature's "architecture of contradictions and inexorable chances" (148), its "wild turbulence of possibilities. / A spiral nebula. / A sea of milk" (146). "A cloud against the dark mountain. / The white of the moon / There is reality. A white flame" (149), he had declared, and in the last line written "There is the sea. It is real" (151). Barrie's *Book 4* opened

> is there a sea
>
> yes
>
> is there a cloud
>
> yes

everything elemental
everything blue

the precision of openness
is not a vagueness
it is an accumulation
cumulous

yes

oceanic

yes &
anything elemental
anything blue is

sky
    sea
        the heart of
the flame

Another aspect of Dudek's poetry that Barrie and I had talked about was his acceptance of prosaic or "functional" passages in his poems; his most important poetic theory statement had been "Functional Poetry," an essay written in poetry in which he had announced that he wanted to reclaim the language of poetry for discursive thought. Although *The Martyrology, Book 3* had contained numerous prose-like passages, *Book 4* would be the first in which Barrie included prose passages typeset as full-justified prose. This was a development that Barrie seemed to be especially pleased about when he sent a passage from it to Gladys Hindmarch and in the accompanying letter wrote that, to his surprise, *The Martyrology* was continuing despite him, that his friends were now going to ignore his habitual rushing up and shouting that it was over, that at last he'd finished the thing, since it seemed he never did. He told her that this new *Martyrology* book was especially interesting to him because of the numerous (for him) technical innovations it contained, especially its shifts

aka{ barrie phillip }Nichol

from one mode to another, from poetry to prose to playscript and so on, which were giving him more "space" in which to write, and allowing more things to flow into one another.

Throughout, however, many of *Book 4*'s passages would be utterly unlike those of Dudek in consisting of close deconstructive readings of individual words. "I began," Barrie would tell Bayard and David in their 1976 interview, "to see the word as a sentence that said things about single letters . . . [T]he word 'word,' for instance, becomes 'w or d' [. . . .] I would read the word as a sentence and in essence I was into an extension of the *Still Water* thing, the *Love a Book of Remembrances* thing, that haiku-like structure [. . . .] [S]ingle letters had symbologies, had contents" (Bayard 39). Barrie wrote multiple sequential pages in *Book 4* in which he disassembled individual words as he had in the visual poems of *Still Water*, using the "sentences" he found thereby within the words to lead him to further sentence-containing words. Again, this was the bpNichol in him writing, bpNichol the ideopoet, punster, language-reader.

> the dull pass of wisdom
>
> w is d
> o ma
> i 'n h and
> the me's restated
> at the pen's tip's ink
> at the tongue's noise
> w in d
>   din
> Blake's vision of
> Golgonooza

In his prefatory note to that privately printed *Draft of Book IV*, Barrie had also written about how preoccupied he had become with the "unification" of his work — "I have, for a long time, been working toward the unification of what have seemed to many . . . as the disparate areas of my concern. The focal point of that unification process remains THE MARTYROLOGY . . ." (2). His remarks in the Bayard/David interview show that by "unification" here he hadn't meant only the physical joining of texts, as in the question of whether the text of *Monotones* should be identified as part of the text of *The Martyrology*. He had meant also a bringing together of method and form. He had wanted the ability to use in the *The Martyrology* the same ways and kinds of writing that bpNichol had used in visual poems such as those of *Still Water*, in the prose of *Two Novels* or his "some afterwords" to *The Cosmic Chef*, or in the 'pataphysical "Probable Systems" texts he had been writing out of Barrie's readings of Wittgenstein — as well as the playscripts he had mentioned to Hindmarch.

The question remains, however, of why Barrie had been so pleased to be able to also believe that *The Martyrology* had ended after *Book 3* — had, as he recalled to Hindmarch, repeatedly rushed to shout to people that it was over, that he'd finished. My guess is that the alternative — as implied by his various notebook meditations on "i" and "we" and by the *Book 3* lines "i am afraid of writing something which does not end / as we does not" — may have terrified him. Earlier in *Book II* he had realized that the end of fantasy leads to the inevitability of death — "dead dead dead" were now his saints. Much like Adam and Eve on leaving Eden, the saints had lost their immortality when they had left Barrie's self-protective dreamworld of Cloudtown.[6] For Barrie in that dreamworld death itself, as whimsical suicide, had been a fantasy. But once outside Cloudtown and in the Therafields' farm garden death, in the shape of the still dog Terry in Visvaldis's arms, was palpable, and in everyone's future. Barrie had titled that concluding section of *Martyrology, Book II* "Friends as Footnotes," and Visvaldis had called the dog the "first friend I've lost in years."

In his 1984 book *bpNichol: What History Teaches*, Stephen Scobie wrote that together with *Book 5, Book 4* of the *Martyrology* was, because of its "drastic dislocations of the very surface of the writing," "forbiddingly difficult and almost defiantly quirky" (127) — but that it nevertheless realized both a poststructuralist understanding of language and "an audacious combination of frivolity and profundity" (128). The profundity for Scobie resided in the poem's illustrations of what it termed "the absolute precision / of fluid definition":

> the precision of openness
> is not a vagueness

aka{ barrie phillip }Nichol

> it is an accumulation
> cumulous

and its choosing of the "imp-art-i-al" over the "partial." As Scobie wrote:

> To separate a part from the whole is to isolate the individual from the community. The redemption of language, whether through the medium of sound or by the open precision of the poem's evolving form, leads out of the loneliness the flesh aches with and back to the ideal of community. "we is a human community," set within history: the city, be it Dilmun or Toronto, is a place to exist as a citizen, as opposed to the "non/man who / believes ONLY in his own self interest" (*Book 3*). VI (130)

BARRIE AND ROB HINDLEY-SMITH AT THE THERAFIELDS FARM, 1974.

The presence of Therafields in Barrie's life, with its hopes to build honest communication between individuals and from there a trust-filled community, is clearly echoing behind both Barrie's writing and Scobie's reading. Also evident again is a psychotherapist's skeptical reception of a client's words — a psychotherapist Barrie Nichol who increasingly in *The Martyrology*, as David Rosenberg has noted to me, has language, poet-persona bpNichol and his lines of poetry as his clients. The therapist watches and directs as the client free-associates. "what you're doing in the situation is not imposing yourself on the person but basically being a catalyst," Barrie had said in that 1976 interview when paralleling his work as a psychotherapist to that as a poet (Miki 2002 147). What the analysand or language says may have more than one meaning.

What was intended may be less than what can be found to have been said. Words are not to be taken at face value. Meanings can often be hidden and need to be "revealed" before they can be "reveiled."

> we work
> the changes
> always
> to reveal
> lest the actual re-veil itself
> a shifting of
> the humus
>   cumulous covers
> poetry's reviled &
> spat upon
>   sweet spit & hhh of breathing

The Martyrology, Book 4, then, marked another sharp intensifying of Barrie's interrogation of his own writing, an interrogation that began in the 1960s when he rejected his "regular" poems because he suspected them of "arrogance," continued in 1972 with his frantic dissatisfaction with *Book 1* even as it was being printed, and led in *Book 3* to the questioning of the AD and BC of the abcdarium and the dismantling of the dream-given "dogma i am god" — where again bpNichol had found more being said than what had been initially evident.

Shortly before beginning *Book 4* Barrie had sat at our dining room table with Linda to catalogue his manuscripts for possible sale to Simon Fraser University's Special Collections. She was writing notes about each page of his early poems. They had come to the manuscript of "Streetsinger," that had appeared in Souster's anthology *New Wave Canada* — an ostensible "love" poem. What bpNichol had written, however, had not been what Barrie Nichol had then thought he was telling the lovely but tempestuous Dace.

> i want
> my fingers
> on your neck

aka{ barrie phillip }Nichol

in your mouth
everywhere to arouse
the sweet singing sound in you
that finds its singer
in me

Barrie had sighed with embarrassment, then ruefully raised his hands slightly apart as if betrayed in the act of strangling someone.

17. Russian Roulette

Six days and seven nights the wind and storm flood.

— *Gilgamesh* XI, 127

Beyond the writing of *The Martyrology, Book 4,* 1975 was an extremely busy year for Barrie. The first of several financial and philosophical crises was erupting at Therafields as the long-term effects of the 1973 oil shortages rippled through North America. Amid rapid economic inflation, work to develop the farm so it could support both therapy marathons and rural house groups was becoming increasingly costly at the same time that the general shift in society toward political conservatism was becoming evident within the membership. Therafields saw a decline in volunteerism and a growing desire among the therapists to have their work viewed as a business — a business that many of them believed should be both financially and socially separate from the farm and Lea Hindley-Smith's community-building aspirations.

In his Therafields history, Goodbrand suggests that he and his downtown therapist colleagues had begun embracing a North American understanding of psychotherapy as an entrepreneurial service provided to individuals, and abandoning Lea's more European understanding of it as an enabler of social awareness, justice, and creativity — what Lacan would call *"le lien sociale"* (1974 51).[1] In a general sense, the latter understanding was at least as old as Freud's *Civilization and Its Discontents*; it had been followed by Lea in her readings of Klein, Reich, and Lindner when she set up house groups in which her clients could learn to live socially. It was now being re-understood by Barrie in his McCaffery-influenced readings of Kristeva, Derrida, Georges Bataille, and Gilles Deleuze and Félix Guattari. It seems very likely that his continued concern throughout *Book 4* with enacting a "we" that both contains and enlarges the "i" was at least in part a product of the Therafields turmoil, as in the passage in which he follows Robert Graves's *bethluisnion*/"alphabet of trees" from *The White Goddess* to write:

> the B gins us
> A's the birth
> tree
> day of
>   celebration
> I
>   the death
> yew
> loss of we
> which is our perfect B
> ginning
>   false pride of individuality
> that i am
>   yes
> but i was of
> came from
>   this soil.

A March 1975 report had noted that Therafields would be $55,000 in debt for the fiscal year, and projected a debt of $150,000 at the end of the 1975–76 fiscal year. A lack of volunteer labour would lead to the hiring of non-Therafields construction workers to complete the 3000-square-foot kitchen needed to feed those expected at the weekend marathons. Nevertheless in 1976 Barrie and the other Therafields directors approved borrowing a further $170,000, with Lea Hindley-Smith's encouragement, to expand the farm's acreage. These figures and expenditures continued to alienate most of the senior therapists, whose salaries, because of inflation, had fallen in purchasing-power by 30 percent since 1973, and increased their resentment that significant portions of the fees they earned were being used to support Therafields administration and the farm development (Goodbrand 170-71). As vice president and member of the board of directors that made most managerial decisions, and as the management person viewed by the therapists as the most reasonable and accessible, Barrie had much of his time consumed by consultations and meetings.[2]

Some indication of the extent and content of the philosophical turmoil at Therafields can be gathered from a front-page editorial in the March 24, 1975, Therafields general circulation newsletter *A Publication* — then being produced in editions of 800 copies by Barrie with four other "coordinators." The editorial itself seemed to contain several divergent viewpoints.

> We have some major areas to reevaluate: 1. Finance, can Therafields survive on its current financial basis? 2. Living arrangements. What is the value of house groups. Were they meant to be more or less permanent living arrangements? Where and how do we want to live? 3. The value of long-term therapy for all. Is theradrama working to the depths it is capable of? 4. What is the place of writing in Therafields? 5. The place of the physical program in theradrama. 6. When an organism veers toward organization and a variety of services (housing, massage, bio-therapy, groups, work and social situations), does that organization tend to attract people whose needs are more for protection by such an all-inclusive umbrella rather than people who need help in discovering their own purposes?

The attempt to transition from a treatment-focussed institution to one that was also an enabler of both creative and lifestyle opportunities was creating not only conflict but also possible therapy contradictions. It was also bringing into focus the fact that while treatment could support itself financially through fees, a new lifestyle environment was not necessarily self-financing. The re-evaluation would continue until the fall, and in early 1976 result in Lea, Barrie, and Rob reorganizing the administration of Therafields so as to reaffirm its commitment to the farm and the idea

aka{ barrie phillip }Nichol

of an "environmental centre."[3] But they would not resolve the continuing financial questions.

Barrie was also busy throughout 1975 creating the serial comic strip "Lonesome Fred" for issues of *A Publication*, and working on a Therafields in-house musical comedy he was tentatively calling "The Ordinary Man"; he had posted a casting call for it in the January *A Publication* for the end of February. He was building for the first time on his early interest in music — in the big-band music he had once danced to with his mother, the Fred Astaire/Ginger Rogers musicals he had attended in Thunder Bay with his sister, the jazz music of his high school and university years, and his own tendency to break into song — usually Herman Hupfeld's "As Time Goes By" from *Casablanca*, especially those lines "It's still the same old story / A fight for love and glory / A case of do or die" — lines that may often recur to a psychotherapist. As well, he also found a way to spend much of May in England where he attended and performed at the Eighth International Sound Poetry Festival, May 14–23 — his first trip to Europe. Other performers included Jackson Mac Low from the U.S., Peter Finch, Paula Claire, Lawrence Upton, Bob Cobbing, and Dom Sylvester Houédard from the UK, Henri Chopin and François Dufrêne from France, and Sten Hansen from Sweden. A letter to Barrie from Houédard dated May 10 indicates that Barrie was already in England travelling with expatriate Canadian poet sean o huigin and planning to visit writers in Cardiff as well as Houédard at Prinknash Abbey in Gloucestershire. Barrie was still in England on May 27, writing a section for his conceptual book *Translating Translating Apollinaire*, attempting to draw with coloured pens masses of *H*s and commenting how, for some reason he does not explain, the entire trip has made him think of overlaid *H*s. On the flight back he wrote notes for the *Martyrology* oratorio he was creating with Howard Gerhart.

In October, my partner Linda sent him on a week-long reading tour of Canada's Arctic, with stops at such cities as Fort Smith and Inuvik, and occasional sidetrips — weather permitting — to Tuktoyaktuk, Pelican Rapids, and Great Slave Lake. It was part of a three-month 10-writer series that she had arranged for the department of education of the then Northwest Territories. The other writers included George Bowering, Margaret Atwood, Al Purdy, Daphne Marlatt, Michael Ondaatje, and

Matt Cohen. It was an expensive tour, but Barrie took Ellie with him, writing about it in the later pages of *Book 4*:

> driving out of Fort Smith
> 30 miles to little buffalo falls
> ruth rees, ellie & me
> watched the water drop
> 　　　　　60 feet into the basin
> the clouds hung grey
> for the seventh straight day
> as if cloudtown lay in ruins above me
> snowbirds flocking up into the sky
> trying to make sense of the wreck around me
> here in the midst of what has never known city

He found himself unexpectedly close to ancient Dilmun with its "crumbled palisades and steeples." He had been, as throughout this pivotal book of *The Martyrology*, alert for glimpses of origins. As a teenager he had hoped to be an archaeologist. At Therafields he had become an archaeologist of his own psyche, of Cloudtown, and of his family. Here in *Book 4* he seems to have had numbers of chance insights into both human pre-history and inevitable decay — wreckage "in the midst of what has never known city" — as well as flashbacks to the demise of his no longer lamented saints. The wreckage could also be a premonition about Therafields, and its potential to become the ruins of a lost paradise.

On his return he sketched in his notebook a table of contents for the book *Art Facts* and wrote a note to himself that he intended to send it to Richard Grossinger of North Atlantic Books in Vermont for possible publication — Grossinger had asked him for a manuscript. Grossinger would later write to Barrie that he was too late in sending it.

His completion of *Book 4* in December 1975 saw him already thinking of beginning *The Martyrology, Book 5*, which would rework some of the *Book 4* lines and extend its "precision of openness" into "chains" of reading that offer a reader numerous reading paths — a concept that he and McCaffery had been discussing in their TRG reports on narrative.

aka{ barrie phillip }Nichol

But his progress in writing it would be slow, partly because of the continuing conflicts at Therafields and partly because he had so many other projects underway. In his notebook he created of list of these, dating it "March 26/76 /May 76," and under each project a sublist of its parts or of tasks he needs to do. The projects included "Probable Systems" (begun 1970, he notes), "Translating Translating Apollinaire" (he dates its start 1972), "Canadian Singers and their Songs" (he calls this work "lines and variations" and dates its start 1976), and "The Martyrology." The sublists indicated that he had written 14 sections of "Canadian Singers and their Songs," between May 1 and May 14, each section beginning with a line from a 19th-century or early 20th-century Canadian poet. By June he would also be writing a series of poems he called "Negatives" — texts that he conceived to be film-negative versions of well-known (to him, at least) Canadian poems. The second is a "negative" of my 1962 poem "Bridge Force." He would eventually include "negatives" of the entire eight-poem "Bridge Force" series in the final manuscript of *Art Facts*.

The *Martyrology* list included *Book 5*. The idea of using chains in this book and footnote numbers to refer to them had come to Barrie early, in a notebook entry on February 7, 1976. He seems to have perceived chains when he noticed that he had begun to write the book in more than one section. By October 29 he had identified three of these — a "main chain" that concerned local Toronto events, a chain that was set outside the city, and one that spanned stretches of time and reconsidered early things he had written. He wrote to himself that the new book appeared at present to be growing out of the subsections he had used in *Book I* and *Book II*, but to be creating a new form of them. Further down he commented that he needed to type the new drafts up so that he could better understand its transitions and check whether or not the work overall was cohering. *Book 5* was emerging as the first *Martyrology* book that was not "processual," that is, the first book in which the sequence of lines and parts was not also the chronological sequence of its composition. Not only was Barrie, by offering his readers a choice of reading paths, encouraging them to read the lines in an order other than the one in which he had written them, but he himself was sometimes writing parts of more than one chain in the same day or week. This change in his writing practice — creating numerous alternative paths rather than following a single chronological one — would allow *Book 5* to be much longer than the other books. It would also result in his working on it over a much longer period.

Throughout the year the philosophical complexities at Therafields increased. In the spring of 1976 the board of directors, now self-renamed as the Advisory Board, had decided that further outreach to the public might result in financial improvements. Lea was to give four public lectures at Therafields' Toronto centre, and hold special marathons at the farm. Members were to be encouraged to set up businesses on Therafields property. Goodbrand quotes from the board's April 14, 1976, minutes:

> There was further discussion about the need to create other avenues of income besides therapy, in which other people who are not Theradramists could also become involved in an income-producing way. e.g., shopping plaza, land, setting up houses for short term living experiences, a Willow Spa, construction company, garage, health clinic, etc.

But these projects were evidently to be done in ways particular to the Therafields understandings of community, for the minutes also quote Barrie as saying, "We are engaged in waging a war against society and are attempting to create alternatives." And Rob Hindley-Smith is recorded as declaring that the farm should have priority over the therapy work done in the city. "He felt the rural centre is the soul of Therafields . . . he felt our perspective was wrong if we saw the Theradramists [therapists] as Therafields and the rural centre as only an adjunct" (Goodbrand 173–74). Such plans and statements of course further alienated the therapists.

In August at the farm Barrie oversaw a week-long work-group marathon, with more than 30 participants. The goal was to address both the members' work-associated difficulties and the need to get farm projects completed at minimal cost. The group's success was celebrated with a front page photo of Barrie and the cheerful participants in the October 18 issue of *A Publication*. The accompanying text was in part a salvo on behalf of the farm in the simmering dispute with the downtown therapists.

> We have laboured to provide for ourselves the facilities required for our therapeutic work. In the process we have discovered that work

aka{ barrie / phillip }Nichol

> situations which demand consistency of effort & patience in striving
> for quality challenge the blocked creativity in people in a way that
> no other therapeutic context can. Many people have gained enor-
> mously from their involvement in "the work scene," but there seems
> to be a lack of clarity at large about what "work therapy" is. [. . .]

It was also an exhortation for more volunteerism.

> Much remains to be done to make Therafields' physical facilities
> adequate for the services it can best provide to people. There is no
> question that the work has to be done & that in some way we have
> to realize it out of our own resources. The question is *how.*

It concluded by listing upcoming work marathons and inviting contribu-
tions to a special issue of *A Publication* devoted to work and work therapy.

Although Barrie's marathon and Lea's lectures and marathons had
all been extremely well attended, the financial deficit had continued to
grow. In the previous year, 1975, a committee consisting of Barrie, Josie
Hindley-Smith, and farm manager John Dean, had begun examining the
farm's financial records and interviewing its staff with the aim of having
it run more efficiently. In the November 29, 1976, issue of *A Publication*,
a front page editorial article announced that this committee, "appointed
by Robert Hindley-Smith and its work . . . approved by Therafields advi-
sory board and the Full-Time Theradramists' Seminar [Hypno I]," had
received the voluntary resignations of "the Entire Rural Staff" and had
redescribed and posted the farm staff jobs. The announcement began,
"What is needed . . . at this time is a new team prepared to take the Rural
Centre through a new and different pioneering experience."

In Brenda Doyle's blog, however, the person whose position was
described as "Hostess at Willow," but whose salary, like the salaries of
most of the farm staff, had been minimal, tells Doyle, "After all the inter-
views we were told that because of the incompetency we would all lose
our jobs and have to be re-interviewed for them." Asked to provide her
"job description," she then wrote down all her tasks — "I wrote reams —
pages and pages. I was doing all of the guys' laundry — 14 or 15 of them.
I cooked three meals a day for them during the week. I cleaned the barn,

kept the records, ordered food for the barn and the Willow, answered the phones, and did work for John Dean. Then on the weekends, of course, I worked steadily at the Willow. On Mondays there I also stripped the beds, washed the sheets, mangled them, re-made the beds and did the vacuuming. I cleaned the mirrors and the kitchen." When Barrie read this, he was evidently astonished. "Barry [sic] just looked at me and said — can this be true? Barry couldn't believe it. He was really upset. I could see that John Dean was looking uncomfortable for the first time." The woman also tells Doyle that she began sending itemized bills to the Therafields accountant Renwick (Rik) Day, for the first time separating the expenses for Lea, Rob, and Visvaldis at the Willow from the other farm expenses.

> Three weeks later I got a call from Rik. He said — is this true? The bills for the Willow were incredibly expensive. There were always beautiful meals and fruit bowls for Rob, Lea, and Visvaldis, chocolates for Visvaldis. At the farm we were eating vegetarian meals. I also did a price of meals and accommodation per person at the barn and at the Willow and it was clear that there was a big discrepancy.

Nothing much appears to have come from the reorganization except that the "hostess" learned that Lea suspected that she was angry at her. Barrie's influence in the committee's work was apparently limited. The woman concludes to Doyle:

> The elitism and Lea's own troubles destroyed everything that we had. After the interviews about our jobs Barry [sic] saw what was happening. One Saturday night after dinner he told me to go home. He called Rob to come and do the dishes with him but Rob wouldn't. Barry was really pissed off with him and was almost crying but Rob couldn't do it. He was like a brat in a tantrum. Barry came and did the dishes with me. ("Thoughts," February 7, 2011)

The incident offers some possible insight into Barrie's thankless administrative role — to mitigate irresolvable situations, mediate between Lea and Visvaldis's now destructive grandiosity and the exploitation of workers such as the "hostess," and delay the financial disaster to which their grandiosity

aka{ barrie / phillip }Nichol

was contributing. It was a role undoubtedly both daunting and stressful, but it was also one that his gratitude to Lea, together with his belief in the ultimate value of the community some of his companions were still hoping to build, seems to have kept him utterly silent about, even in his notebooks or in casual conversations with colleagues in Hypno I. Not surprisingly, one of Doyle's interviewees comments, "I suspect he knew his own integrity was endangered" ("Thoughts," January 28, 2007).

November was also the month that Coach House Press released *The Martyrology Books 3 & 4* — edited for the press by Barrie himself. Although in his notebooks Barrie had been still consistently numbering all the published, unpublished, and unfinished books of *The Martyrology* in Roman numerals, they would now be publicly numbered in Arabic. The change would seem to reflect his therapeutic passage from the imaginary companionship of saints to the everyday companionship of friends, managers, Arctic hosts, and volunteer workers. However, the continuing contrast between the persistent Roman numerals in his notebooks and the published Arabic ones, suggests Barrie's continuing ambivalence about that passage — Cloudtown was still not entirely unattractive.

The most revealing indication of Barrie's inner life during 1976 comes in a draft of the 22nd poem of his new series "Canadian Singers and their Songs," dated May 23, 1976, in his "English Notebook." It began with a line taken from Alfred Gordon's First World War "Ballad of the Forty Silent Men," published in his book *Vimy Ridge and Other Poems* by J.M. Dent & Sons in Toronto in 1918: "day after day no gun had spoken." After a short opening section about two figures locked in boredom and hatred, Barrie abruptly segued to what appears from its internal references to be quite personal material. He writes about being in an Osborne Street barbershop during his teen years — Osborne being the nearest commercial street to his 1957–60 Winnipeg homes — and reading the *Police Gazette*. In it he encounters seemingly "endless" stories of young men who shoot their fathers, for no apparent reason, and finds himself becoming interested, and wondering how strong his own emotions would have to be for him to want to kill, and trying to analyze also whether the angers he's felt toward his own parents, and the arguments he's had with them, could have ever moved him to grab a gun and eliminate them, and himself also, or maybe take off in a murderous rampage across the prairies killing everyone in his path and inspiring lurid headlines about bloodbaths and nightmares and "kill-krazed" kids.

The section curiously combined Oedipal feelings from long ago and a therapist's self-analysis with a parody of how media representations mock and simplify such feelings — reducing them to clichés similar to the ones Alfred Gordon had used when he wrote of the guns of Cambrai and Vimy. One can only speculate on whether the origin of such thoughts about anger here had something to do with his unconscious transferring of "all of his feelings for his mother to Lea" that Doyle will remark on in her October 31, 2010, blog.

A common way of dealing with anger, and avoiding outwardly directed violence, is depression — a way that is arguably more ethical but equally self-destructive. For years this had been Barrie's way — before he came to Lea in 1963 and 1964. In the poem's next section he wrote about how his *Police Gazette* thoughts and fantasies had later changed, how he had imagined that he would die young, perhaps a suicide at age 18 like the poet Thomas Chatterton, killing himself rather than others, and leaving behind such well-fashioned and "exquisite" poems that all would lament his death, the newspaper headlines would offer different clichés, and awards would be thrown after him into his grave.

These lines offered a potentially lethal fantasy of self-pity and narcissism, together with an angry desire for recognition that recapitulated Barrie's familiar feelings that Ma and Pa never listened to him, and still in the 1970s hadn't appreciated his texts or performances. Perhaps Lea and Visvaldis were not listening to his advice now. The lines also connected to his early fears that he might, on a whim, kill himself, or in despair wander carelessly into traffic.[4] As well, they indirectly alluded to his fears in 1971 that he would be attacked for having won his Governor General's Award — that the only awards he could actually be seen to deserve would be ones guiltily tossed after him. Had he outgrown these feelings? Had they been reawoken?

He continued the poem, writing that 15 years after this self-pitying fantasy, despite having published numerous poems and won various awards, he still wonders about the angers that he still remembers. He wonders whether the new poems that he writes defuse those angers, like emptying a gun of its cartridges, or are they part of a game of Russian roulette in which one cylinder still offers a violent end? — and offering as

aka{ barrie phillip }Nichol

well headlines he could never read and talk-show comments about a nice kid who wrote bizarre poems. Moreover, he concludes, he'll never know which was the answer — an emptied gun or a lethal cylinder.

In the overall context of Barrie's writing, it's not a particularly complex or innovative poem — although he did give it a red checkmark in his notebook. It's more a poem by the old melodramatic Barrie than by the later word-questioning bpNichol. The radio talk-show voice could be his mother writing that letter in 1973 — nice kid, but sure writes strange poems. Poems that are expressions of anger — even passive-aggressive poems such as "Streetsinger" — are rare in Barrie's post-1970 work, although his prose often bristles with desperation and rage, particularly the John Cannyside and Phillip Workman texts he was still trying to complete. Russian roulette? Possibly he was playing that game in his willingness to write books that could be misread, in Scobie's words, as "forbiddingly difficult and almost defiantly quirky." Whatever his preoccupation with awards or parental approbation, Barrie had never courted either — never cut his hair to please his father, written prose that could garner a Booker, or even poetry that could interest a jury that lacked a Warren Tallman. Barrie had never wanted to be regulated or socially constrained or compromised — the unspoken goals of juries and their promises of awards, and too often both of parents and employers. "We are waging a war against society." I think, however, that if he had returned to this poem he might have at least altered the last line — a line that may be correct about who can read obituaries but seems glibly pessimistic about his own capabilities for self-knowledge.

18. Strange Years

Engendering, directing, and sustaining the narrative inquiry, an autobiographer's questions are at the heart of his enterprise. While they begin by impelling his narrative, they frequently end by characterizing it. . . .

— Donna Perreault,
"What Makes Autobiography Interrogative?"
Biography, 13:2. 130

Nineteen seventy-seven opened with intense activity at Therafields. Plans were being made for two artists' marathons, a "couples marathon" hosted by Lea and open to non-members of Therafields, a Florida investors meeting, a nutrition workshop partly conducted by Barrie's brother Don, various week-long house group retreats at the Therafields house in Florida, a "Summer Community Feast" in June, a work marathon in July, two open marathons overseen by Lea, a large farm picnic in July, and an August dance to be held on the Toronto Island's ferry *Thomas Rennie* as a fundraiser to assist farm renovations. Some of these events were designed to boost morale and volunteeerism, others — such as the two artists' marathons and work marathon that Barrie was volunteering to co-direct — to increase revenue while serving therapeutic needs.

The first artists' marathon was held January 2–9, directed by Barrie and Grant Goodbrand, and was fully subscribed. There were a large number of artists of various kinds among Therafields members: professional writers such as Barrie, and professional actors, singers, and musicians who performed or were auditioning to perform with institutions such as the Shaw Festival, the Canadian Opera Company, CBC Television, or with various small theatre companies and music ensembles. The marathon was designed to help participants address matters that impeded their artistic work. Goodbrand in 2010 recalled:

> [s]ubjects discussed in the groups included the inability to work, the reluctance to use certain subject matters or materials, the artists' relationship to their audiences — real or fantasized — as well as the implicit audience of the significant persons in their present and past. Sessions touched on their jealousies and rivalries with other artists, and disturbances in their sense of themselves as artists, which of course included their narcissism. This emotional material, which included the artists' dreams, took them back into the formative years of their lives, and delved into experiences that had both inspired and undermined their art. (205)

To some extent Goodbrand's description paralleled Barrie's notebook records of his own therapy. The group of approximately 35 lived at the farm for the week and were given studio space in various farm buildings to write, compose, paint, or rehearse for most of each day, with group sessions held at the ends of each morning and afternoon. On the final evening participants presented some of the work created or learned during the week.

Almost immediately afterward Barrie left to give readings in British Columbia and visit his parents and sister in Victoria. Amid the increasing demands on his time from Therafields and Coach House Press editing (he was editor at this time for books by McCaffery, Ian Hamilton Finlay, John Riddell, and Judith Fitzgerald, as well as his own *Journal*, and the revised *Martyrology, Book I* and *Book II*) his travels were one of few times when he had uninterrupted hours for writing.[1] On January 28, 1977, he stood at the corners of Alpha and Beta Streets in Victoria and wrote a possible *Martyrology, Book 5* passage about the buildings there. On January 29 he copied into his notebook a 1919 newspaper clipping about a great-great grandmother — he had found the clipping in his grandmother's Bible. On

January 30 his mother's predictable return to mourning his long-dead infant sister Donna occasioned his writing the "sometimes I wonder if Donna's speaking thru me" and "Donna today it seemed to me / you could've been a writer" passages of *The Martyrology, Book 5, Chain 3*. On February 1, his conversations with his sister and mother appear to have given rise to recollections of Port Arthur and to his writing of the "sleeping giant" passages of Chain 1. A conversation that he had with members of Barry McKinnon's college class in Prince George led on February 7 to his writing a passage about his saints that he believes will be part of the book's Chain 2.

Over the next few months he would rework and expand this material while also finding time to do his final revisions to the reissued *Martyrology, Books 1 & 2* and prepare for publication *Journal* and the 'pataphysical *Craft Dinner*. But first on February 13–14 he had to give a reading of "the complete Martyrology" as a benefit to help pay for the printing costs of Lea Hindley-Smith's most recent Therafields-published book.[2] He was also taking a leading role in the planning of the summer feast, now a "festival" called "Love/Life," to be held on August 10, and billed as a celebration of the 15th anniversary of the beginnings of what had become Therafields and the 10th anniversary of the purchase of the farm. A large two-colour commemorative booklet was to be printed, and a day of speeches, food, literary readings, music, and dancing planned. Most of the therapists and other long-term members contributed statements or essays to the booklet. In his statement Barrie recalled why two years before he had surprised Therafields members by calling for them to replace the word "community" with "society." "'Community' tends to function as a synonym for 'family,'" he wrote. "Hence the transfer of 'nuclear' feelings into the Therafields situation in the form of being devoured, of never escaping the clutches of <u>them</u> (which must include me since I'm the vice-pres) etc. etc." He was addressing the downtown therapists who had been resisting the policies of "<u>them</u>" — Lea and her Advisory Board — and advising them that their resistance to a long-term Therafields community at the farm has been a neurotic fear of being "devoured." He was also talking about *polis* — about the long history of human attempts to live socially, from Toronto to Dilmun, from the autobiographies of oneself and one's families back through towns like Plunkett and Bronze-Age Britain to Set and Osiris, Cain and Abel, whose still resonant actions he had reached in *Book 4*.

aka{ barrie phillip }Nichol

Now, August 10 1977, Therafields is a society. It is a society of communities. These communities are communities of groups of friends. Depending on the quality of honesty, trust and love that flows within these groupings, between the individuals within them, the communities flourish and the society flourishes. The lacks in the society are lacks in us as human beings, as sensitive perceivers of one another; or they are areas that are not yet awakened, that need encouragement to awaken. What we need now is patience, understanding, and loving confrontation. The tools we have learned to use over these past fifteen years must be utilized in new ways in what is no longer a short-term therapeutic environment but a long-term life commitment.

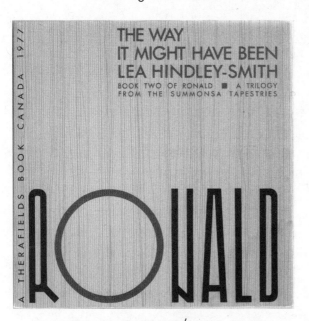

THE COVER OF LEA HINDLEY-SMITH'S NOVEL *THE WAY IT MIGHT HAVE BEEN*, 1977, DESIGNED BY VISVALDIS.

Four hundred and fifty people attended the festival, and for the next few months it would be widely believed to have been a significant success.

Goodbrand comments that most of his fellow therapists, however, ignored exhortations by Barrie such as this festival statement or his slightly later review of Lea's books ("A Brief Introduction to the SUMMONSA TAPESTRIES for the Easily Defensive"),[3] considering him well-intentioned but naive (197). Indeed, the rhetoric that Barrie used in such writing was almost unchanged from when he first began writing for Therafields publications a decade before. In the same period the language and conceptual complexity of his theoretical statements about writing had evolved tremendously — almost certainly because of the increased variety of his reading and the intensity of his ongoing TRG discussions with McCaffery.

Unfortunately, Barrie had no equivalent intellectual companion within the managerial or therapist communities at Therafields. Lea's intellect had been waning as her illnesses grew. Visvaldis, as much as Barrie has tried to make him appear wise whenever quoting him, had had at best a macho folk wisdom. Rob, although impressively literate for someone without much formal education, had — like Barrie — mastered Lea's early views without adding a great deal to them. Barrie's vice president position, created by Lea to insulate herself from being questioned by the older therapists of the original "Catholic group," had kept him from having productive dialogues with any of them and placed him within conflicts that made trust and dialogue difficult. If he could have renewed his Therafields language as vigorously as he had kept renewing the languages of his poetry and other writing, perhaps more people might have listened.

Later in August Barrie and Goodbrand — who was one of the downtown therapists Barrie had called out in his hortatory statement — held a second artists' marathon at the farm and once again drew a cross-section of artists, both professional and aspiring. They would continue to meet at the downtown centre with this group most Sundays for the next year. In the fall, Barrie also began work with composer Howard Gerhard on the opera *Space Opera*, with the libretto based on the idea of a handsome young space traveller becoming marooned on a planet inhabited by xenophobic peoples who communicate only by song. The traveller must, as Barrie wrote, sing for his life. Possibly he was recalling the "ho, ho, ho" "happy kid" that had been his own survival mannerism in the early '60s. In mid-September he was invited by the Governor General to dine with the Queen and the Duke of Edinburgh, who were to be in Ottawa October 14–19, 1977, as part of her Silver Jubilee celebrations. On October 10 he received a note from his mother who was concerned that he might not own a dinner jacket.

During this summer Barrie and Ellie had been making a major change as a couple. For the first time they would be living together on the same city lot, and sometimes under the same roof. This is the "When Ellie and I moved in together" moment that Barrie will memorialize in *Selected Organs* in the fourth section of "The Toes" (48). Barrie and Ellie, along with Rob, his partner Janet Griffith, Renwick Day, and five others, purchased the large Victorian house, 48 Warren Road, and its coach house,

46 Warren. Ellie's space was in the coach house, with Rob and Janet, Renwick, and Barrie in 48.

The Horsemen flew to San Francisco to perform on November 17 at the First West Coast International Sound Poetry Festival. From there they flew to Vancouver to perform at Simon Fraser University and at the Western Front Gallery. At the Western Front Barrie read from *The Martyrology* as well as performing with the other Horsemen. Afterward an audience member asked why the part of *The Martyrology* he had read "contained so many references to God." Barrie replied, "I decided a long time ago that anything that came into the poem I would leave in the poem" (Turner [4]). The questioner was probably responding to the numerous invocations of "father" and "Lord" that Barrie had made throughout most of the poem so far. Barrie's response was somewhat ingenuous. Sequentially reworked passages in his writing are rare, but revision — in the form of deleted or added passages, or of lines that qualify or comment on the ones just written — had been always a possible part of his writing process. His notebooks and manuscripts contain various passages that he has written for the *Martyrology* and either crossed out or ignored when writing the final version for the published poem.

For Barrie the references to an apparent "god" had been in some years merely an acknowledgement of a universal creative force, something akin to Dylan Thomas's "force that through the green fuse drives the flower." In 1976 Barrie told Bayard and David, "I was a very unreligious guy. I was agnostic, bordering on atheistic, until I went through my own personal therapy which had nothing to do with religion. But at the other end of the thing wasn't God; the white-haired one. I just got a sense of the Universe — something that was there and was larger than I was. Sort of an animism, I suppose" (Bayard 17).

But there had been also something consistently masculine, and arguably patriarchal, about this "sense of the Universe." Barrie's addresses to it had always been to "father," "lord," or "god"; the specific holy figures he had recalled and celebrated had been almost all male — Palongawhoya, Buddha, Christ, Horus, Bran, Buamundus. In part this had reflected the male bias of human cultural history, and of languages in which one reflexively mutters "Jesus" rather than "Mary" when tumbling down a staircase. As Barrie would write in *The Martyrology, Book 5*, "Mother / White

Lady / Goddess / the less is known of You / the less is sung." In his own case the repeated cries of "father" had probably been cries as well to his own father whom he has clearly remembered — rightly or wrongly — as largely absent and uncaring in his childhood, unable to protect him from his mother's depressions, and unable also to decisively possess her during his son's Oedipal temptations. The resulting deity implied in *The Martyrology* has been thus much less an animism — or something that just "came in" — than a familiar Judaeo-Christian figure, with or without white hair, that mirrors the father of Freud's "family romance." However, "Lord" has also been often for Barrie a position in language — the "l or d" that finds an echo in "w or d" — language that for him has been almost as miraculous, and fascinating, as creation itself. In *The Martyrology, Book 5*, Chain 3, examining seemingly alphabetic "whorls on ancient stone" at the Lakes District stone circle "Long Meg and her Daughters," he will write of experiencing those whorls

> as if a tone were struck within the brain
> rings the changes
> links the chains of
> thot   history
> mysteries that seem insoluble
> the voluble presence of a silent world

The word "chains" here links the ancient stones and their glyphs to the current "chains" of his writing.

In a Canadian 1970s context of pervasive secular humanism — what my own socialist father called, ambiguously, a belief that "God helps those who help themselves" — and increasing feminism, Barrie's possible beliefs had raised at least a few eyebrows throughout his career. In a notebook entry on February 12, 1972, Barrie had recorded being unsettled by a comment made by a woman at a party about his poetry, that he was always crying for his father, and must have a real fixation about him. He hadn't had an answer — and wrote ambiguously instead in his notebook that those few that dare speak "you" risk being broken. In 1976 Bayard told him that she could "hardly believe" that he didn't "have a very Catholic boyhood" (17). Three months after the Western Front reading, interviewer Ken

Norris would tell him that he felt that both he and bissett were "religious writers." Barrie would reply that there were obviously "religious content and religious concerns" in his writing, and give Norris both the "it just happens" explanation that he had given to the Western Front questioner — "It's a content that's emerged. It's sort of surprised me . . ." — and the teenage-agnostic recollection that he gave Bayard and David (17). Then he would become somewhat less defensive: "But yes, . . . the landscape . . . through which my poetry moves, is inhabited by some sort of God figure or figures as the case may be, some sort of religious backdrop which comes into and out of focus, which is not presented as something you should convert to but rather is presented as part of a reality in which we are interacting, sometimes to our own stunned surprise." He would tell Norris that "[t]hese are phenomena of reality or of living in the world that one has to come to terms with" (Miki 202 244). However, whether these "phenomena" were paranormal or cultural, or involved credence or linguistics, Norris would not get around to asking. Nor would he reflect on how any monumental poetic journey such as Barrie's, back through personal and public history into humanity's social origins, would be likely to encounter things both baffling and awesome.

In his 2008 article "Nichol's Semiology of the Saints," Steve McCaffery's explanation of the religious connotations of some of Barrie's writing would stay close to the saints' linguistic origin in "the production of two words from one." This production was "less a play on words than a play on space which exposes alphabetic combinatory language to an indeterminate number of capricious productions." The resulting gap has created an ironic analogy to the creation of actual saints through torture and breakage, leading McCaffery to suggest that "via the saints language emerges as a surrogate for the Sacred. A saint is born by way of a certain death of meaning, a death to words" (101–102). The saints "are the agents in a game of metaphysics and theophany played out according to a thoroughly material rule" (105). Rather than implying any religious belief referential to signifieds such as God-the-father or the White Goddess, the *Martyrology*'s "ironic ontology" can imply only deities revealed among broken or shifting signifiers, or a belief in powers that can exist only within a language system. His explanation is not inconsistent with Barrie's of a "reality in which we are interacting," or "phenomena . . . of living in the world," although Barrie also has clearly not parsed his poem's ontology with McCaffery's care and analytic dispassion. Or possibly the very implications he has created have unsettled him.

In January 1978 Barrie's main writing projects would be the *Space Opera* that he was still writing with Howard Gerhard and the musical comedy "Ordinary Man," which he had now retitled as "Group: a theradramatic musical," and had engaged musician Nelles Van Loon as a collaborator and eventual performer. Back in 1975 he had conceived of "Ordinary Man" as an in-house Therafields arts project, but the retitling would make it more explicitly a celebration of the group therapy and the collectivity side of Therafields activities. He had already written three acts for "Ordinary Man"; now he had decided to reduce it to a single act, possibly to facilitate its staging in the group room of the Therafields downtown centre. He was also in one of his recurring *H*-obsession periods. Toward the end of the month he began sketching each day designs for various paper *H* sculptures, writing notes about stamped *H*s, burned *H*s, and paper cut-out *H*s, and considering also trying to create an *H* or "Zygal alphabet."

Quite possibly all this *H* activity had been partly due to difficulties he had been having with the current *Martyrology* book. On February 3 he had written in his notebook that Chain 6 of the book was stalled. He asked himself whether *Monotones* could be "filtered" through *Book 5* as a text being reread, or being reconsidered, or being rewritten as a "negative" linguistic image of itself. Or perhaps "Journeying and the Returns" could be somehow made a part of it. This was one of Barrie's familiar "unification" ideas but he was now considering reunification as both a solution to a writing block and an opportunity to introduce new modes of writing to the work. To "reread" was likely the creating of a text that reads closely or deconstructively an earlier text's words and sentences; to "reconsider" may indicate a new text that responds to the earlier subject matter; a "negative" was the method Barrie had used before of creating a "reverse" of a text — a new text that has a relationship to its original akin to a film negative's relationship to its positive print. Here was the planning Barrie Nichol at work, hoping to find new ways to spur *The Martyrology*'s exuberant bpNichol back to his explorations.

In March he was working again on both *Space Opera* and *Group*. In his notebook he wrote a list of the songs that he was keeping for the latter.

These include: "Australopithecus" about family transferences; "Ordinary Man" about psychic masochism; "Great Men Sleep Til Noon" about narcissism; and "I am Obsessed with my Mother's Breasts" about the persistence of Oedipal desire. Around the middle of the month he received word that he had won a $16,000 Canada Council Senior Arts Grant for 1978–79 — an award that would allow him to take a sabbatical as a Therafields administrator and devote most of the next 12 months to writing. Toward the end of the month he went by train to Montreal to give readings, and on the train wrote five new pages for *The Martyrology, Book 5*. Once again, getting away from Toronto had seemed to help resolve a stalled writing project. On April 28 novelist Jerry Lampert died unexpectedly while in Winnipeg at the 1978 League of Canadian Poets general meeting. Barrie had been editing his novel *Chestnut Flower / Eye of Venus* for late spring Coach House Press publication. The unexpected news, learned in a telephone call from Paul Dutton, moved Barrie to a further flurry of *The Martyrology, Book 5* writing, in which he misrecorded the year of Dutton's call and Lampert's death as "April 30 77" while recalling other friends who had recently died and foreseeing again his own inevitable death, and the obligations that the dead leave to the living.

> make my way thru this region of the known
> join them in the un
> country of my birth   death
> carry out this trust been granted me
> those few left who see a worth in the activity
> songs of praise and grief
> songs of joy
> flow from our pens & mouths beyond us

(Chain 3)

Barrie had been invited to perform in early May at the Sound and Syntax Festival in Glasgow — the other performers included Cobbing, Chopin, Dufrêne, Hansen, bissett, Mac Low, Jerome Rothenberg, and Ernst Jandl. Now that Barrie could be on leave from Therafields, he and Ellie had decided to make the festival the occasion for a three-week exploration of England and a visit to the Cotswolds home of Thomas A. Clark and his wife Laurie. Steve McCaffery and four other friends accompanied them for parts of their travels. Barrie did considerable writing on this trip, both on his own and in collaboration with McCaffery, with the quickly forming intention of creating the collaborative book *In England Now that Spring*. McCaffery travelled with them to Glasgow and the Lake District and to London, where he and Barrie had readings at Canada House, before McCaffery left to visit his parents in Yorkshire. Barrie, Ellie, and two of the others drove west through Salisbury, Stonehenge, and Glastonbury to a cottage they had rented in Falmouth, Cornwall, from which they visited Land's End and various stone circles in Cornwall. Barrie and Ellie then visited the Clarks in the Cotswolds before driving to Bath and Avebury. Having already written in *The Martyrology* extensively about early humanity, from Buddha to Gilgamesh, and being strongly curious about origins whether familial or cultural, Barrie was especially focussed on Bronze Age and Roman remains. In his notebook he made a list of the stone circles he had either visited or hoped to visit. His various draft poems, which include "The Martyrology Book 5 Chain 0," contemplated ancient copper mines, the fifth century kingdom of Rheged in Cumbria, Merlin's Cave near Glastonbury, the Nine Maidens plinths in Cornwall, and the stone rings at Avebury. Particularly at the latter two sites he wrote of feeling in the presence of spirituality. At the three circles of the Nine Maidens at Bodmin Moor he wrote:

> i am turning and turning
> o o o
> amid the birds singing & the flowers blooming
> circling under the sky
> under the yellow heat of the sun
> circling and turning   from the many into the one
> into the many many names by which we've known you
> Mother/Father in the vast beyond
> unwritable glyph
> ungraspable conception
> one of the many-named-one i name you
> sky & sun & wind & allness

aka{ barrie / phillip }Nichol

> i invoke you on this lonely moor
>
> . . .
>
> i name you *All* & i invoke you

(*In England Now that Spring*, np)

Perhaps because the plinths are known as maidens, there was unusual awareness here, for Barrie, of the gender ambiguity of the divine — is god, or the universe, a woman, or beyond gender? However he did not include this 24-line passage in his Bodmin Moor writing in *The Martyrology, Book 5*. Later at Avebury, where he experienced a similar "animist" awareness of stones and birds, he reverted to his usual "Lord" shorthand.

> listened to you whisper Lord
> among the stones
> between the calls of birds
> the dull roar of traffic
> the not quite silent moments that come
> your voice hums again
> as it must have always
> a maker who spawned makers
> raised these temples for you
> gestures of their awe
> i've only words
> gestures of my all
> record my awe of you
> my love
> for what it's worth
> i name the places where i found you

(*In England Now that Spring*, np)

He would include a shorter version of this passage in *The Martyrology, Book 5*, Chain 2. The two versions are roughly contemporaneous with ones Daphne Marlatt will write in Avebury in June 1981, in which — following both Robert Graves's *The White Goddess* and recent anthropological research — she will experience the stone monument as one built for a mother goddess, as it plausibly could have been.[4] Even though Barrie's *Book 5* will be dedicated once again to Lea, it was a father that Barrie was continuing to seek, perhaps unconsciously,[5] much like Marlatt, with her own unusual family history, would be seeking a lost and betrayed mother.

When they returned to Canada, McCaffery began work on the Eleventh International Sound Poetry Festival, which he, Steven Smith, and sean o huigin were organizing for October 14–21. Barrie and McCaffery began editing the 112-page catalogue that they had agreed to produce for the festival. As well, they began assembling the manuscript of *In England Now that Spring*, which Aya Press would publish the next year. Barrie himself resumed editorial work for Coach House where in 1978–79 he planned to see published books by o huigin, David Phillips, Richard Truhlar, and Paul Dutton, as well as his own novel *Journal*.

And Barrie returned to the ongoing Therafields crisis, where four fund-raising marathons were planned for the summer, including another eight-day artists' marathon to be overseen by Goodbrand and him, August 6–13. In June there was an acrimonious meeting of the Advisory Board, during which the downtown therapists were accused of paranoia and of being lacking in moral courage and honesty, and Barrie spoke of a cynicism that is "emanating from the concerns about money" (Goodbrand 212). Later in the year the Hypno I therapists who had invested in the farm 10 years before, and who now wished mostly to disassociate themselves from it, were bought out by the Therafields corporation. They then reinvested much of the money jointly with the corporation to purchase houses for themselves near the downtown Therafields centre — causing the residents of the farm to feel justified in embarking on an expensive renovation of the farmhouse. All of these transactions put Therafields further into debt.

Amid these events and developments Barrie managed to arrange the founding of another small press — Underwhich Editions. Several of his writer friends were publishing under their own small press imprints — Michael Dean (Wild Press), Richard Truhlar (Phenomenon Press and Kontakte), Steve McCaffery (Anonbeyond Press) — much as Barrie had been intermittently publishing under grOnk. Barrie thought that by combining these various presses into one they could at least improve distribution, be able to help each other with design and production, and have an annual catalogue. Each "editor" would continue to finance whatever he published. It was another generous Barrie initiative, in as much as grOnk was by far the most prolific and best known of the presses and would benefit the least from the consolidation. The resulting press, Underwhich Editions, founded at a meeting Barrie organized of Dean, Truhlar, McCaffery, Paul Dutton, Steven Smith, Brian Dedora, and John Riddell, went on between 1978 and 2000 to publish almost 90 titles. Two of the first would be Rafael Barreto-Rivera's *Here It Has Rained*, financed by Barrie, and *Sound Poetry: A Catalogue*, edited and financed by Barrie and McCaffery.

In the fall the sound poetry festival and Four Horseman rehearsals for their performance there occupied much of Barrie's time. He attended every event and spent as much time as possible with the visiting poets. Immediately after, however, he and Ellie had to begin packing their possessions, including his meticulously organized book and comic collections, to prepare for a move to another house. After little more than a year, the co-owners had decided to sell 46 and 48 Warren Road because Rob Hindley-Smith and Janet Griffith were separating due to his involvement with — and quick marriage to — another Therafields member, Sheron Fadel, who was now pregnant. Barrie, Ellie, Rob, Sheron, and Renwick were moving to the Therafields-owned 131 Admiral Road, while the others moved next door to the also Therafields-owned 123. Barrie and Ellie's move was complicated by renovations that were needed at the new house and that prolonged the move-in period. For a while Barrie was understandably dismayed by this chain of events that was causing him to unexpectedly lose more than two months of time — all of December and half each of November and January — which his Canada Council grant had supposedly freed up for writing. He had been writing prolifically until the move had interrupted his work. And though he and Ellie had served as best man and bridesmaid at Rob's September wedding to Sheron, to which Barrie had contributed the powerful poem, "Two Words, A Wedding," and were again sharing a house with him, Barrie was finding himself with somewhat less in common with Rob than in earlier years. Barrie's generous poem could be read as implicitly acknowledging this, particularly in its concluding lines, that the newlyweds were necessarily "wedded to the flux of life, because we are words and our meanings change" (*Alphabet Game* 219). Amid the chaos of the move on

December 17 he still managed to write a few pages of what would be *The Martyrology, Book 5*, Chain 8, with bpNichol saying goodbye once again to St. Reat and St. And and punningly reflecting on mortality and the ironies of looking toward the second millennium that was now "seven thousand six hundred & eighty-four" days away:

one more round
in the cycle
    a life
the poem reaches its own end
conclusion
drawn back
into the round of voices
speech and print
word sprint for immortality
'we all die anyway'
human
    counting the days until the second millennium

Between January 28 and January 30 of 1979 he wrote a flurry of letters in which he reflected on the past year — although without mentioning any of the Therafields conflicts. He wrote to British intermedia artist and recent acquaintance Michael Gibbs that it had been a "strange year" for his writing. He'd been doing things like adapting Arthur C. Clarke's short stories to be comic books, creating opera librettos and plays, as well as writing the predictable things — poems, novels, and weird stuff. He'd been just going where opportunities led him. He wrote to Thomas A. Clark that he'd had an unusual summer and autumn trying to make writing the number one thing in his life. He told him that he'd noticed that many of the forms he'd employed in the past — such as the diary-like writing of *The Martyrology* — were ones that were easy to fit within all his other activities and obligations because they were either short or episodic — so now he was attempting different things and learning a ton. But it was challenging and "strange," he repeated. He wrote to his cousin Donna Workman, a nurse who had recently been diagnosed with breast cancer, and with whom over the years he had shared information about his

aka{ barrie phillip }Nichol

psychological struggles. He told her that he was on leave from Therafields and trying to find his way through a "maze" of language possibilities, as well as attempting to end *The Martyrology* before it ended him. He and Ellie were living in new quarters, he added, with Ellie upstairs and the two of them "even" sharing a phone. He joked about what amazing progress in their relationship this shared phone represented.[6]

Indeed Barrie's comfort in his shared life with Ellie had been steadily growing for the past number of years, as her travelling with him to the Arctic and more recently to England reflected. The previous summer they had begun living together in that Warren Road mansion and coach house, and now were actually together in the Admiral Road house. Learning to share his personal space had been a 10-year struggle for him. He sent the same news to his sister Deanna — that he and Ellie were "actually" cohabiting in the same physical building, and joked about what a huge step this had been for him, while being a tiny one for most people. He, alas, he quipped, stepped to a different drumbeat. He then gave Deanna a much more intimate view of his recent attempts to make writing his main activity than he had given Donna or his writer friends. He wrote that trying to dedicate himself to writing had made his emotional life fascinatingly tumultuous, that it had been a struggle for him even to accept having more time for writing, that he'd encountered considerable self-doubt. He'd been tormented, he wrote, by inner voices that had accused him of wasting his time, even though he understood these were speaking to him out of certain childhood matters — matters that he probably didn't need to remind her of.

He then thanked Deanna for having mentioned Ellie in a recent general letter that she'd written to family members, including their mother and father — implying that it was good for them to be forced to see her name in print. He complained with some bitterness that their mother had consistently tried, unconsciously or consciously, to ignore Ellie and his relationship with her — that she appeared to deliberately avoid mentioning her name in letters, as when writing to Don and Liz recently about a photo of the two brothers and their partners and saying that Liz looked beautiful and that Don and he looked good. Note the usual deletion, he wrote. He was finding this more "irritating" as the years passed by. Of course the parental non-responses had been becoming more "irritating" because Barrie now had confidence that his life with Ellie was going to become increasingly meaningful. Deanna wrote back that she didn't think that their mother would ever entirely accept another woman in his life — an interesting reply given the Oedipal troubles Barrie had endured.[7]

Barrie also wrote on January 28 to his mother and father, telling them that 1978 had been the busiest year of his life. He described his trip to England, seemingly mentioning Ellie's name as frequently as he could. He told them about his Canada Council grant, and how he was using it to try to change his life, to try to make writing his number-one activity, and that he'd never thought about it that way before. He described how he was spending his mornings writing, taking a break in the afternoon, and meeting with his continuing therapy clients only in evenings. He advised them as well that he had begun a new novel (although not giving them its working title, "An Idiomatic Tale") based on a family's experiences during Winnipeg's 1950 Red River Flood.

He had actually done somewhat more for Therafields than he was noting in these various letters. Earlier in the month the Therafields crisis had taken yet another turn when Rob and Lea had circulated a tape-recorded joint message in which Rob had abruptly turned his back on the communal values that Barrie had in past years struggled to defend — and to reconcile with the top-down Therafields management of which he was a part. "Since 1968," Rob had declared, "I think we have been constructing basically a socialist state. I don't think you get visionaries coming out of that. I think the way we've been running things is to minimize risk and to maximize security. [. . . .] Right now there isn't a large body of people that's excruciatingly passionate about anything. . . . " Lea, perhaps weakened by her chronic illnesses, or perhaps remembering how the Therafields project had begun from her private therapy practice, had replied, "I think Therafields should become a business." Rob had responded, "I don't think therapists should be employees. I think every-body should have their independent practices" (Goodbrand 213). Together they had showed themselves ideologically somewhat to the right of even the therapists. They had rejected Barrie's "we." Barrie had responded almost immediately in the internal newsletter *Therapost*:

> Our dreams of ten years ago demanded, & still demand, what used to be called 'personal sacrifice.' Which is to say, you don't mind doing

without when you have a firm grasp on why you are doing without. Along with many urban communes of the 60s we had a vision of creating a rural environment in which we could live & work & provide for ourselves; one which recognized our link to the city, . . . & the nature of our work there.

. . .

I believe that we are at a significant moment of synthesis & change where what is necessary in order to move ahead is a reaffirmation of our goals, goals which I still believe to be revolutionary. Never before has such a large grouping of human beings worked so hard to understand so much of what goes into the ordinary daily business of living — work, love, friendship, sex, children, play, the interplay of all these things & the physical and emotional environment they need in order to thrive. But now, at the very point where so much has been realized, we find ourselves strangely divided. The larger purpose seems to be either forgotten or, in some cases, disavowed . . . . This failure of the spirit is one I personally find the most disturbing because it points to the most pervasive levels of emotional blockage. I believe, above all, that each of us, individually, must move to reaffirm why we are here, & whether or not we still support the goals we articulated for ourselves in the late 60s & beginning of the 70s. (Goodbrand 213–14)

This was most eloquent explanation of the communal goals of Therafields that had yet been articulated, but Barrie was making it much too late. His "very point where so much has been realized," however, could also describe the trajectory of his own life. He was ready to continue to "move ahead" but would soon have to do so without Rob, Lea, and many of his other Therafields familiars.

For the remainder of the Canada Council grant term he seems to have worked mainly on "finishing" *The Martyrology.* In writing to David Phillips on January 28 about the Coach House book he was editing for him, he asked him to tell him sometime whether or not he was "pissed off" about the references Barrie had made to him in *The Martyrology,* that he'd heard from someone that he was but would like to know whether that was so. If he was, Phillips would be happy to hear that he thought *The*

Martyrology was now finished — at least, Barrie wrote, he couldn't foresee writing any more of it after *Book 5*, that this book seemed to be the end of the trail. If Phillips replied, he did so orally, when visiting later that year. Barrie wrote to Thomas A. Clark on February 10 that he'd accomplished a major change this past week in how he wrote poetry, moving from a passive stance in which he waited to be inspired to an active one. Consequently, he told Clark with some excitement, he'd been able move past the tonal habits that he thought *The Martyrology* had settled into, and that had been leading him to think that *Book 5* was really the end, and begin something new. Initially he'd thought this new writing might be *The Martyrology*'s *Book 6*, but now he was sure it was actually the first part of a whole new large multi-book work, which itself would be merely the second part of an even larger work to which *The Martyrology*'s five books had been no more than a preamble.

Only two days later, however, on February 12, he had reversed himself, and was writing in his notebook that he had begun *Martyrology 6*, and was drawing up a title page for it that included a dedication to Michael Ondaatje for his having supported *The Martyrology* project "'all the way.'" Possibly he had been talking to Ondaatje about how the new writing had been perplexing him. *Book 6* was to be the first *Martyrology* book not dedicated to Lea. But eventually it would also not be dedicated to Ondaatje.

The problematical new writing that was causing Barrie this perplexity was section 1 of "The Book of Hours" — it was a problem because previously Barrie had totally finished one book of *The Martyrology* before beginning the next. He wrote to Michael Gibbs on February 27 that even though he'd "put a bullet" through *The Martyrology* the poem appeared to have come back to life in a puzzlingly new way along with various new thoughts and visions. He told Gibbs, however, that he quite liked the fact that the poem was asserting its control of where they were going. Later on the same day he sketched in his notebook a plan in which the first five books of *The Martyrology* were to be renamed "Scraptures II," the new "The Book of Hours" was to be part of "Scraptures III," while "Journeying and the Returns," *Scraptures*, *The Captain Poetry Poems*, and *Monotones* were to be combined as "Scraptures I." On March 12 he wrote a fourth hour of "The Book of Hours" and titled it part of "The Martyrology Book VI." Later that day he sketched another large plan in which "Scraptures (The

Books of the Dead/The Books of the Living)" would have four and possibly six parts. Part I would be *Journeying*, *Scraptures*, and *Captain Poetry*; Part II would be *Monotones*, Part III would be *Martyrology Books 1–5*, and Part IV would be called "A COUNTING" and would contain "A Book of Hours" and "A Book of Friends." On April 6 he sketched three new parts for "A COUNTING" — "A Book of Journeys," "A Book of Witness," and "A Book of Politics." On April 25 he wrote to the composer R. Murray Schafer that the new "Book of Hours" texts meant that *The Martyrology* was finished and that he was now writing a new large text, "A COUNTING."

On June 6, 1979, he wrote his report to the Canada Council on his year's work under the council grant. He told the Canada Council he had finished his novel "John Cannyside," had nearly completed *Book 5* of *The Martyrology*, had written 54 pages of a new novel "An Idiomatic Tale," devised 10 new translation systems for *Translating Translating Apollinaire*, completed the libretto for *Space Opera*, four scenes of a libretto for an opera titled "Brother 12," 15 children's poems requested by *Owl* magazine, and four new scores for the Four Horsemen, and had finished his editing of the manuscript of *In England Now that Spring*. He added that the biggest benefit of the grant had not been merely all the work he had completed or what he had learned while completing it. It had been an enormous, more important gift for him to be able to figure out that *The Martyrology, Book 5* was finished, and that a new long work, "A Counting," was underway, to which the books of *The Martyrology* would be but a prequel, and to be able to complete nine hours of that new poem's first book, "The Book of Hours." But although these insights into what he was writing were worth the entire grant, of even greater value, he told the council, had been the opportunity to find out what would occur if writing occupied the primary place in his life.

In a postscript he mentioned that he and McCaffery had co-edited an issue of *Open Letter* on composer R. Murray Schafer and that with Jack David he had selected the texts to be included in a selected writings that Talonbooks would publish, and that he was a bit uncomfortable to be having a "selected" at the tender age of 34. His discomfort may not have been as much with any undue earliness as with what the earliness could portend. Stephen Scobie had recently begun writing a study of Barrie's life and writings for the Talonbooks' New Canadian Criticism Series.

216

When Barrie had heard the news he had written to Scobie, on March 27, 1979, that it all seemed very strange. To have books written about himself, and selected poems published, when he was a mere stripling of 34, and still at least 35 years from heaven. Did it mean that death was just around the corner? he asked. A very cosy corner?

aka{ barrie phillip }Nichol

19. Blown Away

If we're going to write OUR history then it must be
US who write it. After all isn't the work of theradrama
bringing our past lives into our present consciousness
and understanding them?

— bpNichol and Julia Keeler,
"The Autobiography of Therafields,"
A Publication 2, December 8, 1974

At the end of March 1979 Barrie had written to Montreal poet Stephen
Morrissey that life was steadily unfolding as many intriguing revelations
as it ever did, and that he currently had so many irons in his fire that he
worried that he might get burned. This wasn't quite the upbeat report that
he was about to send to the Canada Council, but perhaps slightly more
accurate. As well as working on all the literary projects he had told the
council about, he was also about to draft his defence of Lea's books for the
"easily defensive" readers of *A Publication*; he had written to his mother
telling her that he had begun a new autobiography, titled "Desiring to
Become," and asking her to send him a copy of every photo she had of
him from his first 18 years — receiving the reply that he was welcome
to any photo she had the next time he visited; he had recently received
permission from fantasy writer Jack Vance to adapt part of his collection
The Narrow Land as a comic book narrative. Meanwhile at the Therafields

Florida house, Visvaldis — perhaps depressed over Lea's chronic illnesses, or by the financial uncertainties of the corporation — had relapsed into his alcoholism, "fleeing to Mexico City," Goodbrand writes, "and had sexual relations with women he picked up in the bars" (214). Barrie, who was already scheduled to co-supervise four weeks of summer marathons, then initiated plans for a series of three Therafields Environmental Forums, the first to be held at the farm in July with Visvaldis chairing. Barrie's main goal in these, Goodbrand implies, may have been to return Visvaldis to sobriety and responsibility, although the announced aim was to design a large integrated rural centre to serve the farm members as a communal residence and work space. Barrie himself would chair the following two forums in October, with Visvaldis and other architects on their panels. But by November Visvaldis would have resumed his heavy drinking.

In August Barrie wrote to Janet Griffith, Rob's former partner, and one of the original members of Hypno I, who had now left Canada. He described to her a marathon for therapists that Lea had recently managed to hold, and then wrote that the marathon had caused him not only to think of her, but of all the people he'd begun the Therafields part of his life with and who had left to follow other paths. He'd begun feeling how much he missed them all. He'd realized that when they had all been planning, building, and talking back in the late 1960s he'd imagined that they'd all be together, doing similar things, forever. Barrie was still not an eager writer of letters, and there are no other letters to or from Griffith in his files. He seems to have written this letter on impulse, under the growing pressure of the interpersonal and financial Therafields crises. His nostalgic tone, with its intimation of a lost immortality, seems to have been evoked not only by his memory of Griffith but also by his awareness that many of his present Therafields friends, including those at Lea's marathon, might very well soon also be in his past.

In September 1979 the Therafields farm held a large "fall fair" open house and hosted more than 3,200 visitors. But during the same week Barrie and the other Advisory Board members met with bankers and agreed to split Therafields into three parts — therapy, community, and real estate — and began consultations about the financial arrangements the split would require. Both Lea and Visvaldis failed to attend the meeting. For the next two years Therafields would often appear outwardly to be operating as usual, but behind the scenes house groups were being disbanded, real estate was sold to indemnify members who had been shareholders, and therapists were beginning to operate as private businesses. Barrie himself would be giving much less thought to its future, and much more to his personal and writing lives, although he did expect to continue to help manage Therafields as a corporation that at least provided offices and other services to independent therapists.

He had sent the latest draft of his novel "John Cannyside" to Ondaatje in July, with a note that the Coach House board should publish a poetry manuscript by Sharon Thesen and attempt to get the manuscript of Daphne Marlatt's *Rings* — later published by New Star Books. The previous August he had received a letter from Stan Dragland to write an introduction to an imaginary or "uncollected", "Canada, a Prophecy" anthology, for publication in Dragland's *Brick* magazine — modelled on Jerome Rothenberg's recently published *America, A Prophecy*. Misunderstanding this as requiring him to compile a list of the imaginary anthology's contents, and to do the extensive archival research that would require, and perhaps even to produce an actual anthology, Barrie had delayed responding for a year until again prompted by Dragland. "CANADA: a prophecy" is such a blatant steal, he had replied, but it certainly conveys what you're talking about. He agreed to do some work on it, writing that it would probably be late fall before he could find the time. He told Dragland that he had too many projects underway right now to do any more, but that he'd "really" like to this one. The misunderstanding would continue for a couple of years, but Barrie's willingness to take on such a large task — if he could find the time — demonstrates his continuing concern about canonicity and about keeping alive earlier writing for the benefit of later writers. He had not forgotten how difficult it was when he was a teenager to locate actual Dada texts, or how obscure Sheila Watson's writing had been when he stumbled across it. He went on to tell Dragland that he and Ellie were planning an extended drive out to the West Coast in September, including to Victoria, and that he was planning to work during the drive out on his own *utanikki*, to which he'd given the working title of "You Too, Nicky," and that he foresaw as being a reworking of the "failed" "Plunkett Papers."

Somewhat like the trip he had made with Rob in 1969, their drive took them to Saskatoon to visit Ellie's parents, through Plunkett, and then up to Edmonton to visit Doug and Sharon Barbour, then to Vancouver and Victoria for four days before returning. He seems to have done considerable writing on the trip on the "You Too, Nicky" project, although the notebook in which he did much of it (titled "The Blue Jean Yes Notebook," April 28, 1979, to November 11, 1979) later went missing — and with it his only copy of the original "Hour 8" of "The Book of Hours." In October, after their return, he wrote to Fred Wah to explain his understanding of the history of the word "*utanikki*," referring Wah to Earl Miner's new book *Japanese Linked Poetry*.

November and December saw Barrie do some writing for the still not abandoned Four Horsemen novel project, "Slow Dust," write various passages of poetry that he wasn't sure were part of "A COUNTING" or perhaps a "prologue" to it, write drafts of a text titled "Imperfection: A Prophecy," and begin a series of drawings titled "Interference Patterns." He and Ellie were also concerned that she might be pregnant, something they became sure of in early January 1980. On January 22 he wrote a cheery letter, possibly deliberately cheery, to his parents announcing his impending fatherhood and jesting that it may have been inspired by his and Ellie's Victoria visit. There is no reply to it in his archives — one can but imagine how it may have been received. He told them that he would be in Victoria again in two weeks' time to give a reading at the university.

On Valentine's Day he wrote contrasting letters to poets Ken Norris and Artie Gold. He told Norris that he was somewhat "blown away" because he and Ellie were about to have their first child — the due date was June 23 — and that the event was already opening new possibilities for both poetry and their lives. He told Gold that amid the crush of various events his writing was on the back burner, but that was okay because the changes that were happening were so bizarre and interesting. In his notebooks, however, he had been recording ideas for two novels, one titled "The Notion" and the other "Phone Exchange," a novel that would feature a fictional bpNichol created from newspapers and magazine items, advertisements, and similar things. He'd also written a note about a possible text that would include a biography of "a bpNichol," plus a text for his series "Probable Systems" and a text titled "Realism." Barrie was apparently still very much aware of how he had invented his publicly performing self, and eager both to foreground its invention and to have some fun parodying how readers, reviewers, and journalists had presumed to perceive it — or how a future biographer might. But, more darkly, he also seemed unable to avoid foreseeing bpNichol — along with Knarn — someday dead.

In March he headed west again with the Four Horsemen to give eight performances in 12 days. The tour was an opportunity for him also to visit Daphne Marlatt in Vancouver, whose book *What Matters* he was editing for Coach House. Among the other editorial tasks he would return to were two books in the new Talonbooks Selected Poems Series. He was overseeing the typesetting at Coach House of his own selected poems, which he had now wittily titled *As Elected*, and editing and writing an introduction for my book in the series, *The Arches*. He would send that manuscript to Talonbooks on April 14. Also in April he would write drafts of "The Vagina" and "The Anus" for the series of poems he was titling "Organ Music," and as well performing late in the month at the second International Festival of Disappearing Art(s) in Baltimore.

In May rehearsals began for the production of his musical

THE PROGRAM FOR BARRIE'S MUSICAL
COMEDY GROUP, MAY 1980.

comedy *Group*, now in two acts, and to be performed in Therafields' Dupont Street group room in a six-night public run. It was an elaborate quasi-professional production with a director, choreographer, stage manager, lighting director, three musicians, and a publicist. Several of the performers were professionals with extensive experience in television or on Shaw Festival stages — as well as in Barrie's artists' groups.

For Therafields members *Group* was a warm but poignant celebration of a context and set of beliefs that seemed likely soon to be gone.[1] For outsiders it was an unusually sparkling joining of comedy and wisdom. Barrie was already thinking of restaging it in a larger theatre.

Meanwhile events at Therafields itself had become again more complicated. Although Rob and the corporation's accountant Renwick Day could now see possibilities for financing development of the now independent farm or "rural" centre, resentment among the therapists was making the overall financial untangling of the three Therafields "parts" difficult. Many of the therapists wanted no future dealings with the corporation or its managers. Then on March 8, 1980 *The Toronto Star* published a somewhat paranoid article about "cults," and named Therafields as a prominent example — as a group that "brainwashed" new members into yielding control of their finances and ambitions and insisted on communal thought and living. A politically nervous provincial government promptly appointed the sociologist and widely known human rights advocate Daniel G. Hill to inquire into the charges, which in June he reported to be without substance. But the brief tempest had strengthened the determination of many of therapists to be dissociated from Therafields, and led other members to leave. Goodbrand writes that of the 10 week-long summer marathons that had been in planning, seven had to be cancelled due to lack of interest and that seven of the 17 houses still owned were no longer needed for Therafields' work (220).

In the second week of June Barrie and Ellie headed to the hospital for the impending birth of their baby. Barrie would later, in a letter dated July 16, tell Doug and Sharon Barbour, that when the doctor emerged from the delivery room and told him the news the one thing that went through his mind was the line of Stephane Mallarmé, "Un coup de dés jamais n'abolira le hasard" — "A throw of the dice will never abolish chance." His and Ellie's son had been stillborn. Barrie was initially terrified that Ellie might be dying also. Barrie's mother received the bad news by telephone from Don, and sent Barrie "& Ella" a letter, assuring them that people get over such things with time. Possibly in previously refusing to mention Ellie in her letters she'd forgotten her name. Barrie would generously reply in July that both he and Ellie had thought of her own loss of her firstborn and of Ellie's mother's loss of a three-year-old son. He agreed that the passing of time could help, but suggested that a little "perspective" could also be useful. He told her as well that they were committed to trying to have a family together, and that they were likely to get married next October.

Two weeks after their loss he and Ellie decided to have a brief vacation in New York, where they saw a large Picasso exhibition and took in two Broadway shows. On their return Barrie, with some misgivings, resumed seeing his therapy clients. He wrote to his sister (July 26, 1980) that this wasn't the most ideal work to be doing after such a loss, because a therapist draws so much on his own stockpile of inner joy in order to keep listening to his clients' unhappinesses. When you encounter something so devastating, he remarked, you can quickly run out of resources.

There was even less joy that summer at Therafields as it became clear both that Lea was no longer capable of offering any leadership ideas and that both Rob and the therapists were in their own ways refusing the ideals on which most members, including Barrie, believed that she had founded its therapies. Barrie regretfully but tersely wrote to his colleagues in July "Whatever the term 'Therafields' described when Lea first coined it, it no longer describes the same physical reality. The Therafields of summer 1980 is not the Therafields of summer 1967. [. . .] We should honour the term by retiring it until we can use it in a way that won't pollute the original feeling of challenge, joy, and promise we felt around it" (Goodbrand 220-21). Barrie's brother Don had recently severed his ties to the corporation, and Barrie probably would have as well if he had not had responsibilities to oversee its debts and financial obligations to the therapists. In mid-August he and the other managers encountered yet another credit crisis and were forced to sell more houses.

In September he began teaching part-time at York University — a second-year creative writing course that he would teach, often with an additional senior course — until 1988. Barrie was already foreseeing the possible end of his paid work at Therafields, and I was coordinator of York's new creative writing program and controlled its part-time hirings.

On October 11 Barrie and Ellie married, holding a reception at the Vivaxis restaurant. Their invitation — hand-drawn by Barrie — requested "A.L.S.A.P.U.T.C." ("As Little Sentimentality As Possible Under The Circumstances"). Barrie, however, could not comply. He reported to Steven Smith, who was in the U.K. for the year, that he had been unable to

aka{ barrie phillip }Nichol

keep from weeping, while Ellie had managed to appear calm throughout. He joked that they had reversed sexist stereotypes, while perhaps creating a few of their own.

The next weekend Barrie read at the three-day Canadian Poetry Festival in Buffalo, a festival co-organized by Robert Creeley and Duncan-scholar Robert Bertholf and attended as well by McCaffery, Wah, Marlatt, Tallman, and bissett. On his return he and Ellie began another mammoth move — from 131 Admiral Road into another large Victorian house, 99 Admiral Road, which they and Renwick Day and Grant Goodbrand were now jointly purchasing from Therafields. As well, Barrie was bringing home 25 cartons of books and other possessions from his room at the farm's lavish "Willow" house, once Lea's principal residence, which was now largely unused and likely to be sold. The move out of 131 had been occasioned, as had the one a year earlier, by Rob and Sheron. This time it was Lea's interference with the care of their new baby that was the catalyst. Lea was now back living in her nearby house on Admiral with companions who attended to her failing health. Sheron narrated the story to Brenda Doyle:

> I took it for about four weeks because I didn't know any better. When the baby was born, Lea called and said, "I'm sending (one of her companions) over to stay with you for six weeks because you have no instincts." She said she was very concerned about the baby because I was his mother. [But t]here is never a time that you are more intuitive than when you give birth to a baby. She was into this whole thing about only feeding the kid every four hours. [. . .] After a few weeks I said to Rob that it was all crazy. The child was crying and Lea's companion was walking him up and down and he needed to be fed. [. . .] It was horrible for me. I hated her at that time and didn't want her in the house. I felt like she was insanely jealous of me, that I had stolen Rob from her. ("Thoughts," December 5, 2010)

The moves took only two weekends, but the sorting required to fit everything into the new space — Barrie and Ellie had only the ground floor — consumed most of the next two months. He told Smith in January that he had tossed out or sold "tons" of accumulated magazines and various books and become more organized than he had ever known himself to be. During part of this time he also was commuting with Steve McCaffery to London, Ontario, for rehearsals of his friend R. Murray Schafer's musical/theatrical pageant *Apocalypsis*, for which he and McCaffery had advised and done small bits of writing, and in which they were now part of a cast of 500.

Again the new house and move were not things Barrie had desired. The move separated him from Rob, who moved with Sheron to King City, north of Toronto, where his sister Josie and her new husband Adam Crabtree were also now living. It may also have complicated his relationship with Lea. With each move the number of people sharing their house was becoming smaller, paralleling the shrinking of Therafields and collapse of its dreams of communal living. From the Admiral-Road-area house groups of the early 1970s most long-term Therafields members were now heading toward nuclear households.

Because of the various Therafields crises and changes, Barrie had been finding very little time this year for writing, except for drafting a few parodic dice-based board games — a Four Horseman board game, a TRG board game, and a "Time Times Time: the Eternity Boardgame" which he had begun in Victoria during his Feburary visit. He had also begun collecting board games. While working with me on an *Open Letter* project to collect Louis Dudek's previously uncollected lectures and papers, he had encountered Dudek's notes for a similarly parodic Monopoly-like "The Poetry Game." Whether it was this encounter, or his general feeling that events in his life, particularly at Therafields, had become irrational, beyond any individual's capability to influence or predict, dice-based board games had begun to dominate his thinking — to the extent that when his son was stillborn it was Mallarmé's throw of the dice that he had recalled. It was an odd thought to find comforting, he had told the Barbours in that July letter, but it seemed reasonable to him. Then he had added that two or three weeks ago he had had a dream in which he was playing a board game, which seemed to be his own life, and there he was, dice in his hand, all ready to play again.

The one important work that Barrie would write in 1980 was "Hour 13" of his "Book of Hours." He flew west in November with Ondaatje, taking a three-day break from unpacking and sorting his books, to give readings in Lethbridge and Camrose. Being away from Toronto and from

Therafields business seems to have again released him to write. "Hour 13," written while they were in Lethbridge, is the extraordinary "the heart does break" hour in which he ponders the meanings of his child's stillbirth.[2]

He had also finally decided, somewhat before his trip to Lethbridge and Camrose, that he hadn't really completed *The Martyrology* — that the new writing that he had thought was part of his new book, "A Counting," had been actually an extension of *Book 5*. In a letter dated January 23, 1981, he explained this change of mind to Scobie, who had recently sent him the first chapter of the bpNichol book he was drafting, writing that he had now come to view "A Counting" as *The Martyrology, Book 6*. He had realized this, he told Scobie, only when he had finished "Imperfection: a Prophecy," the first section or "book" of "A Counting," and had noticed that all of the references that he had worked with there had come directly out of the Bran and Brendan material in *The Martyrology, Book 5*. Instead of having begun a new work — which, because of Barrie's belief that he never worked on more than one work of discursive poetry at a time, would have meant that the *Martyrology* had ended (to his great "relief," he joked), he had begun writing book sections "spawned" by the chains of *Book 5*. He predicted to Scobie that each of the 12 chains would give rise to a new *Book 6* section, or "book," and this *Book 6* would be a "set of books." He continued the letter by bemusedly reflecting on his repeated eagerness to have seen *The Martyrology* terminated, and by suggesting that it was more likely that its continuability was unlimited, that it could go on "forever," so long as it "renews itself." The letter, together with his now year-long puzzlement about whether his writing was extending *The Martyrology* or beginning a new project, showed the extent to which he had now separated the desires of Barrie Nichol from the assumed desires of his poem and its bpNichol writer. He was treating the poem much like Barrie Nichol would a therapy client — not directing its life but attempting to find out, and enable, what it "wanted" to do. The unrealistic optimism of "forever" aside, *The Martyrology* had become suddenly one of very few things in Barrie's life apart from his marriage that he could realistically expect to continue. He was finally accepting it as a possibly "lifelong" companion.

The new work that had moved him toward this view, "Imperfection: A Prophecy," was an example of the new kinds of writing he had hoped *The Martyrology* might contain. It began as playscript or masque, with the apostles addressed by Paul in Romans 16:7, Andronicus and Junias, fleeing Jerusalem while lamenting the personal imperfections that had caused them to do nothing to stop Christ's slaying. In Britain the poem brings them together with the legendary and playfully promiscuous giant Buamundus as successful Christian missionaries, but who soon must flee westward into different and equally (im)possible story lines. The voice of this later part of the poem is the mischievously solemn bpNichol of Barrie's "probable systems" texts of *Zygal* and *Artfacts*. In one "possible" storyline Buamundus becomes the "Sleeping Giant" of Port Arthur, and Andronicus and Junias the models for some Mayan carvings. In another Buamundus freezes in the Arctic while Andronicus and Junias disappear into the Pacific Ocean. The playful hypotheses continue the blending of deities and cultures — Horus, Brun, God, et cetera — that Barrie had begun in *Book 5,* Chain 3, and tip his theology sharply toward the multicultural and 'pataphysical.

what it all adds up to

. (the end)

Andronicus — apostle ⟶ ?

Junias — apostle ⟶ ?

Buamundus — giant ⟶ ?

the known guessed at

thus conclusions
and/or theories
viz: science and history
          myth and legend
some sense of
the components of
reality

("Book I," *The Martyrology Book 6 Books*)

aka{ barrie / phillip }Nichol

Barrie's concluding deconstruction of the word "religious" into "a region of the real / uncharted ⸗ (largely) // open to misconstruction / and fanaticism" offers a semantically rich rebuke to readers who have classified him as a "religious poet," suggesting that he was a poet of an even larger metaphysical curiosity. Even the scholarly possibility that Junias — whose name was also recorded in early manuscripts as Junia — may have been a female apostle is left open here. Nowhere does the text assign either "her" or Andronicus a gendered pronoun. ·

20. Eric Von Daniken Meets Kurt Schwitters

He dashed off comic books, hatched operas and banged out television scripts. He futzed with fiction, tinkered with radio plays and monkeyed with children's verse. As a member of the sound-poetry ensemble Four Horsemen, he chanted and nasal-droned for audiences across North America. He favoured collage, comic books, typefaces, puns, doodles and blank pages, and had a soft spot for the letter "H."

— Carmine Starnino, "Does bpNichol's once-revolutionary wordplay have staying power?" *Maisonneuve*, July 5, 2011

Nineteen seventy-nine and 1980 had been extraordinarily stressful years for Barrie. His son had been stillborn. He had been forced for the second time in two years to lose two months work in moving to a different house, with both moves kindling memories of the numerous dislocating moves his family had made in his childhood. Both moves had been caused by unexpected and abrupt changes his best friend Rob had been making in his own life — while also increasingly disagreeing with Barrie on the goals of Therafields. Therafields itself — a context that over 16 years had provided Barrie with self-knowledge, an extended family life, idealistic goals, employment, and a host of friendships among both its therapeutic and artistic communities — had been slowly imploding. His numerous friends from Hypno I were now regarding him as little more than an impediment to their hopes of disentangling themselves from "the Smiths" and a financially impractical rural community. Illness had so reduced Lea's spirit and intellect that she was no longer recognizable as the charismatic healer who had once saved him. Yet Barrie was continuing to treat all those involved with civility and attempted understanding, and to describe the Therafields' changes mildly to others. Therafields is enduring even more turmoil than ever, he had written in a letter to his sister in July 1980, elaborating that huge changes seemed to be imminent, making all parts of his life unpredictable. And he wrote that he had continued to move his various writing projects forward, although never at the pace he desired. In February 1981 he wrote a letter to Steven Smith about Underwhich Editions sales and revenue. On top of everything else he was managing Underwhich during Smith's absence in Britain. Barrie wrote that beyond such mundane matters his own life rushed on, that there wasn't enough time in any of his days, and that if he became tired he worried that he was wasting time.

Much of his creative time in the first part of 1981 was spent preparing for the "Clouds and Water" exhibition of paper works and sewn cloth visual poems that he and Ellie would hold in March at the Vivaxis café. The highlights of the exhibition were the multicoloured cloth works, which Barrie designed and Ellie sewed as partly quilted wall hangings, some as large as 40 x 30 inches. In February he also managed to find time to draft "Hour 14" of "The Book of Hours" and "The Tonsils" for "Organ Music." That month the six volumes from the Talonbooks Selected Poems Series were released, with celebratory launches planned for April and May at Harbourfront in Toronto and Robson Square in Vancouver. While in Vancouver for the latter, Barrie drafted another section for "Organ Music" called "The Toes." In June he drafted "Hour 17" during a visit with Ellie to Point Pelee National Park.

June was the required time for the Therafields corporation to purchase back the shares of those members who no longer wanted their money so invested. According to Goodbrand, to make this repurchase the board had found itself having to borrow $863,000, with the loan secured not only by the assets of the corporation but also by the personal assets of Barrie, Rob, and Renwick. Earlier in the spring the three of them had scrambled to launch various money-making plans. Rob had become a representative for Amway. As a board they had bought additional properties adjacent to the Dupont Street centre in the hope of replacing all the buildings with a large business complex. They had commissioned Visvaldis to design a $10 million spa, complete with a private airstrip, to be built near the Willow. But their hopes of selling unused Therafields houses to help finance these were thwarted by declines in Toronto real estate values. Meanwhile Lea's health had declined to such an extent that she could no longer care for herself; Rob had to create a separate corporation to handle her affairs (Goodbrand 223). How committed Barrie himself was to the various development plans is unclear. Quite possibly he was outvoted by Renwick, an accountant, and the increasingly right-leaning Rob. Certainly, the enterprises being planned were unlike any that had ever interested Barrie. The only things that the record makes certain are that he was ethically committed to repaying Therafields investors, and determined also to be able to support what he was confidently calling to close friends his "petite famille." He had begun considering what he might do as a writer to replace his Therafields income. For Ellie was pregnant once again, and being closely monitored for an expected November delivery.

In July Barrie had Canada Council supported readings scheduled in Vancouver at Simon Fraser University and the Octopus East bookstore. He and Ellie flew west for the readings and then on July 27 took the train back, with Barrie hoping to write a journal-poem along the way. The result was *Continental Trance*, the third book of *The Martyrology, Book 6 Books*. Barrie thought this text might be a replacement for the "You Too, Nicky" one that he had vainly hoped to create during their drive west through Saskatchewan in September 1979.

A little more than a month later, on September 16, their daughter, Sarah Kathryn, was born 10 weeks premature. She would not be released from hospital until November 28, with both parents during the interim making daily trips to the hospital to be with her. In this period he wrote and delivered a paper — with handouts — at the Toronto 'pataphysics conference, "The Symposium on Linguistic Onto-Genetics," wrote a draft of "Hour 18" of "A Book of Hours" on the birth of his daughter and a draft of "Hour 19," prepared and mailed the manuscript of *The Martyrology, Book*

5 to Jerry Ofo for him to begin creating its visual images, and mailed as well a complete manuscript of *Scraptures* to Charles Alexander for possible publication by his Black Mesa Press. He also began work with musician John Beckwith on the 12-minute CBC-commissioned *Mating Time*, which would be broadcast the next year. Dutton notes both the importance of such collaboration to Barrie, and how he brought Beckwith "a ream of obscure '20s and '30s pop-song sheet music" to work with. Quite possibly these new performance collaborations — with Van Loon, Gerhard, and Beckwith — were partly replacing both the various cooperations Barrie had

been involved with at Therafields, and the to-Barrie disappointing Four Horsemen collaborations. They were not especially lucrative ventures, however.

The first sign of financial discomfort came in a letter dated January 2, 1982, that Barrie wrote to Gwen Hoover, the Canada Council officer in charge of its public readings program. He was lamenting how long it had been taking

BARRIE PERFORMING IN R. MURRAY SCHAFER'S *WIZARD OIL AND INDIAN SAGWA*, 1982. *(Marilyn Westlake)*

her office to process his reports and issue cheques for his poetry-reading expenses — which were often around $700. He told her that he never had cash on hand for these, and had to either leave the amount on his credit card and — at current rates — pay $60 in interest, or cash in an investment and lose $60 in interest, making his profit on the reading marginal at best. It was a complaint he would make several times that year, with Hoover soon attempting to give him a travel advance for most of his readings. Later in the month he performed in Kingston in R. Murray Schafer's new musical pageant *Wizard Oil and Indian Sagwa*, and while driving to Kingston encountered near Port Hope the Choate Road scene that inspired on January 21 his beginning of the "Inchoate Road" section of *The Martyrology, Book 6*. In February the choral work "Mating Time," music by John Beckwith and text by bpNichol, and commissioned by the CBC, was performed by the internationally celebrated Elmer Iseler Singers. This appears to have been one of the first new paying tasks Barrie had encountered. He was also considering writing children's books — both for his new daughter and profit. The previous fall Black Moss Press had published his first children's book, the collection of poems *Moosequakes and Other Disasters*, in a small edition. The press was also interested in him attempting a more commercial text.

In February he became the point man for a rather strange project that he, Mike Ondaatje, and Margaret Atwood had conceived. Much like Irving Layton and Eli Mandel in 1970 had raised money to give a "peoples poet" award to Milton Acorn because, in their view, he had been unjustly deprived of a Governor General's Award when it had been awarded to George Bowering, Ondaatje, Atwood, and Barrie were setting out to raise money for an award to Phyllis Webb to compensate her for her book *Wilson's Bowl* not having won, or even been shortlisted for the Governor General's Award, which had been given in 1980–81 to Stephen Scobie. Timothy Findley sent them $500 and a note saying that the book was damn good. Scobie also contributed and magnanimously apologized for his book's having won the award over Webb's better one. In a letter to Atwood Barrie asked whether they were going to hold a public award ceremony — possibly he was recalling the much advertised ceremony at Grossman's Tavern, complete with imitation medal, that had accompanied Acorn's compensatory prize. By April they had raised almost $3,000, which they had Barrie convert to a money order and send to P.K. Page with instructions to present it privately. Ironically, within a year Webb would win the actual award for her 1982 selected poems, *The Vision Tree* — a book that contained 30 pages of poems from the rejected *Wilson's Bowl*. Or perhaps there was no irony — possibly Barrie's efforts along with those of Ondaatje and Atwood had acted as a discreet but effective lobbying campaign on Webb's behalf. Perhaps that was at least what one of them had hoped for. All three, along with Scobie, would have understood that such awards are as much political statements as literary. Daphne

Marlatt had written to Barrie in late 1981, sending him $30 for the fund, and mentioning that her partner Roy Kiyooka perceived the project as mere "literary maneuvering" that he had little interest in.

Overall, the spring of 1982 was a lively time for Barrie, as he undertook somewhat more travels than usual because of the fees they would earn him. In the second week of February he did several readings on the West Coast with Steve McCaffery. He later wrote to Toby McLennan, whose first book he was editing for Coach House, that he had just returned from giving readings in British Columbia, including Nanaimo, North Vancouver, and the Sechelt Peninsula, and then added that she probably knew how such trips went and typed the words *travel, eat, read, drink, sleep* more than 35 times. In March he undertook a week-long residency at David Thompson University Centre in Castlegar, British Columbia — a residency that the centre was combining with a weekend conference. Here he wrote a note about his still languishing novel "bpNichol by John Cannyside" and further drafts of "Inchoate Road" and "Inchoate World," writing one of the latter in his notebook and recording that it had been written on the road between Salmo and Creston in the company of Stan Bevington, Nicole Brossard, Nancy Jean Thomson, and Joan Hoogland, all hoping to arrive in time to catch a plane to Calgary. In a brief mention of this trip to Page in the letter in which he later enclosed the Webb money order, Barrie complained for the first time in print of having back pain. Explaining his delay in sending the money, he wrote that it had included one out-of-town-trip, a messed-up back, and a period for recovery. The recovery period had been almost three weeks.

With that letter to Page on April 7, 1982, Barrie's letter-writing came to a temporary halt, as did his notebook entries — although in May he did oversee the staging of a revised *Group: A Therapeutic Musical* for the Toronto Theatre Festival. He had been writing quarterly "Toronto" reports for the magazine *cviι*, and on August 7 wrote its editor to apologize for having missed the last deadline. He told her that just after his last letter (March 29) his world had exploded around him, engulfing him in a series of urgent meetings about a particular business matter. The emergency had continued into early July, carrying him well past her June 15 deadline. Because of the nature of the blow-up (he comments that he is using that word deliberately) he turned to do some intensive "personal writing" rather than resume replying to letters. A few days later he wrote less hyperbolically to Gilles Morin, an acquaintance who apparently knew the Therafields scene, telling him that the ongoing debates seemed to be in endless disorder, whether about how to change or dissolve the corporate structure of Therafields, or how to create something new to succeed it.

Barrie had actually resigned from most of his Therafields positions, and ceased working as a therapist sometime in May, and at that point wished himself fully separated from it. Goodbrand suggests, however, that because of the financial arrangements under which he had pledged his assets as security for the corporation's bank debt, Barrie was obliged to remain, at least legally, a Therafields director until that debt was retired in the fall of 1983. The turmoil or blow-up that Barrie mentioned in his August 1982 letters may have been the collapse of Hypno I at the end of March, or the bank's threat shortly afterward to recall the Therafields debt and seize the corporate and personal assets that had secured it. In consequence of that threat, Rob and Renwick had been forced to give up their dreams of a $10 million spa and a downtown plaza — dreams that it's unlikely Barrie had shared. In July the three directors began laying off employees and selling corporation real estate and other assets (Goodbrand 226). Rob and Renwick had been of course following the one path they had felt most capable of following. Barrie had hoped mainly to emerge from the Therafields debacle with a clear conscience, time to write, and some way of supporting his "petite famille."

How bad was his situation? He would describe it on May 13, 1983, in a letter to David Phillips as having begun when he and Rob, as directors, had launched an austerity program to rid the Therafields corporation of various unneeded elements, one of which happened to be Barrie's vice presidential job. He had been forced to fire himself. The change had occurred much more quickly, he wrote, than he had anticipated or wanted, even though in some ways it was welcome. He had thus been forced to support his little family that summer of 1982 by spending savings, doing freelance writing and, he told Phillips, selling much of his treasured and lengthily-assembled collection of historic North American comic books and newspaper comic sections. Steve McCaffery tells Peter Jaeger in 1998 that he recalls "this as a time of great depression for Barrie but was not privy to the details" (Jaeger 88).[1] Goodbrand notes that the Therafields transformation seriously "weakened" Barrie's friendship with Rob, who "had a new coterie of friendships allied with his entrepreneurial ambitions and he and Barrie would [now] meet only on the occasions when Barrie and his wife Eleanor were invited to a party at Rob's house" (253).

That July Barrie had made another trip to British Columbia to read at Simon Fraser and visit various friends including Bowering. There, as usual during travels, he had done considerable writing — a long section of "Inchoate Road" — and thought again about his Winnipeg flood novel, "An Idiomatic Tale." Late in the month he listed in his notebook the three writing projects on which he most wanted to work: a rewrite of "John Cannyside," "An Idiomatic Tale," and a "mystery novel." His ambition to write significant novels was a long-standing one and, in the light of his success with poetry and recent successes as a script writer, plus his sense that he had now only limited time for writing, oddly persistent. His "John Cannyside" or "bpNichol by John Cannyside" project was now more than 13 years old and, with his current plan to "rewrite" it, seemingly no closer to completion. On August 7 he wrote to Bowering about trying to resume writing "An Idiomatic Tale," saying that he was enjoying the writing of it but wondered whether anyone would enjoy the result. He told Bowering he was creating the whole narrative out of a series of images that would constitute a two-week period in the life of a family, a period in which, as one would expect, nothing is resolved. The reader enters and leaves the narrative in the middle, and "hopefully" will experience a resolution through the leaving of it. The images will be all that the reader knows about it. That's why he's calling the novel "idiomatic," he told Bowering, because it's the normal "family" story. The explanation, however, seemed to say as much about Barrie's understanding of family, or about what is usual in a family, as about the novel. On the Labour Day weekend he entered the Arsenal Pulp Press Three-Day Novel competition, writing a text he called "Still."

By September 1982 he had an invitation to write potentially profitable scripts for Henson Associates' popular television series *Fraggle Rock*. Aware of the income-earning transitions he was attempting to make, both poet Dennis Lee and Barrie's s fellow Coach House Press board member David Young, who were already writing for the Henson series, had encouraged Barrie to make contact with its producers. As well, through another acquaintance, actress and playwright Marye Barton, he had the possibility of co-writing a musical comedy for a theatre company in nearby Cobourg, Ontario.

But Barrie spent much of September composing and rehearsing new work for two performances the Four Horsemen were to give at the beginning of October in Nanaimo and Victoria. As usual, he was less than enthusiastic about his Horsemen role, and on September 26, after an unsatisfying rehearsal, wrote in his notebook a long and reflective analysis of the group's limitations. Again he perceived himself as doing little more than supporting the work of the other three. He wrote that when the group had begun he had already reached the end of his interest in solo sound poetry, but had been enthusiastic about blending a variety of voices. However, once in the group, he believed, he had moved much too far from a solo position, and allowed himself to be merely the one who "underlined" the voices of the others. He had become mere glue for the group's words and emotions, when he should have been trying to help create pieces in which four strong creative personalities collided. Instead, all he did was mask or harmonize the differences among the others, so that the group never had to confront its aesthetic and emotional conflicts. His improvisations, he reflected, had worked toward a blending of voices, rather than trying to achieve interesting discordances or dissonances — peace at any cost. He recalled only once allowing himself to use techniques or make sounds that might bring him into visible conflict with another member. That was when he had proposed a solo piece, "Eric [sic] Von Daniken Meets Kurt Schwitters" and all of the others had disliked it, McCaffery so much that he had mocked it. The incident, he thought, had made him retreat in terms of composition, so that now he would make no substantial personal initiatives involving collaboration, but instead write safe four-part texts that he knew the others would accept.

Barrie went on in this note to blame himself for this retreat, although his account also portrayed his fellow Horsemen as rather dysfunctional in their communications. Competitive sarcasm as a kind of sibling rivalry, at times seemingly designed to impress Barrie, and at times to embarrass him, had characterized their public interactions during at least a few post-performance receptions or parties. Each was a great friend to Barrie individually, but not always when gathered together. He wrote that his problem in the group had been that he responded too strongly to ridicule, allowing it to silence him when it should be precipitating vigorous argument. That his weaknesses as a composer and improviser had sprung directly from an inner need to avoid discord — that his preference for harmony had not been aesthetic, it had been personal. The note recalls the seemingly happy-go-lucky Vancouver teenager who once concealed his desperate emotions under resolute cheerfulness.[2] It also perhaps sheds light on his interactions on the Therafields corporation board with the more financially experienced Renwick and Rob. It makes it difficult to believe that he could have strongly disagreed with their plans — or could ever have resisted Lea's decisions, whatever the risk to his perceived integrity or the financial health of the corporation.

After two more trips west, once to read in the Winnipeg area and once for several readings in Vancouver, Barrie returned his attention on December 2, 1982, to his "John Cannyside" or "bpNichol by John Cannyside" project. In this he was possibly influenced by the fact that an actual "bpNichol" book by poet-critic Stephen Scobie was now well underway, and that Scobie had been asking him questions similar to those the fictional Cannyside had more crudely asked of his "bpNichol." In his revision Barrie was considering having Cannyside do a "taped interview with bpNichol" and changing the text to make the dates in the life of the novel's "bpNichol" correspond to those in Barrie's own. Later on the same day he pondered the idea of framing the novel within a story about its having been discovered in the Simon Fraser University archives by "two editors" who argue about its interpretation, one emphasizing chronology, the other pop psychology. Scobie had also been consulting the Nichol papers at the SFU archives.

Barrie's devotion to this repeatedly uncompleted Cannyside project, and to autobiography in general, was now close to obsessive. Quite possibly he experienced pleasure in writing about himself in the third person as "bpNichol" and viewing himself, as his "two editors" were, from a post-death perspective. It was a perspective he had taken in his first notebook when he had speculated about whether it was offering much of value to a future biographer. Perhaps unconsciously he did not want ever to finish "Cannyside." In it "bpNichol" was much more clearly a fiction than it was in Barrie's everyday life in which his friends usually thought of "Barrie," "bp," "beep," and "beeper" as constant and interchangeable beings. But Barrie seems in the "Cannyside" projects to know and enjoy the fact that he has invented "bpNichol" — and to sometimes tease or mock himself for having done so. Of course he had also invented "bpNichol" as part of his struggles to reinvent and save "Barrie Nichol" — but he never appears to joke about that. Most recently he had used the third person to write the cover blurb for bpNichol's *The Martyrology, Book 5*, which would be released in December 1982 by Coach House: "in *The Martyrology, Book 5* bpNichol maps his own life in the present, and the saints and giants who inhabit his imagination's past."

Barrie's parents flew to Toronto and stayed with him, Ellie, and Sarah over Christmas. It was the first time they had visited him. When they left he began drafting his first *Fraggle Rock* proposal, "Invasion of the Rat People" — a title that he had almost certainly chosen before their visit, which had gone unexpectedly well for all parties. He wrote David W. Harris (now calling himself David uu) on January 17 of the new year that this had been the first Christmas he had spent with his parents in 20 years, and that his *Still* had won the Three-Day Novel Contest.

aka{ barrie phillip }Nichol

21. Unable to Rest

When a writer is most strongly engaged with what he is doing, as if struggling for his identity within the materials at hand, he can show us, in the mere turning of a sentence this way or that, how to keep from being smothered by the inherited structuring of things, how to keep within and yet in command of the accumulations of culture that have become a part of what he is.

— Richard Poirier, *The Performing Self*, xiii

Barrie would spend much of 1983 getting accustomed to being primarily a freelance writer. He applied to join the Performing Rights Association of Canada, listing "Phillip Workman," "bpNichol, "B.P. Nichol," and "Barrie Nichol" as pseudonyms. He set aside time, July 11–August 8, for the rehearsals of the play he and Marye Barton were beginning to write — now provisionally titled "Tracks"[1] — for the Cobourg theatre. He discussed with his lawyer the contract for "Tracks," and with both his lawyer and his accountant Renwick the negotiations for the sale of a second accumulation of his manuscripts to Simon Fraser.[2] He finished three new children's books with Black Moss Press, *Once Upon a Lullaby* (published that spring in editions totalling 13,000 copies), *The Man Who Loved His Knees*, and *To the End of the Block*, and prepared to pass two weeks in New York in April watching the production of his first *Fraggle*

Rock script. In February he wrote about some of this work to his father, telling him that he had "lots" going on, and that his finances were healthy, but was unlikely to have enough travel money or time that year to be able to take another trip to the West. It was only with difficulty that he could accommodate a request from Roy Miki to speak in early July on "poetry and the sacred" at a colloquium Miki was organizing at Simon Fraser University. Miki managed to find enough money to expand Barrie's visit into a more lucrative week-long residency.

For the remainder of the year Barrie would mention in almost every letter he wrote how hard he was working, and sometimes how little time he had for writing poetry. In May he told David W. Harris that he had been "overly" immersed in writing, teaching, and trips to readings. He told Bill Griffiths that his editing work for Coach House had been delayed by the demands of his own writing and the need to make a living for his little family. He told David Phillips that what with the *Fraggle Rock* scripts and the Cobourg play for the past seven months his typewriter had been "smoking." In June he asked Roy Miki to tell his graduate student Irene Niechoda, who was hoping to create a source-book to his *Martyrology, Book I* and *Book II* as her M.A. thesis, that it was only writing that was keeping him from writing to her. He told Judy Copithorne that he was finding little time to work on *The Martyrology*, that he was mostly working on scripts, which he was enjoying, in order to earn money to support himself, Ellie, and Sarah. In October he would tell the editor of *Dandelion* that he was not currently writing a lot of poetry. His life was further complicated in June when Sarah was hospitalized with a puzzling illness, creating anxieties that only some tests, months later, would dispel.

It was also complicated when, at the Coach House Press editorial board meetings, the recently appointed Sarah Sheard moved to limit the number of books Barrie or other editors could edit in any given year. Until this time the eight-member board had aimed to publish every year approximately 20 titles, two each chosen individually by the members and four by the board collectively from unsolicited manuscripts. But several of the members had often had difficulty finding manuscripts that they liked. Rather than see the press fall short of its 20-book goal, Barrie would regularly volunteer to find and edit extra titles. Sheard's proposal puzzled Barrie — why would she want to curtail his generosity? Why were David

Young and his old friends Stan Bevington and Michael Ondaatje supporting her? He wrote to Copithorne on June 27 that Coach House was going through some bizarre upheaval that he couldn't figure out.

In July he received an invitation to read at the University of Hawaii, and again replied by pointing out how inflexible his current activities had made his schedule. He had a nine-reading, nine-day promotional tour booked for August for his novel *Still* and at least two weeks in September taken up by the shooting of his second *Fraggle Rock* script — which meant that he'd be working his buns off in the rest of September. Meanwhile, since his return from his Simon Fraser residency he, Ellie, and Sarah had been living in Cobourg for the rehearsals and opening of *Tracks*. Despite this being a working summer, Barrie had found small city life relaxing, and had written to his father that they might someday move to Cobourg, where housing was astonishingly cheap. However, in September, despite all his other commitments, he accepted Gwen Hoover's invitation to join the Canada Council's Committee on Public Readings and attend several Ottawa meetings a year.

Later that fall some of his financial worries would be diminished, although without any increase in the time available for his working on projects such as *The Martyrology* or "An Idiomatic Tale." His fellow Therafields directors succeeded at last in fully retiring the corporation's indebtedness; Barrie would be able to write to his British friend Bill Griffiths on October 23, 1983, that all of his savings had been inaccessible for the past two years because of various legal complexities, but now matters had finally been sorted out. He was at last free of his remaining Therafields connection. He had had two more *Fraggle Rock* script proposals accepted, his fifth and sixth. He also had received an invitation from Ottawa-based MSN-TV to submit script proposals for its animated series, *The Raccoons*. Barrie had replied by sending the requested resumé and script proposal, but suggested as well that because of *Fraggle Rock* he might have a "time problem." Nevertheless, in January 1984 he would send *Fraggle*'s Jerry Juhl two further script ideas.

To facilitate undertaking all these new freelance projects Barrie had bought his first computer, an Apple IIe, the previous March. In his letter of October 23, 1983, to Griffiths he had enclosed a small visual poem that he had created by playing with its Gutenberg word-processing program, and mentioned that he was now also stealing bits of time to learn Apple's

aka{ barrie phillip }Nichol

programming language, Apple BASIC. Barrie's computer play and study of Apple BASIC would enable him to create by the middle of 1984 a suite of twelve "kinetic" visual poems — ones written as computer programs that generated changing formal arrangements of words and letters on a computer screen. In September 1984 he would publish through Underwhich Editions 100 numbered copies of these "digital" poems, under the title *First Screening,* on 5.25 inch floppy diskettes — viewable, however, only on an Apple IIe. But because of lack of time, changing technologies, and anxiety that he was already not working enough on more personally important projects such as *The Martyrology* and the ever-languishing Cannyside narrative, he would never add to this remarkably pioneering attempt at computer-programmed poetry.[3]

In February 1984 he made his long-awaited reading trip to Hawaii and managed to free up time to spend a week there. Here he did extensive revisions to the "In the Plunkett Hotel" section of *The Martyrology, Book 6* and drafted "Hour 26" of its "Book of Hours." On February 26, he mailed the former to Scobie for possible publication in *The Malahat Review,* and gave him a summary of how much he had recently accomplished. He was working hard on *Fraggle Rock* scripts, he told Scobie, had done a really big revision of his first children's book, *Moosequakes,* and had completed the sixth section of *Martyrology, Book 6,* "The Grace of the Moment." He had only two more hours to write for "The Book of Hours," and then he would have a complete version of all of *Martyrology, Book 6.* Entire, finished, he added, to emphasize how pleased he was, and that he'd actually sketched a possible title page for *Martyrology, Book 7.* But he wanted to have all the parts of *Martyrology, Book 6* published — in magazines or booklets — before it appeared as a gathered work and was having, he wrote, good luck with that too.

All this productivity, however, was partly accomplished by avoiding writing letters. A number of Nichol letters were sent out that month, but almost all were written by Ellie, who apologetically told each correspondent that bp was extremely busy. Another silence in Barrie's writing in these months concerned Visvaldis, who had jumped to his death from his apartment balcony in early December. In none of Barrie's future writing would there be a direct reference to him.

"In the Plunkett Hotel" was one more element in the "unifying" hopes that Barrie now had for *The Martyrology*. His various "Plunkett" projects, including his "The Plunkett Papers," dated from the same 1965–70 period as *Scraptures* and *Monotones*, and he also hoped to make them part of his now ever-continuing poem. The Plunkett writing had begun as a factual inquiry into his family origins — dates of emigration, places lived during decades-long journeys from Europe to Saskatchewan, locations of farms, genealogical tables. The text he had now produced was a kind of meta-commentary on the superficiality such research can create. Origin now was a complex and enduring mystery beyond dates and names and their implied Biblical series of begat's:

> moving reservoirs of cells & genes
> stretches out over the surface of the earth
> more miles than any ancestor ever dreamed
> . . .
>
> tribal, restless, constant only in the moving on,
> over the continents
> thru what we call our history
> tho it is more mystery than fact,
> more verb than noun,
> more image, finally, than story.

("Book V," The Martyrology Book 6 Books)

The iconic Plunkett Hotel, several times for origin-wishful Barrie a pilgrimage destination, was no family Grail Castle or Church of the Holy Sepulchre. "in the Plunkett Hotel / no trace remains of what my grandparents did"; "from the Plunkett Hotel / the roots run everywhere: / Minnesota . . . ; / Vermont . . . ; / England . . . ; / Saxony . . . "; "in the Plunkett Hotel / we became what we really are, / transient, temporal, i's in motion / crossing the flickering division lines of history." Wistful since 1944 for a fixed and reliable place beyond his distracted parents and their shifting residences, once believing it might be found in "family," and its records and physical residue, he was finding it here in transience itself, and in the mysteries of motion and mortality of which his body had been increasingly a reminder — deconstructively:

aka{ barrie phillip }Nichol

        singing 'ifamly

                fiamly

                faimly

                    family

                        famliy

                            famlyi'

In the middle of March 1984 he had an unexpected reading in Winnipeg, to replace an ailing Miriam Waddington, and at the end of the month a reading in Edmonton and a meeting with a graduate class. When he returned he told Ellie that he had experienced severe back pain. He went to see a chiropracter, Mary Ann Franco, whose office was next door to the old Therafields Dupont Street centre. She suggested an x-ray, but he declined. She then suggested that he needed to try to rest, and he replied that he was unable to rest lying down or standing up, only sitting up. Most likely he had been quietly in pain before either of these trips. Like many in the Therafields community, Barrie was skeptical about treatments offered by mainstream medicine, and disliked most synthetic medications, including painkillers. He had often treated himself for fatigue and weight gain by going on several week liquid-diet fasts, saying that these purged his body of "toxins."[4] His extra weight — which in *Selected Organs* he was joking about as inherited from the Workman-family hips — had usually returned quickly after the fast.[5] In his commitment to fasting he was quite possibly emulating Lea, who since 1968 had intermittently attempted to control her diabetes through diet and weight loss rather than medication (Goodbrand 82–83).

By August he was writing scripts for *The Raccoons* as well as for *Fraggle Rock*, but he was unhappy that the *Raccoons* contract he had signed was not an ACTRA one — a fact his lawyer had pointed out while scolding him for having signed it. The company, Evergreen Raccoons, was enthusiastic about his scripts, however, and so the matter seems to have been quickly resolved without legal formalities. This month saw Barrie and Ellie buy out the co-ownership in 98 Admiral from Renwick and his partner Louise, who had decided to move to San Francisco; they would rent much of the newly empty space to ex-Therafields friends. Barrie described the event in a letter to the American poet-publisher Karl Young on August 21. Barrie's theme was again how busy and "full" his life was, beginning with how much there was to do when he and Ellie had become sole owners, and how afterward he had moved his studio to a different room and converted his old studio into a living room. Busy, he repeated.

The next day he wrote Young a longer letter, telling him that he had now written a few little pieces of *The Martyrology, Book 7*, and was about to start revising *The Martyrology, Book 6* — doing a close rereading of all of its books and editing them in terms of all he'd learned about the overall book while drafting it. He also mentioned having performed recently with the Horsemen in Quebec City and preparing to leave for a reading in Victoria the next weekend. He seemed to be finding ways to both earn money and be productive. However, three days earlier, August 19, he had written differently to the Canada Council's Gwen Hoover, telling her that he still hadn't got a grip on how to be a freelancer — that he seemed always to be off-balance, that tasks seemed to come up in ways that no one could plan for.

Stan Dragland had been in touch again that spring and summer about his "Canada, A Prophecy" uncollected anthology suggestion, apologizing for his confusing explanation of it, and wondering whether Barrie was still considering it. It's unclear whether Barrie now understood that he was being asked only for an essay on an "alternative" poetry canon, and not for an entire anthology — his reply on August 21 suggested that he may have thought that both tasks were almost equally large, i.e. that the essay would require the same identifying of poets and poems as would the anthology. He told Dragland that the scope is "HUGE!!" and asked whether it would be possible to do it justice. He said that he couldn't be out and about doing "that" amount of research — where would he find so much time? They'd end up getting the project "out" when they were both in their 80s and far past their prime. The letter indicates the time pressures he was under, his conscientious commitment to alternative writing, and the kind of work he might have done if he had indeed lived longer or enjoyed longer the financial flexibility of his Therafields years. He had also talked to others, including myself, of someday editing an open form anthology under the anti-Yeats title "Mere Anarchy."

That month he also returned a fiction manuscript to a friend who had asked him to publish it through Coach House, saying not only was Coach

House behind schedule but that he could no longer put his energy into editing prose — that he had only so much energy, and was spreading it too thin as it was.

In November he created some drawings for a "Bestiary," and did a little more writing for *The Martyrology, Book 7*, possibly beginning work on a new "You Too, Nicky," to "replace" or be about the poem of that title he had set out to write in 1979. He also drew in his notebook the title page of a "Martyrology: Book of Sources" in which both the complete *Scraptures* and *Monotones* would be republished, and added at the bottom of the page that *Monotones* in this printing would be done "properly," with all the blank pages included. Much of this activity was little more than planning and note-making. His substantial writing time that fall seems to have been taken by scripts for Evergreen Raccoons and Henson Associates; one of his Evergreen scripts he was co-writing with playwright Carol Bolt.

In February 1985 he flew to California to participate in the What's Cooking Performance Festival at the University of San Diego. He wrote to Barbara Caruso to apologize for having to miss a meeting with her, and commented that he was not happily anticipating the plane flight, that he still had that "pinched nerve" in his back and that spending hours sitting down was not great for it. Nevertheless, he would not only take part in the festival but travel to it through Oakland to visit Renwick Day and Louise, and their newborn baby girl Morgan. In Oakland he began the *Martyrology, Book(s) 7&* poem beginning "wandered the streets of downtown Berkeley / all morning / the pain in my leg / so intense at certain moments i could not stand / the pain," a poem he dedicated to Charles Bernstein.[6] In Del Mar near San Diego while "climbing the hill from the beach" he continued this poem, noticing that its lines were arriving "like waves beating on the shore of some knowledge," or like "waves of pain," and that his "processual" poetics were having him drag not only his leg up the hill but the entire *Martyrology*. "Imperfection" — the implacable cause of both the entropy that sees planets be born and die, and of his own poetics — was putting all the lines of his life at stake.

> that imperfection
> the whole reason for such decisions
> notion of the processual

or this talk of doing
to be included with the doing
hauling my leg up the hill
even as this line drags every other line with it
the whole of the Martyrology trailing behind
its failures its successes

The text had the startling tone of a requiem for a long poem still in process.

Barrie talked to Ellie about the pain both before and after the trip. When visiting friends he was now standing much of the time rather than sitting down, because of pain. He had a similar difficulty at Coach House Press editorial meetings, sometimes pacing beside the table while discussions proceeded. When he got around to reporting his San Diego travel expenses to Gwen Hoover in April he reported also those for two other readings, one in Montreal, and one six months before in Simcoe, Ontario. He apologized for having taken so long to send her these, explaining that his bad back had now been causing constant cramps in his left leg, that on most days he could hardly walk, and that it was also painful to sit down to write. But he'd had to keep the old income incoming, which meant that letter writing just didn't get done. Things were getting better, however, he assured her. He had taken a plane to the Montreal reading he was reporting, but the pain had been so bad that he had had to return by train, renting a bedroom. He explained to Hoover that Via Rail had had nothing else available in terms of beds — just a bedroom. If the expense was excessive, he hoped she would tell him, adding that the hour and a half he had spent on the plane, unable to lie down or walk around, had been excruciating. He joked that he must be getting old, or that perhaps the title of his magnum opus was becoming his destiny.

Three days later he wrote an even more detailed account of his suffering to Barbara Caruso, while finding new signifieds in his initials. Just a brief message from the "b(um) p(edestrian)" he began, telling her that he was continuing to limp along. His back and hip were a little better but in his left leg once-dead nerves seemed to want to be reborn, and were causing continuing spasms and making it impossible for him to know when he might be able to sleep or walk. As a result, he continued, he and Ellie had needed to make various planned purchases — such as a new bed — much earlier than they'd anticipated, and had run themselves a few thousand dollars short, requiring him to cut back temporarily on the Underwhich titles he was financing. He outlined all the activities he nevertheless was committed to — a two-week trip to Europe, another to Banff, three weeks in Cobourg for rehearsals of another musical comedy he had written, the editing of an issue of *Open Letter* on Caruso's work, a week workshopping an opera, and several script projects — commenting that although his body had slowed down, he hadn't. But he had cut down on venturing out. He was spending as much time as possible lying down. He was trying to save as much energy as he could and then throw it all into his writing.

By the end of April his "rebirth" optimism about his leg nerves seemed to have faded. On April 27 he wrote to the organizer of the What's Cooking Festival that the bad leg and back pain that had been afflicting him in San Diego were still continuing unchecked. He offered a mild complaint about his accommodations: that his painful back and leg had virtually imprisoned him in his hotel room, and that it sure would have been easier for him if he'd been housed closer to the campus — but he guessed that was now obvious. This almost weekly shift from realism about his affliction to optimism about recovery and then back to realism had been characteristic of Barrie throughout the spring of 1985 as he struggled to work at what was for him a normal pace.

BARRIE ANOINTING MICHAEL DEAN WITH "PLASTER DE PARIS" AT L'AFFAIRE "PATAPHYSIQUE, 1985.
(Marilyn Westlake)

He ended this letter with explicit hope — writing that he had "hope" that they would invite him back sometime when his body was working properly.

In May he made a substantial contribution to the satirical Toronto conference L'Affaire 'Pataphysique, a conference partly organized by members of the Owen Sound sound poetry group. Erecting a booth for his "'Pataphysical Hardware Company," he offered for sale a company catalogue, and a variety of paper objects including *Critical Frame of Reference* (eight pages plus an acetate sheet), *Plaster de Paris* (including a plastic bag of talcum powder), *Open Verse* (one page of instructions), *Closed Verse* (one page of instructions), and *Tho(ugh)t* (a silkscreened thought balloon, a "thought holder" headband sewed by Ellie, and a "thought suppressor" — a 1½ -inch pin). His elaborate presentation, relatively trivial in the context of his other creations, and produced amid continuing time-demands and pain, constituted a huge gesture of support for the younger Toronto writers who were enthusiastically expanding and publicizing concepts that had been important to him since his first encounters with Dada. He was once again — despite or perhaps because of his pain — thinking of the "we" that must survive the "i."

Also that May he wrote a conclusion to his latest revision of his John Cannyside novel — a conclusion now being "written" by the character Harry Gardenia. Set in a bar seemingly borrowed from a Spillane novel, the manuscript had four characters — Gardenia, Cannyside, Nichol, and an indeterminate "I." Gardenia has been reading Stephen Scobie's recently released *bpNichol: What History Teaches* and is enraged that Scobie has not only dared to write it but has published before he or Cannyside. Then "I" abruptly intervenes, seizing the narration, killing bpNichol by striking him with a pipe, so he can end "his" novel and get it published. Who "I" may be remains inconclusive; "je est un autre" had been for Barrie since the late 1960s a watchword quotation. Beyond the metafictional narrative highjinks, and the playful jibe at Scobie, there is serious parody being attempted here of literary power struggles — critics battling for control of an author's meanings, authors vying for control of what their lives and works "say," and quite possibly Barrie battling for control of who readers may think bpNichol is. At conferences Barrie would often snicker when a critic used that deadly phrase "what the author is trying to say," with its probably unconscious implication that authors are usually less articulate than their academic readers. Parody, however, was not the easiest mode for Barrie to write, no more in the Cannyside novel than it had been in *The Captain Poetry Poems.*

Because of the continuing pain in his back, hip, and leg and conflicting commitments, he cancelled his August plans to participate in the New Poetics Colloquium in Vancouver where several of the L=A=N=G=U=A=G=E poets would be speaking and reading. In the second week of that month he performed in the Banff Festival's three-day production of R. Murray Schafer's opera *Princess of the Stars*, on one day to an audience of over 3300; on August 13 his musical *The Gargoyle* opened in Cobourg.[7] On his return he consulted again with his family doctor, who obtained for him a November appointment with a well-known Toronto surgeon who specialized in such ailments. He resumed teaching at York and working on various television scripts. In late September, in preparation for the appointment, he had x-rays and other tests. He described these in an October 9 letter to Renwick Day. He told Day that he was still limping. That although his back seemed better, he now had a swelling in his foot. The swelling had begun in May, and while it had now gone down quite a bit, it was still visible. He'd had the usual array of blood tests and x-rays and so forth, and was now told that there were no tumours, kidney problems, or visibly pinched veins or arteries but that the pain might have something to do with his sciatic nerve. He was now waiting to see a specialist who could figure all this out. So, he wrote, life hadn't been as generous as it could be. He wrote that when you're unable to walk normally you're likely to become depressed. But, he laughed, life marches on, and he kept limping on behind it.

On December 6, 1985, he was admitted to Toronto's Mount Sinai Hospital for a CT scan and possible surgery. He wrote to Gwen Hoover on December 8 that he was out on a weekend pass from the hospital waiting for his CT/T scan to be read and his surgery to be scheduled. He had the operation on December 11. The surgeon recorded in his hospital report that he had expected to find an L5-S1 lesion but was unable to. He told Barrie that he should feel better. On January 1 Barrie wrote to his brother Bob, who had asked for his help in arranging to receive copies of *The Toronto Star* to sell in his small Victoria store, that his back was continuing to improve, and that even his foot was getting better. He was heading off to Halifax to spend three days working on a new kids' TV series that he'd agreed to do. After a February follow-up appointment, the surgeon wrote a "Final Diagnosis" in which he remarked that the patient was "surprisingly relieved of leg pain." Ellie, however, wondered whether the relief could be due to Barrie's getting increased rest and taking heavy doses of painkillers since the surgery.

Barrie's biggest achievement that year had been writing the sixth book of *The Martyrology Book 6*, "The Grace of the Moment" — especially given what little grace the moments of this year had seemed to have. It was a theme that instantly engaged the punning, swerving bpNichol:

> the real ride is the present tide
> pulls you   out
> mark the me's
> mar or are the sub
> stance or text of
> a life
>
> so that even <u>this</u> vocabulary
> changes with the pull of the present
> words entering the ear or eye
> their current's currency
> carries them
> into the unmarked reaches of your future
> poem
> [. . .]
> no st algia here
> just the bare longing of the moment lingers

The poem was suffused with fears of death — "death brackets endlessly." His cousin Donna had died of her breast cancer, reminding him yet again of his dead sister whom he once thought might be writing his poems.

> Donna
> dead of cancer   October 21ˢᵗ, 1983
> cousin born the same year as me
> carried my dead sister's name

aka{ barrie phillip }Nichol

death brackets endlessly
being ing be finally that aside
that drop in voice
notated in
death's presence
the dread flicks past
all light & motion
[. . .]

we carry the red ribbons mark us for death
the blood of being flooding out or
leeched
    brief bright ribbon we wrap the present in
    this human grace

The lines offer the paradox of their own joy —

this singing is a small instance of a being
holy alive
& holey
    wholly here

juxtaposed with a prescience even Barrie could not have known —

this pain words wear
carry within them like a spine
involves the very line its
twists & turns

                ("Book VI," *The Martyrology Book 6 Books*)

Brilliant and fearless, the singing of the poem, and the irrepressible bpNichol "joy" in its language play — holy, holey, wholly indeed — create a disturbing contrast with the implacable information that the words, rapt in their "bright ribbon," are bringing "like a spine" to the mortal Barrie Nichol.

22. The Waste of My Words

His imagination was so vast, his skill level so accomplished, that he would help you to completely reimagine what you had written in multiple ways, so that it suddenly dawned on you that you had infinite choices, abundant options, as opposed to the one way you thought the poem inevitably had to be written.

— Ken Norris, interviewed by Kevin Spenst,

Prism International

In the spring of 1986 Barrie and Ellie, unhappy about difficulties in keeping boarders, decided to take advantage of the changing Toronto real estate market by selling 98 Admiral in what was becoming a fashionable downtown district, and purchasing a smaller house at 114 Lauder Avenue approximately a mile northeast. The house was coincidentally less than a block north of one that Rob and therapist Gus O'Brien had purchased two years before to house the now nearly blind Lea Hindley-Smith. Unable to move without help, Lea would die following heart surgery 15 months after Barrie and Ellie's mid-June move. What with her weakness, and Barrie's back and leg pains, they would have rarely seen each other. In April Barrie had written to poet Clint Burnham that he'd had a bad year, his back fucking up, having to have an operation just before Christmas, and a pile of mail accumulating on his table. He was unable to pack or lift boxes or otherwise help the move into the new house, and was consulting again with his family doctor. The small house was the first residence that Barrie had not shared with Therafields friends since 1964.

In his next letter to Phyllis Webb, August 8, 1986, he wrote that he was finding his new living situation "okay." It was just his little family and he was enjoying that. Family living was more intense, he thought, than living with others, but good. Anyway, he told Webb, he figured he'd more than done his communal bit. As well, he wrote, starting a family is like starting one's own commune. His remarks would have been greeted as provocations had they been published years before in a Therafields newsletter. But in fact they pointed to the overall journey his life had been taking, from his confusions of 1964, through therapy, house groups, joint ownership of houses with Rob, Janet Griffith, Sheron Fadel, Grant Goodbrand, Ellie and Renwick, owning 99 Admiral and renting space to others, to the present.

The actual move, however, with its familiar recapitulation of all the other moves he had experienced, still dismayed him. He had written to Robert Kroetsch on June 18, while thanking him for having agreed to recommend him for a Canada Council grant, that he loathed moving, and hoped that they would be in this new house for many many more years. He hated being surrounded by a chaos of books stacked on top of books stacked on top of books. He believed in Gertrude Stein's advice, he told Kroetsch, that "to be extraordinary in your writing you must be ordinary in your living," and this chaos sure wasn't ordinary.

Amidst the physical pain, household adjustments, and script writing for Nelvana's *Care Bear* series, he was still working on *The Martyrology*, overseeing the publishing of *Book 6*, and working at least on the conception of *Books 7* and *8*. In a letter to Robert Bertholf, co-organizer of the 1980 Buffalo Canadian Poetry Festival, Barrie had written that he was busy with writing *Books 7* and *8*, and explained that *Book 7* was to be a "shuffle text," and *Book 8* would use both an ode and the concept of "paragogy" as its organizing principles. Eight, he wrote, would appear at random among *Book 7*. By "shuffle text" Barrie meant that the book would be unbound and unpaginated, most likely boxed, so that its parts would have no fixed relationship to one another, somewhat like those of his first Canadian book, *bp.*

He wrote several letters that spring to writers hopeful of publishing books with him through Coach House — Diana Hartog, Douglas Barbour, and Clint Burnham — advising them, as in the Hartog letter, that because of recent editorial board changes there was at best a slim possibility of his getting someone's poetry book accepted there (March 10, 1986). He was also getting into royalty disputes over both *Fraggle Rock* scripts and one *Raccoons* script — the one he had co-written with Carol Bolt. In March he wrote to *Fraggle* actor Karen Barnes about an episode in which he and Phil Balsam had written the music and lyrics and that had been mistakenly labelled in its videotape release as having "music and lyrics by Phil Balsam and Dennis Lee." This was the second instance of such careless labelling by Henson Associates. He told her that he felt simultaneously impotent, frustrated, enraged, and despairing about being able to stop this from reoccurring. He thought it could affect both his royalties and his reputation. In April he and Bolt wrote to three of the Evergreen Raccoons principals demanding that producer Kevin Gillis withdraw the co-writer credit he had given himself for a script, "The Intruder," which they had written. They argued that it was a normal part of the script writing process for producers to ask for things to be included, or parts of a script to be rewritten if they didn't seem to work, and that it was utterly wrong for them then to think that just having done their job had made them into co-writers. They were considering complaining to ACTRA. The fact that both of them continued to write for the series, and that there was no further written correspondence, suggests that the dispute was resolved amicably.

Beyond these complexities, Barrie was also still enduring the pain occasioned by travelling. In June he went with the other Horsemen to perform at the Future Indicative conference at the University of Ottawa. Afterward Barrie had misgivings about both the performance and the travel, and wrote to organizer John Moss that he didn't think they'd been especially good, but that they were grateful to have had the opportunity to perform. He commented that it might have been their last performance, and that Moss might want to record the moment for posterity, adding that he had said much the same to the other Horsemen (June 18, 1986). The same day that he wrote to Moss he also wrote a note to Judy Copithorne to accompany 25 copies of her book, *A Light Character*, which he had recently edited for Coach House. He told her that his back was better, but his foot was still getting increasingly puffy throughout the day, and that he was still limping and not writing much new poetry. But he was hoping all this would improve with time — that he'd decided no longer to pursue the muse, and simply let poetry come to him when it did. He was still doing other things, "of course." The other things — scripts, children's books — he was very much pursuing. In a June 13 letter to Dick Higgins, he asked the American poet to blurb *Martyrology Book 6*. Very shortly after this letter, however, he changed the book's name to *Martyrology Book 6 Books*, using this title in his July 31, 1986, afterword — presumably in recognition of the "set of books," which, five years earlier, he had told Scobie it was going to contain. The book had come all the way from being titled *A COUNTING* to being called a book of six books, but in small letters the words "a counting" would still appear mysteriously on its fly leaf.[1]

An invitation to the Horsemen to read that September in Amsterdam, however, changed his mind about both travel and performing. Obtaining funding from the cultural branch of the Canadian Department of External Affairs, Barrie and Rafael flew to Paris in early September, to be joined later in Amsterdam by Steve McCaffery and Paul Dutton. Barrie spent a week at a hotel on rue de Caumartin working on new text for *The Martyrology 7*. In Amsterdam they performed at de Meervaart Theatre to a very small but entirely Dutch audience as part of a festival of Canadian culture. Barrie reported back to External Affairs that the publicity for the festival had been ubiquitous — that the official maple leaf had glowed from lampposts, construction barriers, the covers of weekly entertainment magazines, et cetera (October 28, 1986). But the visit had contained incidents. In Amsterdam Barrie's wheelchair — he had rented one in each city to get around — broke down, making it difficult for him to get to the theatre. And one night a man drowned in the canal outside their hotel while they slept. Barrie wrote a passage about it in his notebook (now one called the "Four Years Later Notebook") for *Martyrology 7* — about being troubled that night by things that couldn't be reached, by someone calling out to them, and by a terrible silence — but does not appear to have included it in the *Martyrology* manuscripts he would leave for publication. On adjacent notebook pages he also made notes for a computer game, "Trial of Champions," and for another TRG board game.

The *Fraggle Rock* series had ended earlier that year. Barrie felt wistful about the excitement and camaraderie he had experienced in helping to create it, and also missed the income his writing for it had generated. He still had Nelvana *Care Bears* and other assignments, and in October managed to get a small Ontario Arts Council grant on the recommendation of David Lee's Nightwood Editions. He reported to the council that it would allow him some time free from "commercial work" and that he would work on "The Martyrology Bo(o)ks 9 (vi(8)i)," his "Organ Music" series, a new work called "Unsigned," and the John Cannyside manuscript — which he'd be delighted to finish off he wrote (November 24, 1986).

In the October pages of his notebook he penned a note about writing a book on his sound poetry of the past two years, a book with the title "S Ays." In it he told himself to try to think of those poems not as sound poems per se but as essays that had incorporated what he had learned about sound. On the same page he wrote a note about undertaking "The Bard Project": which he saw as a project that would formalize how to talk about technical matters in writing. He wanted a work that moved forward through the history of literary form — possibly by successively employing historical forms — with the goal of creating a poetry Frankenstein, a bardic Frankenstein that would re-enact in literary terms the doctor's original corruption by the illusion of possible immortality. Barrie would build a (presumably satiric) bard rather than a monster — thus a "bard project." The note was somewhat ambiguous about whether this was to be primarily a poem written in a Frankenstein-inspired combination of historical forms — the poet as Dr. Frankenstein — or whether it was to be an essay written in various verse forms — a kind of "Essay on Criticism" for all time. It was to be part of *The Martyrology*, Barrie wrote, but he wasn't sure exactly what part — possibly it would be *Book 10*. What was not ambiguous was that these were large ideas and that he expected to have the time to explore them.[2]

That month he had been booked to take part in a joint reading at Harbourfront with George Bowering, Sharon Thesen, and Michael Ondaatje — a booking that, unbeknownst to him, was part of a much larger event. When he arrived he was impressed to find the Brigantine Room packed with an overflow audience of more than 500, and somewhat puzzled to see many of his out-of-town or even out-of-country friends — Stephen Scobie, Robert Kroetsch, Fred Wah, Douglas Barbour,

Bob Cobbing — present. Paul Dutton greeted him, commenting on the large turnout. Barrie beamed and replied, "Yeah, George is always a great draw." The evening got underway with Barrie as first reader, but when he started to speak his microphone cut out — by prearrangement having been turned off at the sound board. Dutton and Steven Smith rushed from the audience on the pretext of helping to fix the "malfunction." Barrie, however, unaware that the microphone wasn't working, assumed that Paul and Steve must want to join him in doing a trio, to which he had no objection. Dutton took over the mike, its volume now restored, and presented him with a 270 pp. bpNichol Festschrift issue of *Open Letter* — an issue that he and Smith had covertly edited over the past year, even sneaking some of Barrie's own photos out of his house for quick duplication. Shocked to incredulity, Barrie could only stare at the volume in his hands and repeat in amazement, "Holy shit! . . . HOLY SHIT!! . . . HOLY SHIT!" Thereafter the evening unfolded with a panoply of readers whose work he had long admired and who were among the many contributors to the Festschrift, including those he'd been surprised to find in the audience when he had arrived. What also astonished him was that a hundred or more of his friends in the audience had come not because of the regular Harbourfront advertising but because they had been told of the clandestine arrangement — and had been able to keep that arrangement a secret. His brother Don was among them, and was also astonished. He had expected a gathering of a few dozen, and had at this time no inkling that Barrie's writing had such large and often affectionate national and international audiences. For the editors and contributors this was a well-earned mid-life tribute and celebration; none of them saw his "bum leg" or "pinched" sciatic nerve as ominous.

In general, this fall was a productive one for him, although not necessarily for the writing he most wanted to do. He gave readings in Detroit, Quebec City, Castlegar, Nelson, and Victoria. In Detroit he shared the bill with Gary Snyder; in Quebec City he read both solo and in duo with Steve McCaffery as TRG, doing two sound poems in French. He completed the children's manuscript "Shopping with My Aunt," and planned a children's collection to be titled "Tiny Commotions." He did more rewriting of his ever-present "John Cannyside" novel, working especially on how to conclude it, and deciding to add a section that would debate the morality of detective fiction. Perhaps not surprisingly, given his medical condition, he drafted "The Hips" for his "Organ Music" series. "You can never forget about your hips," he wrote, in a prose poem in which he created a genealogy or biological lineage of hips that moved from his own hip pain back into family memory.

> And now most days I feel this pain in my left hip, if I sit in a chair that isn't made just right, I feel this pain in my left hip, and I think about Maw, I think about Grandmaw, I wonder if all their lives too there was there this little nagging pain saying I won't let you forget about me. And you don't let me forget about you do you? You're there reminding me, every time I stand too long, reminding me, every time the chair's too soft or too hard or too wrong. You're never going to let me forget about you. Are you hip? (41)

Barrie's hip of course was not at all "hip," and no "nagging little pain."

In November and December he sketched in his notebook approximately 30 pages of visual poems — something he had not done in his notebooks for many years. And as he often had done near a year's end, he wrote a brief personal retrospective for one of his correspondents. It was in a letter to the British poet Lee Harwood, whose edition of Tristan Tzara's selected poems, *Chanson Dada*, he was supposed to be guiding and partly financing to joint Coach House/Underwhich publication. The past year had been a trial for him, had been "wierd," he began, listing how it had included the leukemia death of a niece, his back "op," selling their Admiral Road house, moving to a smaller one, having once-trusted long-term sites of income disappear and thus having to find new ones, and having to be out of town too much doing readings. He then addressed the various delays at Coach House. These were one of the reasons he had been getting increasingly discouraged, he said; he was finding it hard to keep his enthusiasm up when a book took as long to push through to print as the one he was editing for Harwood. In such situations, he wrote, misunderstandings were almost inevitable. "Wierd" — a word (along with "concious") that Barrie had chronic difficulty in spelling — is not quite accounted for by the events he lists. Cheerful Barrie was still not one who could easily bring himself to complain. In both "The Hips" and the

Harwood letter he was grossly minimizing the pain that had required him to obtain bedrooms on intercity trains and wheelchairs at readings — much as he was reducing a key word when he wrote about his back "op." He was minimizing also his discouragement with Coach House — his editorial contributions having been capped at two titles, poetry titles been given low priority, the culture of the editorial board having become increasingly commercial and unfriendly to literary innovation.

He also did not mention an even greater commercial woe he was encountering. For several years he and other *Fraggle Rock* writers had been dismayed by the unexpectedly small amount of the residuals payments they had been receiving despite the overall success of the series. They had vainly requested a complete and transparent accounting. In November Barrie had co-signed a letter with David Young and three others script writers to Henson Executive Vice President Diana Berkenfield, and copied it to other *Fraggle* writers, expressing their "collective dismay with the way we are being treated by the Henson organization" and asking her to organize a meeting to resolve matters.

> Since the show went out of production we have had to make repeated calls . . . about the status of these payments. When the cheques arrive they are months late and, to be blunt about it, rather less than we expected. Despite repeated requests over a period of years we have never received ANY clarifying information as to what gross receipts have been or how our residual payments have been arrived at. When we ask pointed questions the answers are vague, incomplete, and cloaked in mystery. At the best of times we feel bewildered — in our worst moments we feel positively patronized. (November 26, 1986)

The meeting would occur the next year on June 22, but accomplish little. Barrie learned there that many of the shows listed Jerry Juhl as "Head Writer," thus making Juhl "the credited writer" to whom all residuals would go. He then screened each episode and discovered that almost all of the ones that he had been contracted to write or co-write had been credited onscreen to a "Creative Producer" (all shows) or "Head Writer" (four shows) — in each case either Jerry Juhl, Jocelyn Stevenson, or (in two instances) Duncan Kenworthy, with possibly all of the residuals in the "Head Writer" instances having gone to Juhl or Stevenson. In Barrie's contracts, however, there was no mention that the show he was writing would have a "Head Writer" above him. And none of his many letters from Juhl were signed as "Head Writer"; the only title Juhl had used in any of these was "Creative Producer." Barrie also had three "FRAGGLEROCK Contract Sheets" from different dates that listed Juhl only as "Creative Producer" and Stevenson as "Senior Script Editor/Writer" or "Senior Script Consultant/Writer."

Complicating matters for Barrie was the fact that during the production of the series he and Juhl had become close friends. Barrie was careful in all his correspondence not to blame Juhl for what appears to have been a substantial diversion of funds, ascribing it instead to Henson Associates' inattention to contracts, carelessness about screen credits, and weak accounting practices. He would write to Juhl in September 1987, beginning his letter by saying that he was very sure that he already knew that Barrie and other writers had been challenging the Henson corporation's calculations of royalties. He wanted to assure Juhl, he wrote, that he didn't begrudge him a penny of the money Henson had paid him — Juhl was probably worth twice as much. But he detested the accounting fictions he believed Henson had devised in order to rationalize its royalty distributions, and how the Henson accountants had seemed like sharks gorging on prey whenever the writers had questioned them about money. So Barrie and the other writers had formally filed a grievance, and were looking forward to having everything reviewed by someone who was objective. He signed the letter with "love" from his whole family (September 8, 1987). There is no return letter from Juhl in Barrie's files; he quite possibly returned the message by telephone.[3] The ACTRA grievance would eventually be resolved in the writers' favour. That same month Lea Hindley-Smith died. Barrie made no mention of her death in his notebooks or letters, but of course most of his letters now were to non-Therafields correspondents.

Barrie began 1987 with three large new projects in view. He had eight episodes of CBC Television's children's series *Under the Umbrella Tree* to write for production that summer. He had a two-week residency being arranged for late April at the University of Turin, during which he would teach workshops on poetry, plus a possible one-week residency afterward in Rome. And through an actor friend he had made at *Fraggle Rock*, Terry Angus, he was involved in writing a double pilot for a new children's TV animation series, *Blizzard Island*, and likely to be its head writer if it were sold to a network and put into production. By February, he had completed his work on those two scripts and was travelling to Halifax for a read-through by the actors. He had also been writing outlines and notes for the Ron Mann film, *Comic Book Confidential*, at this point known to him as only "the Comix movie." His numerous February 1–9 notebook pages show him approaching the task with the same care and detail he gave to his own projects. He out-

BARRIE SPEAKING IN TURIN, 1987.

(Flavio Multineddu)

lines the various reels and 'chapters' of the film, assigns topics and relevant writers and works to each, and adds notes that outline his personal understanding of the history of the comic book genre. He drafts the "chapter headings" that will later appear in the movie. He and Mann had been friends since The Four Horseman had performed in his 1982 movie *Poetry in Motion*. During Mann's 1985–86 period in Los Angeles, Mann had consulted with him about entire screen plays.

February also saw Barrie again troubled by Coach House Press events and again apologizing to writers who hoped to publish there. He told Endre Farkas that December at Coach House had been "stormy" and January more laid-back, but February was finding them hopelessly in conflict. As a result, he wrote, the press can make no commitments whatsoever about new books (February 8, 1987). He would tell Daphne Marlatt and Betsy Warland that things over the past eight months or so at the press had gone in every possible direction — and then a few more (April 11,

1987). The ongoing reorganizations would soon have him off the editorial board entirely and briefly on the new board of directors.

In early April he mailed to Marty Gervais at Black Moss Press his autobiographical prose poem "Organ Music" manuscript under the title "Selected Organs: Parts of an Autobiography" — minus an "unselected" part "The Lily," a poem that is about the penis and that contains a long third section about Barrie's father. He had, however, already published this poem in the Vancouver periodical *Writing* (issue 5, Spring 1982), which he assumed his father was unlikely to encounter.[4] In the covering letter to Gervais, Barrie mentioned having begun a new poem — part of a new book of *The Martyrology*. It began in rhyming couplets, he told Gervais, and kept moving through a variety of other rhyme forms. This was very likely part of the "Frankensteinian" bard project that he had sketched the previous October in his notebook.

On April 22 his literary editorial role at Coach House Press ended. The now right-dominated board voted to replace itself with genre-specific editors and transfer ownership of the press from Bevington to a non-profit corporation with a board of directors separate from the editors. Barrie, concerned about the philosophical/aesthetic directions the new corporation might take, volunteered to be a director rather than an editor. As a director he could at least initiate one of the four "workhorse" commercial titles that his colleagues now wanted the press to publish each year.

Ellie and Sarah accompanied him to Italy. They landed in Venice on April 25, 1987, and spent one day there, with Barrie writing a text he titled section "vii" of *Martyrology, Book 7*. The next day they went by train to Turin. There on April 30 and May 1 Barrie drew 23 visual poems in his large format notebook, leaving the backs of the pages blank as if he were intending the drawings to be removed and framed. The first six he had titled "Six Turin Texts." On May 6 he wrote a new passage for "Ad Sanctos," which he subtitled "Martyrology Book 11." Later that day he sketched a two-page plan for *The Martyrology*'s Books 7, 10, 11, 12, 13 and 14. *Book 7* was to be "Gifts" (which he planned to be unbound), *Book 10* was to be "St Anzas: bases & basis" (to be interleafed among *Book 7*), *Book 11* "Ad Sanctos" (to be bound sideways), *Book 12* "IM: mortality play" (his new title for the bard project), *Book 13* "J" (a novel with James, the younger brother of Jesus, as the main character), and *Book 14* "A Book of

Days" (modelled on his "The Book of Hours" — with each section composed in a different 24-hour period). He'd arrived at this numbering plan through his experiments with base-8 mathematics — 8 being his favourite number because of the symmetrical visual shape that it shared with the letter *H*. In conventional base-10 terms, *Books 10, 11, 12, 13,* and *14* would have been *Books 8, 9, 10, 11,* and *12*. The next day he drafted a text that he titled "from the Martyr Bk 7 (+10)" — which would later be included in *Book(s) 7&* as the untitled prose poem beginning "the waste of my words & works. . . ." Two days later in Milan, May 9 and 10, he drafted 10 pages toward "Ad Sanctos." Again, travel, and time away from commercial commitments, had given him hours of substantial productivity.

"[T]he waste of my words & works" had been triggered by the sight of Turin's great Renaissance buildings "turning to dust around us" — as if foreshadowing his own decay or the fading into oblivion of his writing that might, like these buildings, become "inappropriate for another space or head." In this poem the characteristic bpNichol/Barrie Nichol ambiguity of the *The Martyrology*'s speaking voice was created by both the ambiguous second-person pronouns — did they address Barrie or the reader or both (Barrie being a reader)? — and by how the verbs "fades, fade" were made to jointly serve the text's words and a human subject's life.

> our bodies, our sounds, words, this page, even as you read,
> even as your vision, your life — uneven, even — fades, fade.

The final four words both enacted the disappearance of letters, the *un* and the *s*, and mimicked the continuing disappearance of Barrie's bodily agility. As so often in the later books of *The Martyrology*, Barrie achieved an unsettling portrayal of personal loss foregrounded against a millennia-spanning vision of inevitable entropy, foreseeing simultaneously Barrie Nichol's death and the much slower fading to black of "bpNichol" and other ostensibly pathetic relics of human culture. Knarn was still yet to vanish.

Back in Toronto, except for drawing 15 new visual poems he appears to have spent most of the rest of May back at work on television scripts. The *Blizzard Island* concept had been sold to the CBC and twelve shows needed to be outlined, written and produced. In June 1987 he attended the *Fraggle* writers meeting in New York, wrote notes for a *Blizzard Island* episode, and in his notebook drafted a criticism — addressed to Steve McCaffery as part of a dialogue for inclusion in Roy Miki's collection *Tracing the Paths: Reading . . . Writing The Martyrology* — of what he perceived as the latent imperialism of the American "Language Poetry" school that had emerged out of the 1978 founding by Bruce Andrews and Charles Bernstein of the magazine *L=A=N=G=U=A=G=E*. He wrote that the fact that many of those writers considered to be "Language" writers were skillful both at writing essays and at getting them — along with their writing theories — into print had permitted their poetry to enter U.S. literary history as the work of a U.S. "movement," even though many — including both McCaffery and one of the earliest L=A=N=G=U=A=G=E writers, Charles Bernstein, had often appeared to consider them neither specifically American nor sufficiently similar to one another to be considered a movement. In part Barrie blamed Ron Silliman for these misconceptions, particularly his 1986 anthology of Language writers *In the American Tree*, as well as Bernstein and Andrews's 1984 anthology of essays that had appeared in *L=A=N=G=U=A=G=E*, *The L=A=N=G=U=A=G=E Book*. In both of these, he argued, the editors seemed to have deliberately ignored their writers' non-American indebtednesses. They appeared to have been claiming Language writing — an area of the mind much larger than a nation — as an American writing, like a conqueror planting his nation's flag on a new territory. Seems rather imperialist to this guy, Barrie wrote. He went on to accuse the three editors of hypocrisy. How could they advocate a poetry that questioned the power relationships between writer and reader, he asked, when they themselves were claiming the power of national authenticity, and failing to challenge the blinkered tradition and selective historical thinking on which earlier exceptionalist theories of American writing had been constructed?

From the beginning of his work as writer and editor Barrie had been internationalist in his understandings of aesthetics, traditions, influence, and modernity. For him Silliman's *American Tree* had been mostly a political manoeuver designed to consolidate Language poetry's national reputation. The group itself — if it was a group — had roots in poststructuralism, in European psychoanalytical theory, in Dadaism, in Stein's Cubism-derived emphasis on the materiality of an artist's materials — much like his own writing — which Silliman's "imperialist" tree had inevitably elided.

aka{ barrie / phillip }Nichol

However, he had misremembered the Andrews-Bernstein essay collec-tion that, although preponderantly populated by American writers, had included ones such as McCaffery, Christopher Dewdney, Brian Fawcett, David Bromige, Alan Davies, and the British Eric Mottram and Cris Cheek.[5] Perhaps because of this oversight, or his own second thoughts about the questions his comments raise, his views on "Language" did not find a place in the published dialogue.[6]

In late June and early July he taught at a one-week workshop in Red Deer, Alberta, and gave a reading at Simon Fraser, with Ellie and Sarah accompanying him for family visits in Saskatoon and Winnipeg. On their return Ellie began teaching a course for George Brown College's aca-demic upgrading program. Barrie went back to his family doctor to again seek help for his painful hip and repeatedly swelling foot, and was referred to a second specialist. He drafted another section of "Organ Music," "The Nose." He did more work in his notebook toward Ron Mann's "Comix" film, sketching various "intercuts," listing various themes that could be ironically invoked, suggesting the title "Comic Book Crazy," and sketching on July 28 a "new opening sequence." Mann recalls that he was also recommending visual artists who could work on the film, selecting much of the music for it, and would provide from his personal collection the majority of the film's examples of comic books. He was doing all of this out of friendship and belief in the importance of the project.[7] And he continued both his commercial and small press work. He described these to Steven Smith, writing that in the past weeks he had been working fran-tically, trying to finish doing outlines for 12 episodes of the *Blizzard Island* series. He was writing four and the rest he would be editing as the series' head writer — plus he had a script to finish for the *Under the Umbrella Tree* series and some skits and continuity for a new CFTO children's show. "Whew!" he added. As well he had the usual editing work with Coach House Press books that he still had to get into print, two sound poetry cassettes to get produced for Underwhich authors, and two Underwhich books to get produced before the end of the month. But so what, he asked Smith — implying that this was the normal life he had come to expect — just the regular crazy routine (September 8, 1987).

He had also recently received a $5,000 grant from the Canada Council to collaborate with composer David Mott on a music-theatre work to be titled "MEME" and to be performed outdoors in three parts.[8] There was a possibility too that Barrie's *Space Opera* collaboration with Howard Gerhard might receive a professional performance. As well, he was considering doing more individual work in sound poetry. In his letter to Smith he had remarked on the perpetually awkward issue of whether the Four Horsemen were still officially a group, and regretted that he'd linked his own activities as a sound poet so much to whether the "horsies" would continue. He indicated that he would prefer to extricate himself to the extent that he could do his own reassessment of sound poetry as a medium, and of the strength or weakness of the work he'd done so far. He told Smith that there were a number of works that he'd created in recent years for the group that it had never agreed to perform, and that rather than abandon them he'd like to perform and record each voice of these himself, and mix them into multi-track recordings.

He then commented on the possible negative effects on his reputation that the current critical interest in *The Martyrology* might be having, and how perhaps returning to solo sound poetry could be a way to remind his audience of his multi-dimensionality. Dutton and Smith's bpNichol Festschrift had contained at least six articles on *The Martyrology*, and Roy Miki's collection *Tracing the Paths* was in press for 1988 with many more. Barrie told Smith that now that the attention being given to *The Martyrology* had become "obsessive," and along with it arguments that he was a "major" writer (whatever that might mean, he added), he probably should go back to emphasizing all the other kinds of writing he'd been doing at the same time as the *Martyr*. He would rather be multidimensional than major, he implied — if those were the only choices. In conversation he was telling other writers that he wanted to focus more on writing "ugly," less aesthetically or thematically appealing poetry, such as his recent 'pataphysical writing, or the numeric lines of "St Anzas V" — he felt he needed to take more risks. As in the 1960s when he'd deplored "coterie" magazines that he believed published only fashionable poetry, he was suspicious of popularity, and preferred to be publishing an unfamiliar, difficult writing rather than one that readers found pleasurable or comfortable. He also told poet Gerry Shikatani that he hoped some day soon to be able to edit and publish 15 or more single-author collections of Canadian visual poetry, to create a "library" of work in this still academically neglected and non–popular genre. Shikatani recalls,"the point was that it would take up all this shelf-space, that it would have this big physical presence that would sit there — and not just be ignored as if this kind of art didn't exist" (letter, January 4, 2012). Barrie was evidently still envisioning those Sigmund Samuel Library shelves.

There was considerable irony in Barrie's literary situation. His writing was receiving the most attention it had ever received from readers, critics, and academics, but he now had the least time, and the least energy, that he'd ever had to work on it or change or enlarge its directions. In his note-books he was often writing more plans for new work than he was writing actual new work. Ellie's going back to teaching was one possible solution, one that could reduce his need to do commercial television work. He was also considering giving up the usual two writing courses he'd been teaching at York University. He had applied to the Canada Council for a Senior Arts fellowship, similar to the one he had held in 1978–79.

In October he and Shikatani began planning a Coach House Press "workhorse" title. Barrie tried to parody recent Coach House rhetoric when he described it in his notebook as "Percheron Book" from Coach House Press; its title was to be "Toronto Walks," and it would feature accounts of favourite walks by Gwendolyn MacEwen, David Donnell, Christopher Dewdney, Gerry Shikatani, and four to six others. One of the walks would be a 'pataphysical walk recounted by some of the "Wild Culture" writers who had planned and hosted the L'affaire 'Pataphysique conference.

There was some irony here also in Barrie, with his bad hip and leg, working on a "walking" anthology. Possibly the concept was nostalgic — Barrie after all had once been a successful middle-distance runner. He had again become optimistic about recovering some mobility and — with mainstream medicine doing little for him — had turned to the bioener-getics and homeopathic remedies offered by his brother Don. He wrote to Phyllis Webb on November 18 that his hip was surprising him by seeming to be getting better, that he'd been doing some "work" — the Therafields term for both physical and psychological therapy — with his brother Don in which he and some others attempted to heal his "energy body" and that in the last few days he had begun feeling a lot better. So he hoped that although he might always have to limp, he might not have to always endure a painful hip. On the same day he had written to British poet P.C.

Fencott, telling him that whereas a year ago, when his back was at its worst, he had for many weeks been fortunate to get even one hour's sleep in a night, he had been now been getting treated by his brother, who had begun practising holistic medicine, and he was feeling a whole lot better.

23. Unbound

For the general public until now, he has been largely measured by his diverse body of work, and is only just beginning to become clear as a vulnerable body behind the incandescent character he created, bpNichol, and most particularly the character of bp as the "writer" of The Martyrology.

— David Rosenberg,
"Body By Nichol," *Open Letter* 14:1, 10

Despite Barrie's optimism, 1988 did not begin well. Most of January was taken up by writing two troublesome half-hour scripts, teaching at York University, drafting eight pages for "MEME," and curating that month's activities of Toronto's Music Gallery, including a mini-festival of Toronto sound poetry. In February his weakened hip caused him to slip on the ice while at York and sprain knee ligaments in his bad leg. He was unable to teach for two weeks, and — as he explained while apologizing in mid-March to writer Lesley-Anne Bourne whose Canada Council letter of support he had failed to write — he had mostly lain, sat, or limped around ruminating on how he had been spending his life. However, he had managed to draft 10 more pages for "MEME" on February 8, draft a section of *Martyrology, Book 8* the following week, and put the first three *Blizzard*

Island scripts into the mail on February 27. But his rethinking had led him to a number of big decisions.

He was going to take at least two years off from teaching, he told Bourne — so that he could have more time for the literary writing he wanted to do. The past year had given him very little time to do his "own" writing — writing that clearly did not include television scripts (March 13, 1988). He had resigned a few weeks before as a Coach House Press director, to avoid both editorial calls on his time and the various financial risks that corporate directors necessarily accept. After less than a year he was already not sure that the new corporation could stay out of bankruptcy. He had also decided to "narrow down" his television work to just the *Blizzard Island* series. An additional reason for these decisions to cut back may have been the large amount of travelling that he had recently been invited to do, including reading at a festival in Tucson later that month. Some of his thoughts while rethinking may also have been anxious. The day after writing to Bourne he wrote generously long replies to questions from a Italian student he had met at Turin, and then concluded the letter by telling her that her questions were all really big ones, ones that he would likely be still pondering when workers were sealing shut his coffin (March 14, 1988). Late in March he learned that his application for the Canada Council Senior Arts fellowship had been denied.

On April 15, 1988, he and Ellie and Sarah flew to Saskatoon, where Ellie's parents still lived. Barrie proceeded to nearby Weyburn where he spoke at two workshops and drafted plans for a "Take Two" issue of *Open Letter* in which he hoped to have Margaret Atwood write about *Survival*, Dennis Lee about his essay "Cadence, County, Silence," Lionel Kearns about his essay "Stacked Verse," and various other writers, including Douglas Barbour and Phyllis Webb, who would also offer second thoughts about one of their early books, essays, or statements. On April 18 he returned to Saskatoon to give a reading. With Ellie and Sarah he then flew to Winnipeg for another reading and to visit his sister Deanna. Back in Toronto, he had rehearsals with the Horsemen for a Brown University performance in Rhode Island, which they flew to on May 2.

On their return he resumed work on the *Blizzard Island* series, amid yet more serious back and leg pain — most likely brought on by his recent travelling. He wrote to a *Blizzard* co-writer Andrew Cochrane that he thought he was in the middle of a new "arthritis" attack — that he'd been told that his ailments might progress this way. He told Cochrane that the pain was anything but fun, and that he was now trying to get by on painkillers — things that he had never wanted to consume. He joked that those cliché lines about age not withering and years not condemning didn't apply to him, at least not yet (May 10, 1988). A little more than a week later, in a letter to James Reaney about "EAR LICK," a Canadian songs-by-poets series that Barrie and Ondaatje had been trying to interest CBC Radio in airing, his thoughts turned again to mortality. He commented to Reaney that this life seemed to offer only a finite amount of time, and that it might be the only life one got, adding parenthetically that he had never made a final decision about whether that was so — that it seemed foolish to try to make a call on that until the moment arrived (May 22, 1988). But in a few days he was flying to Calgary for a week-long residency, and on May 29 was in Vancouver for the launch of the Miki-edited collection of *Martyrology* essays,

ONE OF BARRIE'S LAST FORMAL PORTRAITS.
(Marilyn Westlake)

Tracing the Paths. Barrie then journeyed to Victoria for a four-day visit with his parents. There he wrote a new draft of "The Nose" for "Organ Music," and new texts for *Martyrology, Book 7* and *Martyrology, Book 10*.

Back home in June he appears to have worked mostly on getting *Martyrology, Book 7* ready for publication. He was now calling it "Gifts,"

and drafting and sketching the "Middle Initial Event" with which it
begins. He was also consulting with McCaffery about the peculiar "base
8" numbering system he had been toying with for *The Martyrology*'s
later books. McCaffery did not care for it, and Barrie decided to seek
Fred Wah's advice at the Red Deer workshop where he would again be
teaching. Barrie was also pondering an invitation that the Horsemen had
received to perform in the last week of July at the prestigious Rencontre
Internationale de Poésie at Tarascon in the south of France.

He spent the first week of July with Wah and Red Deer College Press
publisher Dennis Johnson at the Red Deer workshop. As in the year
before, the workshop was held at Sylvan Lake, a resort where Barrie's par-
ents had spent their honeymoon in 1933, and where one of his uncles had
played in the dance band. At both workshops Barrie found himself inside
an unintended return to an origin, amid memories of ancestral memo-
ries — "re-membering" — and amidst the *i*'s those memories had once
engendered. This time he began writing a poem he would call "read,
dear," which would become the second text of *Martyrology, Book(s) 7&*.

fam-**i**ly
fam**i**-ly
fam-**i**ly
fam**i**-ly
fam-**i**-ly
    -**i**-ly
    -**i**-
    -**i**-

One of these *i*'s was his long-dead sister Donna, and in the seventh part of
the poem he rewrote from memory a decade-old poem about her death.
In the following part the "sylvan" lost 1930s world of her death confronted
him with his own losses, or the bpNichol narrator of the poem did, seem-
ingly addressing him — "you," "we" — with ominous news.

things remembered or recalled

the way that old song refuses to leave the mind

alone

conversations with gone friends
how it seemed you would all go on
foreverie

/frag/mented / memory of   /
beginnings   stories of
the world before you came to be

we are all
somebody's dead
baby

Echoes here of Donna and of Barrie and Ellie's lost son — along with ones very likely of the also dead Lea, Visvaldis, cousin Donna, Jerry Lampert, and others — showed that this unsought visit to a past was pointing Barrie toward a much-too-nearby future. And then in the tenth part the narrator would tease him with the news that "i signs / i signifies / i sings." Very personal pronouns were shifting all around him. The final part began as if it were speaking to him:

at sylvan lake
certain things begin
or it is another
arbitrary point from which a line gets drawn
story has its start
its impulse
to unravel
. . . .
sometimes you think you see it all in the
mirror   rim
but then the light's dim or
your eyes fool you

When Barrie returned to Toronto, once again in severe pain, he

visited his family doctor, who referred him for x-rays. The x-rays surpris-
ingly showed a clearly visible shadow across his lower spinal column, and
his doctor quickly booked him for a magnetic resonance scan at Toronto
General Hospital. The three other Horsemen travelled to the Tarascon
festival without him. Barrie worked on readying the manuscripts of *Art
Facts* and *Martyrology, Book 7&* for publication, and on preparing for a trip
to Halifax for the shooting of the *Blizzard Island* episodes. In mid-August
he telephoned me in France, where I would be for the next year. I had
entrusted him with the management of our journal, *Open Letter*. He gave
me a progress report on the fall issue, told me about the x-rays and that
he now expected to have new surgery. He seemed more relieved to have
found a cause for his pain than anxious about the operation.

He had the MRI scan on August 26, and was referred to a surgeon, who
saw him within two days. There was a large non-malignant tumour in his
sacrum. The surgeon was hopeful that it could be removed, but warned
Barrie that the lost feeling in his leg could not be restored and that some
paralysis was possible. On August 30 he readied a revised diskette of his
Apple IIe computer poems *First Screening* and sent it to Dennis Johnson for
Red Deer College Press to publish.[1] He also mailed the final manuscript
of *Art Facts* to Charles Alexander of Chax Press in Tucson. He wrote the
first two of his "body paranoia: initial fugue" or "bp:if" poems — pun-
ning one more time on those "bp" initials. Punning also on the two
bodies, the poem's and Barrie's, and pondering the now 24-year-old rela-
tionship between the initials and that body with its anxieties and "awk-
ward bits" that surgery awaited. The puns brought the unfortunate Barrie
and bp together in terror — "sayn't / n't ready" — terror that theirs might
be a relationship that doesn't "work out," that "we" might not grow older.

    awkward bits

    relationships
    that don't work out
    (between words &

    where does fear fit in all this?
    anxiety?

> terror that we might not
> grow older

bp of course would, and will, grow older. Around September 5 Barrie flew to Halifax for the *Blizzard Island* shootings, returning September 9. From there, having heard that Paul Dutton was upset about the impending surgery, he had phoned him "to reassure me that it wasn't a question of 'the big D'" (email April 15 2012). On September 10 he wrote the fifth of the "bp:if" poems and the instructions that they be left out of the binding of *The Martyrology, Book 7&* — "interleaved into the final bound copy of *Martyr 7 &.*" Barrie wanted bp to have open possibilities. Even if.

These were not, however, the only works he was creating. Readers of *Gifts* could get the impression that Barrie was preoccupied with his surgical prospects to the exclusion of all else, or was writing his last poems from a hospital bed. On September 2 and September 4 he drew 'pataphysical items — the second one titled "the shirt off my back." On September 10 he wrote several pages of what appears to be a poem for voices, entitled "Radio Work," and added additional sections on September 11 and 12. Also on September 12, he wrote a memorial poem for Robert Duncan, who had died earlier in the year. These are all entries in his notebook, which he used mainly when travelling. There could well be other work in his manuscript files. Paul Dutton visited him on the 12th and was moved to hear him, amid his pain and anxiety, express sympathy for the distress his doctors were clearly suffering when having to give him such troubling news and limited possibilities. However, Barrie also reassured him that "the worst-case scenario is that I will have to be in a wheelchair." Barrie also gave him his Christmas present — a book about the Dutton name — under the pretext that the present was "just too good to wait that long for" (email, May 15, 2012). Philip McKenna recalls yet another expression of Barrie's selflessness from this period. Barrie confided to him that during one of his moments of anxiety he had sighed "Why me, Lord?" But then almost immediately he had heard a voice replying, "Why not you, son?"

On September 13 Barrie attended the premiere of Ron Mann's film *Comic Book Confidential* at Toronto's Festival of Festivals, and at the after-party met one of the comic book legends whose books he had collected, Will Eisner. Barrie had recently created what Mann describes as a "collectors program/promotional comic book" that would accompany the film, and had also recorded a commentary on the film for CBC Radio — both as gifts to Mann.

On September 14 and 15 he typed at least six letters, most of them about business matters, but one was to Fred Wah who had written that he had heard from George Bowering about the upcoming surgery. Puzzled by how vague news about it had reached Bowering (it had come to Bowering through me), Barrie wrote a detailed reply. He wrote that after having spent three and a half years trying to find out what his problem was, he had been told that it was not arthritis but instead a tumour, in his sacrum. They call it a "cordoma" he told Wah, querying the spelling, and saying that of course the little bastard had been growing and messing up his nerves, etc. He explained that the good news, if there could be such a thing, was that it wasn't one of those incendiary metastatic kind of tumours — once they went in and got it that was the end of it. But, he continued, no one knew for sure how much damage it had done or what nerves were involved, and so couldn't tell him how much movement he would have, below the waist, after the surgery. He was going to have tests about that next Tuesday, and the surgery likely a week after that. It would be 12 hours of surgery, with the surgeon coming at the tumour from two sides, and a recovery that could take 10 days or two months. He told Fred that the positive side of all this was that he might soon be walking without pain, something he hadn't experienced in years. That'd be great, he reflected. But there was also unavoidable anxiety — "attacks" of it, he wrote (September 14, 1988). On September 15 he wrote a similar letter to British sound poet Paula Claire and a cover blurb for George Bowering's book *Errata*.

On September 21, after the additional tests, Barrie saw his surgeon and learned that the tumour was even larger than had been previously thought. The choice, as he said to Ellie, was either to let the tumour grow and quickly kill him — possibly within two months — or risk the surgery. As when three months old, he was choosing to live. On the next day — his last before entering hospital — Gerry Shikatani, recently returned from Europe, visited him for the afternoon; again they discussed the difficult publishing situation of visual poetry. They went out briefly to a nearby Future Shop where Barrie — limping ahead as much as walking — bought a Walkman CD player to use in hospital while recovering. They

returned to Lauder Avenue where on the back porch he bid Gerry fare-
well, telling him that he'd see him on "the other side" of the surgery. In
the evening Barrie visited his old friend Rob Hindley-Smith.

The operation began on September 23 but was so complex that it had
to be paused and resumed on September 24. The surgeon later described
the tumour, a sacral chordoma, as being the size of an oven roast, and its
involvement with other tissue so extensive that the bones of the sacrum
had to be sawed and removed.[2] The extent of the surgery caused such
blood loss that supplies had to be borrowed from other hospitals and a
recovery machine employed so that the blood being lost could be re-
transfused. Near the end all the blood of his type in Toronto had been
exhausted. Barrie died on September 25.

aka{ barrie phillip }Nichol

24. The Afterlife of bpNichol

*it's precisely this borderline between the real life of the
i & the i's existence in narrative time, any narrative's
time, that was one of Stein's central concerns.*

— bpNichol in Miki,
Meanwhile: The Critical Writings of bpNichol, 318

*I realize that I lived with a person who wrote, as con-
trasted to living with a writer. Actual writing took place
separately: emotionally and physically. Barrie laughed
over an incident in Vancouver at one of his readings when
an old high school chum that he had not seen in many
years was waxing eloquently to me as to how exciting
it was to live with a writer. Lacking in tact, I guess, I
told her it wasn't like that at all, but that he went into
a room, closed the door and wrote — hardly exciting.*

— Eleanor Nichol, "The Ordinary Man"

The 1995 issue of *West Coast Line* magazine in which Ellie Nichol
responded to a request to write about "The Influence of Therafields
on bp's Writing" was guest-edited by George Bowering, who titled his

introduction "The Sound of the Beep" and wrote there that he was not about to do an issue without some Nichol in it. As well as Ellie's contribution, "The Ordinary Man,"[1] the issue contained a short essay on *The Martyrology* by Steven Smith, a brief recollection of Therafields artists' marathons by Philip Marchand and 10 pages of songs and dialogue from Barrie's first musical *Group* — the songs' first publication. The table of contents listed the latter as "From 'The Group.'" The issue was one of many signs that bpNichol was very much alive to various readers and editors even though Barrie Nichol was no longer entering his writing room and closing the door.

Ellie's choice of "The Ordinary Man" as her title, and her recollections that she lived with a person rather than a writer, that it had been Barrie with her in Vancouver at the bpNichol reading, and that whatever exciting bpNichol writing had come into being behind that closed door did so within a "hardly exciting" domestic context, recalls the Gertrude Stein advice he had cited in his 1986 letter to Kroetsch — that to be extraordinary in your writing you should be ordinary in your living. It also, however, reflected a tendency in Ellie to underestimate Barrie's "extraordinary." His passing through the door to his study to recommence bpNichol's writing had not been as dramatic as Clark Kent's rushing into a phone booth to become Superman, but had been at least equally productive. One had to be "ordinary" — reliable, punctual, careful about income, mortgages, and *Fraggle Rock* contracts, caring of one's family members — in order to maintain the everyday rooms that supported the special doorway. One also had to be ordinary in order to nourish the continuing life of the work — stuffing envelopes with copies of *Ganglia*, rushing to make sure that bpNichol was included in *New Wave Canada*, booking airline tickets for multiple-reading tours, overseeing book publications, ensuring that manuscripts became ready for publication, consulting with doctors in hope of a continuing life, resisting the weariness-creating pain of his mortality. Inside the room would appear that "extraordinary" literary character bpNichol, the "Martyr-poet" as Roy Miki evidently came to call him (Swail 181–82), continuing his interrogations of the present moment, going through the hours, following the chains, journeying in search of a return. Inside the room and inside the books.

With Barrie's death the potential scenarios that he had often anxiously foreseen had opened, as the *Martyrology*-poet bpNichol had revealed to him in the apocalyptic final hour of "A Book of Hours" in *The Martyrology, Book 6 Books*:

> (in the library stacks the shelves grow fuller, the buildings forced to expand, the budgets cut, nonexistant [sic], of course the voices become more muted, even tho they are screaming, even tho they have things to say, things you might want to hear, the words disappear into the dust, the darkness, the books closed and noone here to read them, noone here to take them from the shelves, anything any one of us might say becoming simply what it is, ink on yellowing pages, disappearing into this wait of words, the unvoiced endless hours)

Here the authors may be dead, but the books still have voices — "muted, even tho they are screaming." It is those still living who cut budgets, close books, and mute voices, or who allow humanity to so decay, as in H.G. Wells's *The Time Machine* — a book that Barrie knew well — that there is eventually "noone here to take them from the shelves." The gloomy "Hour 28" had been a kind of visit to the underworld, or at least to the afterworld in which the afterlife screams of bpNichol would have to resound:

> the old notion of immortality seen for what it is
> a preening in the bleak light history reflects

For bpNichol saw, in this last "Hour," that his own textual body was, in its own way, as material as Barrie's bleeding body would be: "ink on yellowing paper," dependent on shelves, buildings, and budgets, and the endurance of human culture. As much as this dusty library passage had echoed Wells's view of the Darwinian future, it had also spoken of Barrie's experience with libraries, first working at the Sigmund Samuel where thousands of books rested on their shelves undisturbed since acquisition, and latterly visiting Simon Fraser's Special Collections where 50 or more boxes of his own manuscripts rested in a windowless vault.

Re-establishing care for the now Barrie-less bpNichol nevertheless would require the assistance of such "ordinary" public institutions.

aka{ barrie phillip }Nichol

Ordinarily. Whatever their susceptibility to neglect and budget cuts, public institutions on average have much longer lifespans than individuals — even the lost Royal Library of Alexandria. It was to Simon Fraser University that Ellie, as Barrie's executor, trustee, and default literary executor, quite reasonably turned for advice about how to deal with the contents of the room beyond that once opening and closing door; she was referred to Irene Niechoda, the Roy Miki student who had recently completed her source-book for *The Martyrology, Book 1* and *Book 11*. In three months in the summer of 1989 Niechoda sorted and organized the room and, on the basis of Barrie's notebook and other sometimes ambiguous instructions, created a plausible and publishable manuscript of *Book 7&*. Niechoda then resumed her doctoral studies, working toward a dissertation that would create a source-book, or "sourcery" as she was calling it (fancying herself something of a bpNichol), for other *Martyrology* books. Her not completing this latter project repeated Barrie's own inability to create more than hints of *Books 10* and *11* and signalled once again the fragility of human expectation. It also showed that institutional longevity is not immune to the vagaries of individual lives.

Coach House Press published *Gifts: The Martyrology Book(s) 7&*, conceived by Barrie as *Book 7* with *Book 8* variously embedded within it, in 1990, and *Ad Sanctos: The Martyrology, Book 9* — words by bpNichol and music by Howard Gerhard — in 1993. By the latter date the press was no longer affiliated with Barrie's friend Stan Bevington, who was now taking legal action to reclaim the original Coach House logo. Much entropy. Longtime Barrie Nichol friend and Coach House author Christopher Dewdney was listed as the editor responsible for the production of both; another longtime friend of Barrie's, David McFadden, was listed as typesetter. Collectively with Niechoda and Ellie Nichol they were standing in for Barrie to provide the supervisory oversight he had given each of the previous volumes. These were posthumous publications of Barrie Phillip Nichol but definitely not posthumous work of bpNichol. Even the board of directors of the recently incorporated Coach House Press, most of whom Barrie Nichol had never met, and who had hopes of making the press a successful bourgeois publisher, were contributing to keeping bpNichol alive because of their sense of a historical obligation to Barrie. But this was not necessarily a sense of obligation to those things Barrie had spent his life serving — the endurance of poetry, story, and self-reflection, and their news that individual lives could have meaning and that the journey from Dilmun could continue.

> carry out this trust been granted me
> those few left who see a worth in the activity
> songs of praise and grief
> songs of joy

bpNichol would continue publishing and being published about. *Art Facts: A Book of Contexts* would be published by Tucson-based Chax Press in 1990, a press operated by Barrie's longtime poet-friend Charles Alexander. *Truth: A Book of Fictions*, edited by Irene Niechoda, would appear in 1993. In 1994 *An H in the Heart: bpNichol a Reader*, edited by Barrie's old friends George Bowering and Michael Ondaatje, would follow from McClelland & Stewart — a press Barrie had once said he "would never publish with."[2] That

BPNICHOL LANE, TORONTO. *(Stan Bevington)*

year also the City of Toronto would agree to name the alley on which Stan Bevington's print shop was located "bpNichol Lane," and Bevington and his colleague Rick/Simon would engrave in its concrete the Nichol poem "a lake / a lane / a line / a lone." After the unsurprising 1996 bankruptcy of Coach House Press, Stan Bevington and his recently established Coach House Books would volunteer to keep all *Martyrology* volumes in print, and later make all volumes available online as attractive but unsearchable

aka{ barrie phillip }Nichol

facsimiles of the original books. Installation artist Gil McElroy, who had met Nichol once in 1981, but had remained in tenuous friendly contact, would then begin work to curate the 2000 exhibition *St. Art: The Visual Poetry of bpNichol,* and edit the accompanying catalogue with informative essays by Paul Dutton and Barbara Caruso. *bpNichol Comics*, edited by Carl Peters, another Miki student, would appear in 2002, and include Barrie's 21-page mixed-media memoir about the late Toronto comic strip dealer George Henderson, mistaken by Peters as a version of Barrie's "John Cannyside."

Some of those standing in for Barrie would do a better job than others. Also in 2002 would appear the carefully researched, almost 500-page *Meanwhile: The Critical Writings of bpNichol*, edited by Miki himself. *The Alphabet Game: a bpNichol Reader* would appear from Coach House Books in 2007, edited by Darren Wershler-Henry (now Darren Wershler) and Lori Emerson as a kind of 336-page rebuke to the Bowering/Ondaatje "reader"; to extend it and accommodate Barrie's sound poetry and colour-based visual work, they established the companion website bpNichol.ca. *The Captain Poetry Poems Complete* would appear from Jay MillAr's Book Thug press in 2011, but without any explicit statement of who had edited or "completed" it (MillAr was most likely the bashful stand-in). But of a "complete" or "unified" one-volume edition of *The Martyrology* there has not been discussion.

In 1992 Niechoda would publish her *A Sourcery for Books 1 and 2 of bpNichol's The Martyrology* — to complaints that her commentaries rendered parts of the poem pedestrian. Roy Miki and Fred Wah would publish a collection of student essays about *The Martyrology*, titled *Beyond the Orchard*, in 1997; some of the student contributors would worry whether the poem was worth studying when Barrie himself had been male and white; many appeared to have read only two or three of *The Martyrology*'s eight books. I would publish a "bpNichol + 10" issue of *Open Letter* in 1999, Lori Emerson guest-edit "bpNichol + 20" and "bpNichol + 21" *Open Letter* issues in 2008 and 2009, and David Rosenberg a "*The Martyrology:* Survivors' Retrospective" issue of *Open Letter* in late 2009.

In *The Martyrology, Book 9, Ad Sanctos*, 12 pilgrims — including several of Nichol's paragramatically discovered saints — journey to Rome hoping to die and be buried near the grave of St Valentine. Once there, one of them discovers the grave offstage to the right, and another discovers it offstage to the left. After highly charged arguments about which is the "true grave," groups of them depart in each direction, leaving three characters — "i" bracketed by St Agnes and St Ranglehold — to go in neither direction, and ambiguously singing "one and one makes one zero." The critical response to bpNichol since 1988 has been somewhat like this scene; most critics have tried to situate themselves beside the grave of the "true" bpNichol. Some have seen this bpNichol as the *Martyrology*-poet — humanistic but postmodern, possibly religious, playful, generous, much like the once smiling Barrie Nichol, and paradoxically yearning for an ontological certainty he knows impossible. Others have ridiculed this view, suggesting it to be the work of "disciples and exegetes, mystics and sycophants" (Wershler-Henry, "Argument for a Secular *Martyrology*" 43); "*The Martyrology* is, sadly, not pomo because, despite all its alleged efforts to subvert humanist ontology, the text nevertheless reiterates the spiritual anxieties of modernism, substituting a poetic gain for a mythic loss . . ." (Bök, "Nickel Linoleum" 64). The latter have argued their true bpNichol to be the visual poet and 'pataphysician, the author of *Zygal*, *Art Facts*, *Love: A Book of Remembrances*, *Truth: A Book of Fictions* — books that wittily assert and demonstrate the semiotic constructedness of being. Somewhere in the middle of the stage a few, such as Steve McCaffery, have seemed to offer Deleuzian "both/and" readings. McCaffery argues *The Martyrology* to be a paragrammatic text that misses various opportunities to be entirely free of a lyrical humanism. But, he writes, "the core issue of *The Martyrology* coincides with the core issue of postmodernism: to achieve a finite inscription of writing's infinite combinatory motions" ("The Martyrology as Paragram" 202). Such an approach would likely, at the end of *Ad Sanctos*, read "one and one makes one zero" as meaning both "one and one makes one zero" and "one and one makes one [plus] zero." Also near the middle has been Roy Miki, who by 1998 had come to see "the Martyrology poet" as a textual being, as having become at the beginning of *Book 4* "*The M* poet who signs himself into the text, simultaneously dying into language and being reborn as bp — no longer the imperial/empirical Nichol but a textual entity" ("Turn this Page" 122).

David Rosenberg's readings of both 1998 and 2011 were somewhat similar, viewing "bpNichol" as the mercurial writer within the text and

aka{ barrie / phillip }Nichol

the clock-time Barrie Nichol as the "parental" author "watching over the shoulder of the bp who writes at a table in his room, comprehend[ing] the difficulty of separating from his created character — just as most parents and children experience" ("Body by Nichol" 12). Or, as in the dedication Barrie wrote for *Book(s) 7&:*

for Ellie

outside these books

that life

McCaffery too has sometimes implied such a view of a split *Martyrology*-Nichol — Barrie the parental watcher and bp the impetuous breaker of words into new meaning. "Nichol does not indulge in all-out logophilia, but rather censors, arbitrates, selects, and through restriction — (why not a St Upid?) regulates the plastic disposition . . . to which all alphabetic combinatory language is predisposed" ("Nichol's Semiology of the Saints" 103). Rosenberg, a widely read Biblical scholar and translator as well as a poet and essayist, author of *The Book of David* and of *Abraham: The First Historical Biography*, and co-author with Harold Bloom of *The Book of J*, has brought to Nichol a view of literary history that is considerably larger than the modernist ones with which critics have usually framed Barrie's work. Rosenberg has notably differed from most other readers on the possible humanism and ontological yearning of *The Martyrology*. So what if a resonant humanist modernist epic has been written in a historical period understood by many to be postmodern and — in terms of Aquinas's framing of ontology — resolutely nominalist, he has seemed to say. In *The Martyrology* bpNichol has transcended the difficulties with fragmentation that had limited Pound, Williams, and Olson, he argues, and created "a classically epic journey through the history of civilization, from Sumer to modern Canada, and through the personal history of a journey out of hell and into the saving methods, systems, traps and graces of human language and the cloudily grandiose thinking it puffs up" (8).

This epic had not been invalidated by the poststructuralist theory some anti-humanist critics had attempted to use against it. Rather it had superseded "French and continental theory and philosophy; psychoanalytic commentary; continental and American avant-garde poetry, north and south; modern and ancient epic; and the nature of authorship and created character in Spanish and English-language literature back to Cervantes and Shakespeare" (9–10). Implicit in the arguments of Rosenberg — whose own work has had a lifelong focus on elucidating the implications of authorship — has been the suggestion that in its overall nine books *The Martyrology* may be the most significant English-language poem of the past century. McCaffery has endorsed at least a small part of Rosenberg's comparison of the *Martyrology*-poet Nichol to earlier modernists, while continuing to affirm the poem's anti-humanism: "For Nichol content is an extension of rupture and hence marks a radical departure from the processual poetics of Olson and Creeley" (2008 102).

Most of these current critical custodians of bpNichol have agreed on the overall importance of his writing (though few are as strongly evaluative as Rosenberg and McCaffery) but usually have disagreed about the relative importance of *The Martyrology* versus his visual, 'pataphysical, and conceptual creations. However, most of those who have preferred the latter as Barrie's "true" postmodern works, such as Bök and Wershler-Henry, have had little to say specifically about them. This biography has also had little to say about them, partly because Barrie himself had little to say about them, was seldom asked to comment on them, and included few hints about his own life within them. For the most part his life was indeed "outside these books."

As well, Barrie took a much more casual and patient approach to these collections of visual, 'pataphysical, and conceptual works than he did to either *The Martyrology* or his fiction. He was not worried by publication delays. *Zygal*'s publication was delayed by various typesetting considerations from 1973 until 1985, and that of *Art Facts*, also conceived around 1972, held back until after his death by the delays with *Zygal*. As Niechoda notes in her "Additor's Note" to *Truth*, all of these books had been accumulatively constructed, with one-of-a-kind or series items dropped into the relevant file folder as they were created. Items that did not fit easily into one might be moved to another; some might accidentally be placed in more than one. Barrie was not troubled either by delays in his adding to a series or to a folder, as he was with whether or not he was adding to or still writing *The Martyrology*, nor by questions of unity or disunity, or of whether he was ending a continuing project such as "Probable Systems" or "Negatives" or completing a book. He appeared to assume there would always be more. Yet this series of books was as much "ended" by his death as was *The Martyrology*.

As a result of his low-key approach, except for the interim publication of individual items in magazines or as short-run pamphlets or as gift cards to friends, only two of the five projected collections were published in his lifetime, and one — "Ox, House, Camel, Door: A Book of Higher Glyphs" — still awaits publication. It would be perhaps unfair to say that Barrie was less invested in these personally than he was with other work — his notebooks reflect him creating or conceptualizing such drawings and texts almost every month of his life, sometimes in bursts such as the 23 drawings he created in Turin. But he was much less anxious about them than he was about either *The Martyrology* or "John Cannyside," and much less "parental" — to borrow Rosenberg's term — in his assisting them into print. These, however, were definitely bpNichol creations, ones that had their inception in the 1964–65 months in which Barrie had reinvented his writing self as the non-arrogant "bpNichol," "ideopoet."

> if i am i i am
> if i is i i is
> (*Love*)

The four-book series *Love, Zygal, Art Facts,* and *Truth,* along with similar work such as his *Konfessions of an Elizabethan Fan Dancer, Still Water, ABC: The Aleph Beth Book, Unit of Four, Alphabet Ilphabet,* and *The Adventures of Milt the Morph in Colour,* has tended to fall into a gap between the literary and the visual. Much of their contents has been more appropriate for display on the walls of art galleries — where the work of bp's Seripress collaborator Barbara Caruso hangs — than on the pages of books. Literary critics have been much less comfortable writing about them than they have been about his work that was more obviously textual, while most art critics have not seen them as part of their field. Sotheby's Canada is yet to offer a bpNichol creation at one of their auctions.

Barrie's life's work had predicted this overall carnival of signifiers, losses, and significations — a carnival that was already well underway in his lifetime. In the opening fragment from "The Chronicles of Knarn," *The Martyrology* had begun with both an ending and a dispersal of fragments:

> i've looked across the stars to find your eyes
> they aren't there
> where do you hide when the sun goes nova
> i think it's over
> somewhere a poem dies
> inside i hide my fears   like bits of broken china
> mother brought from earth
>   millenniums ago

Whether this "Knarnian" ending that precedes, together with its very early — or late — Knarnian bpNichol "i"-narrator, comes into being before the saints reach Cloudtown or after *Book 9* has been written, or resides somewhere in an Einsteinian circularity of time and space, both preceding and succeeding, is never resolved. "it's too late to say anything and too late to have anything to send." But the passage's apocalyptic and spiritually empty images resound throughout the various books. "i wish i could scream your name" the speaker calls, foreshadowing or recalling the books that will scream, or will have screamed, in the deserted library of *Book 6 Books*. "a long time ago i thot i knew how this poem would go," the speaker laments, foreseeing the thousands of times *The Martyrology* would surprise its writer with content he had no idea its words could contain. "i wish i could scream your name & you could hear me out there somewhere where our lives are," he calls, somehow mysteriously echoing the dedication Barrie would sooner or later write for *Book(s) 7&*: "outside these books / that life." Knarn is a lost home or an about-to-be-lost home, or perhaps a closed book, depending on one's position in time. It's a home about to be taken away, much like a home in *H* section, Wildwood Park, was taken away from young Barrie, or Cloudtown taken from his saints, the stone circles of Britain taken from their deities, Eden taken from the first couple, or Barrie from his neurotic fantasy-life of 1964 into his journey as bpNichol.

Each loss, each expulsion is from a fantasy of no future, no time left, or no time. If you are not planning the new, you are on the side of death, Barrie had written in 1972 with Lea Hindley-Smith and therapists Stan Kutz and Philip McKenna. After Cloudtown and its community of saints collapses, Therafields collapses. And after Therafields, the Coach House

aka{ barrie phillip }Nichol

Press. Each time Barrie struggles against the changes, like a saint. Each time there is something more beyond the gates of Paradise to journey toward.

His final series of poems, the "Assumptions" of *Book(s) 7&*, forecasts in its punning reference to the upwardly rising Mary (bp's last great ecclesiastical pun) other possible journeys. Assumption into what — an afterlife of language? or something beyond g & d, l or d? — had endured throughout *The Martyrology* as its major critic-troubling ontological mystery. Mary's own afterlife of bodily assumption had itself been written into partial being in the sixth century, and become an official Church policy with a written proclamation by Pope Pius XII only in 1950. Institutions can last almost as long as the *ars longa* of Hippocrates, and write their own memories into cultural memory. Spider-Man can be both the white Peter Parker and the black/hispanic Miles Morales. The institution of Christianity is almost as old as the institution of Western literature and, as Northrop Frye argued in *The Great Code*, culturally almost inseparable from it. bpNichol's own institutional future is more precarious than that of Frye, his fellow Canadian, who is indisputably at the moment a world literary figure, much like bpNichol was in 1967–70. Such futures are largely political, produced year by year by things such as the race and gender anxieties of Miki's students, the right-wing humour of poetry columnist Starnino, the nationalist opportunism identified by Barrie in Silliman's *In the American Tree* or interventions by other writers such as Miki, Rosenberg, McCaffery, Wershler-Henry, and Emerson.

bpNichol's future is further complicated because Barrie wrote deliberately — like Frye and like Barrie's other early Canadian contemporaries Sheila Watson and Louis Dudek — in an international modernist context, no matter whether one considers him a 'pataphysician or the *Martyrology*-poet. His first homage was a sound poem to Hugo Ball, and his first critical focus, and literary "mother," Gertrude Stein. In visual poetry his peers were Houédard, Finlay, Gomringer, and the Garniers; in sound poetry and performance Bernard Heidsieck, Henri Chopin, and Jackson Mac Low; and in the long poem Charles Olson, David Jones, Basil Bunting, Robert Duncan, Robin Blaser, and Ed Dorn. He was also one of very few significant poets, possibly the first, to be also a professional psychoanalyst, and to write implicitly as an exponent of Freud. *The Martyrology* is, among other things, the epic life-journey of a psychoanalysis, the psychoanalysis of a text, complete with analyst and analysand, an analysis, as Freud had written in 1937, "both terminable and interminable." It effectively attempted to translate Freudian analysis into the company of Homer, Virgil, Dante, and Milton as a primary survival and discovery narrative of Western literature. What is entwined with the bpNichol future is thus much less the history of any one national literature than the ongoing history of a modernism founded in Freud and Darwin and elaborated first by Stein, Dada, H.D., and Pound, and later by Bunting, Olson, Mac Low, and Duncan.

Barrie wrote and left that last writing to be "interleaved" among other texts, leaving the rest to the reader and the human future.

> The lines arrive
> like waves
> beat at the shore of some knowing
> some continent behaviour of your own
> like waves of pain
> pass thru this body
> and the body & the pain & the words & the days simply are
>
> (from "Assumptions," *Martyrology, Book(s) 7&*)

That interleaving, however, was much more a metaphor for the care of literature, and specifically of the *Martyrology* as itself a lifetime affirmation of the importance of literature to culture, than it was a final clever postmodern gesture. Barrie had not spent most of his adult hours writing, editing, worrying about how to write, caring about the various ways language could signify — and caring also about the future of dusty libraries — in search of personal aggrandisement. He had been a therapist in his life as well as in his profession — one who had hoped to be an unobtrusive catalyst both to individual understanding and the enlargement of civilization. His early decision to be a non-arrogant "ideopoet" had been analogous to his decision to take up psychotherapy — as when he conflated the two roles to Caroline Bayard, "what you're doing in the situation is not imposing yourself on the person but basically being a catalyst." For bpNichol the next significant act beyond that *Book(s) 7&* interleaving will be the publication of a one-volume collected *Martyrology*. It will be a gathering that has

aka{ barrie phillip }Nichol

already happened to many similar 20th-century projects — Blaser's *Holy Forest*, Silliman's *Alphabet*, Zukofsky's *A*, Pound's *Cantos* — and one that is implicit in both Barrie's life and his writings about his work.

Those who fault *The Martyrology* for being insufficiently postmodern, or valourize it for being successfully so, are overlooking the possibility that, in adapting to the dominant international aesthetic of his period, Barrie may have both incorporated and transcended it. He created an Odyssean epic narrative that both completes itself and stays open, and within it a vivid literary character who voyages with him from teenage breakdown, through therapy in Toronto, through years of professional practice as a therapist, personal commitment to communal living, various searches to reclaim family, and a continuing struggle to write or not write a "lifelong" poem, to a reclaiming of wholeness and family, as in *Book(s)* 7&'s "You Too, Nicky," a family that "was there before we began." Both bp and Barrie seem to speak in many of the *Martyrology*'s later passages of lives that are books, and books that are lives.

> And if i tries to retain a kind of loyalty to ideas, not blindly, but allowing them, always, to evolve under the scrutiny that time permits, it is simply that struggle with constancy, to stick with what makes sense until it no longer makes sense, to not be swayed by infatuation's blind calling. It is what binds books together, these motifs and concerns, the trace of a life lived, a mind.

There is often an implicit sense of summing up in such passages; as usual the writing moves its searching forward but with a strong awareness of the earlier *Martyrology* books — the books its new lines dragged up that Del Mar hill. Readers of *Book(s)* 7& and the other late books who have not experienced all the ones preceding, as bp and Barrie have, are not reading the text in the fullness of its significations, much like someone who has read only a random chapter of Joyce's *Ulysses*. Barrie Nichol's particular journey from imagining the "Sailor from Mars" comes, despite the tragedy of everyone's mortality, and despite the aesthetic expectations of Barrie's period, not simply to a postmodern irony of five pieces of paper that may or may not be interleaved, but to a meaningful end.

To expand McCaffery's observation, *The Martyrology* may not be "postmodern," but it powerfully testifies to living, writing, and hoping within postmodernity. Part of its saga-end meaning resides in the contrast between the irrepressible bpNichol's continuing Odyssean life, created like a "sayn't" out of language, and his author's own mortal "imperfection" — "gone beyond the reach of talking." Part lies also in Barrie's facing that imperfection with interrogation and analysis, in his asking repeatedly what human life could be without poetry, and in asserting and revealing poetry — as in "You Too, Nicky" — as news from the core of civilization.

notes

1. This debate occurred in issues 2 and 4 of the journal, with Coleman's letter being published in issue 5.

2. Nichol helped organize and host the Eleventh International Sound Poetry Festival in Toronto in October 1978.

3. Nichol's interest in the work of French Dadaist poet Alfred Jarry, who had defined 'pataphysics as "the science of imaginary solutions, which symbolically attributes the properties of objects, described by their virtuality, to their lineaments" (*Gestes et opinions du docteur Faustroll, pataphysicien,* 669), led him in the 1970s to imagine the founding of a Canadian "pataphysics (with the double apostrophe intended to denote its Canadianness), which he helped "document" in issue 4:6-7 (Winter 1990–91) of *Open Letter.* The issue was co-edited by Steve McCaffery and him as the "Toronto Research Group." That interest was manifested again on November 20–21, 1981 in Michael Dean and Richard Truhlar's The Symposium of Linguistic Onto-Genetics, the papers of which Nichol published in *grOnk* Final Series, Number 5 (1985).

4. The manuscripts of all these works, together with the notebooks in which many of them were first outlined, are in the Contemporary Literature Collection of the Special Collections department of Simon Fraser University's W.A.C. Bennett Library.

5. This overlapping and confusing numbering of notebooks seems to have resulted partly from his frequent travels, particularly those to the Therafields Florida properties in the 1970s. His main notebooks were large and hard covered. He

used them at home, at the Therafields farm, and while travelling — if he remembered to take the current one with him. If he did not remember, he would buy small a soft cover booklet in which to write while away, and apparently guess at its number in his "small" notebook series.

6. In a June 1968 note titled "Further," Barrie cites R.D. Laing's *The Politics of Experience* (Miki 2002 25) about how to create a "history" of phenomena. Laing writes in the opening chapter, "My experience and my action occur in a social field of reciprocal influence and interaction. I experience myself, identifiable as Ronald Laing by myself and others, as experienced by and acted upon by others, who refer to that person I call 'me' as 'you' or 'him,' or grouped together as 'one of us' or 'one of them' or 'one of you.'" Such ideas would not only not only have been contributing to Barrie's growing sense of the importance of community at this time but also to his later understandings of the 'repicrocal' relationship between 'me' and 'we.'

7. One of Ellie Nichol's principal objections to this book is that it takes seriously Barrie's various declarations that much of his work is built on autobiography. She has indicated to me that she believes that all of his seemingly autobiographical writing was fictional, which of course it would be in the sense that all autobiographies, like all understandings of "who we are," are acts of self-imagining and self-construction.

Chapter 1: Birth, Death, and Life, 1944–48

1. I interviewed Deanna at her home in Langford, British Columbia, on February 5, 2011. All quotations are from this interview. My impression throughout was that Deanna does not see her birth family as particularly unusual or her mother as having been especially unhappy. Barrie's recollections of his parents seem to be, in her view, particular to him and quite possibly to his position as the youngest in the family, and have little connection to how the parents actually were.

2. In conversation about "The Vagina" Barrie would also recall the baths light-heartedly, sometimes quipping about them being among the more "steamy" episodes of his childhood.

Chapter 2: *H* a Section

1. Wildwood Park was a planned community modelled by its developers on the Radburn, New Jersey, experiment of 1929 as a community for the age of the automobile. Many of the Radburn ideas have been retained by later subdivision

planners — self-contained neighbourhood units on crescents or cul de sacs, and the elimination of through traffic, although not in as radical a way as in Radburn or Wildwood. See http://en.wikipedia.org/wiki /Radburn,_New_Jersey

2. See for example Quentin J. Schultze and Robert Woods, *Understanding Evangelical Media.* Downers Grove, IL: InterVarsity Press, 2008. 194, or Scott McCloud, *Reinventing Comics.* New York: Harper, 2000.

3. Recurrences such as this, or those of his Red River Flood narratives, suggest the considerable extent to which "The Autobiography of Phillip Workman by bpNichol" is autobiographical of Barrie.

Chapter 3: Port Arthur, 1953–57

1. The adjoining Ontario cities of Port Arthur and Fort William at the western end of Lake Superior became amalgamated as Thunder Bay in 1970.

2. In 1987 he told interviewer Flavio Multineddu that "in certain sections of *The Martyrology* I've been talking about my personal life; I've been talking about things that happened to me personally: that letter 'i' sometimes is me and sometimes on the other hand it clearly isn't. One of the things I like best about *The Martyrology* is that 'i' reads as my 'eye' whether I'm talking about my life or something which is really fictional" (6). Punster Barrie would have been aware of the multiple meanings that word "really" was carrying.

3. Stein wrote several "autobiographies" of others, including the extremely "we-full" *Everybody's Autobiography.*

4. A remark he makes in his 1969 notebook essay "Comics as Myth," that the Oedipus myth continues to be "interesting" "because we'd all like to get into our mothers" suggests that one result of his therapy will be that he manages to forgive himself for his Oedipal desires by ascribing them to all men — or at least to all men who were poets. He wrote, "In fact, if we were to agree with [Edmund] Bergler, we'd have to say that by definition a poet is a mother-lover" (Peters 83). The remark indicates one of the ways in which Barrie intended the title of his first sound poetry recording, *Mother Love*, to be read.

Chapter 5: Vancouver, 1960–64

1. Paul Huba had died in 1959 at age 46, from a lung condition, believed to have been silicosis and caused by his art. Two of his larger works, a sculpture in red

granite titled "The Postman," and an untitled ceramic mural, are on permanent display at the Vancouver Post Office, 349 West Georgia Street.

2. Creeley's statement, quoted in Charles Olson's "Projective Verse" (*Human Universe and Other Essays* 52), had been "Form is never more than an extension of content."

Chapter 6: Lea or Dace

1. Barrie tells Niechoda that it took him four years to overcome his "compulsive" attraction to Dace following their separation in 1966. During the first three of these years he was conceiving and writing "For Jesus Lunatick," first published in August 1969 as part of *Two Novels*. Barrie's other writings for or about Dace include the visual poems "Bouquet for Dace," "letter to a loved one," and "The End of the Affair," all in the 1967 British edition of *Konfessions of an Elizabethan Fan Dancer*, and reprinted in the 2004 Coach House Books edition edited by Nelson Ball.

Chapter 7: Becoming bp

1. Among the papers Barrie left with my late partner when she was acting as his literary agent in the early 1970s are three carbon pages of a book manuscript dedicated to Sybil & Dezso Huba "who got me thru to here." It is "by bpNichol" and titled "poems for the end of summer"; the table of contents lists 14 poems including "1335 comox avenue" and "fourth letter to barb shore." Sybil Huba does not appear to have written to Barrie except in 1964.

2. Barrie would encounter such misprisions of his writing name throughout his career, the most amusing being a letter — a response to telephone inquiry he had made — addressed to "Mr. B. Peanuckle." One of my last mementos of him is a White Swan paper towel that was lying on my dining room table when we were talking and joking in the spring of 1988 about the base-8 numbering system he was considering adopting for the books of *The Martyrology*. ("8" was for him the numerical version of H — a resonant figure that looked the same from front or back, whether right-side-up or upside-down.) On the paper towel he printed the results of our jests: "Book (10)$_8$," and then, centred below, a self-satirizing "bp(sic)Nichol" and then below that a "[bp(sic)]sic."

3. In his 1961 essay "Ideas of the Meaning of Form," which he had quoted from during his summer lectures that year in Vancouver, Duncan had proclaimed that poets should no longer aim to write as masters and create "masterpieces" but

only to record "testimony"; that poets' only "mastery" should be in being "obe-
dient to the play of forms that makes a path between what is in the language and
what is in their lives"(61) — an extremely apt description for much of the middle
and later books of *The Martyrology*. Barrie mentions to Flavio Multineddu, in
his 1987 interview, reading Olson's actual essay, "Against Wisdom as Such,"
in Toronto in 1964, during his "ideopome" and "bp" self-transformations. He
summarizes Olson's essay as advising that "we should never sit down to the occa-
sion of writing . . . to be 'great': we should just sit down to write. We shouldn't
set out to be wise when we write, but he says: if wisdom comes up as part of the
writing, that's fine: just don't do it as the first thing you set in to do" (34).

4. "Communications Therapy" — largely at Barrie's urging — had become at
this time the official name of the therapeutic approach that Therafields offered.
He was one of the producers of the pamphlet, *Communications Therapy*, which in
the very late 1960s was given to each new or prospective client.

Chapter 8: Ideopoet

1. Barrie had probably been reading Williams's contribution to *Our Exagmination
Round His Factification for Incamination of Work in Progress*, a gathering of com-
ments on the then unpublished *Finnegans Wake*, published by Shakespeare and
Company in 1929.

2. The untitled and unbound poem prints the words "pane," "rain," and "pain"
in a large column of light blue letters on a dark blue background, evoking —
possibly ironically — the familiar pathetic-fallacy association of sadness, rain,
and blues. The poem is also included in a plain text version, under the title "hi
coo," in *Konfessions of an Elizabethan Fan Dancer*.

3.Barrie's 1964–65 desire to give up "arrogance" in his poetry, to give up writing
as the lyric poet who "knows," anticipated by five years Lacan's identification in
his Séminaire XVII (1969, published 1991 as *L'envers de la psychanalyse*) of the limi-
tations of the *discours du maître* (the "master's discourse") and its contrasts with
the other three of his four discourses, the *discours de l'université* (the "university
discourse"), the *discours de l'hystérique* (the "hysteric's discourse"), and the *discours
de l'analyste* (the "analyst's discourse"). He would go on to effectively write much
of *The Martyrology* in the latter two discourses without, in all likelihood, having
encountered Lacan's namings. *Seminar XVII* would not be published in English
until 2007. Duncan's "Ideas of the Meaning of Form" had of course anticipated
Lacan's comments on presumed "mastery" by almost a decade.

4. Barrie most likely read some of Bergler's writings on psychic masochism

himself shortly after entering therapy with Lea. As well as his 1965 notebook reference to reading Bergler's *Parents Not Guilty of Their Children's Neuroses*, there is the title of one of his visual poems in *Konfessions of an Elizabethan Fan Dancer* — "Homage to Edmund Bergler." In the poem a diffident, possibly maternal voice — "oowhat   d e   a   r" — is "reduced to nuisances."

5. Dutton remembers Steve McCaffery telling him that when still living in Britain and first reading Barrie's poetry in British magazines he had assumed that he was 50 or so years of age, much like Bob Cobbing or Ian Hamilton Finlay, and that when meeting him in Canada he "had been fully expecting to meet an old man."

6. The letters have been published in *bpNichol Comics*, ed. Carl Peters, pp. 52-61.

Chapter 9: Captain Poetry

1. Barrie had also explained the concept of the book to Geoff Hancock in an interview three years before (1975), telling him that "In the mid-sixties, the most common male poem was from the *courier de bois* tradition. The poet comes in from the woods, slams his ax on the table, and declaims a poem about his sex life. That has its own boredom" (36). Outside of Barrie's own Canadian English "courier de bois" would more likely be spelled "coureur de bois."

2. See www.chbooks.com/cart/add/338?destination=node%2F958.

3. Goodbrand's *Therafields: The Rise and Fall of Lea Hindley-Smith's Psychoanalytic Commune* is the only major source of data and organizational information about this large influence on Barrie Nichol's life. The book has some limitations, however. Record-keeping at Therafields appears to have been inconsistent, despite Barrie's own attempts to create and maintain an archive. What archives survived its dissolution were only partially rescued by Goodbrand before their planned destruction by the officers of the Phoenix Community Works Foundation, which had inherited them. Goodbrand himself was familiar mostly with the Therafields downtown Toronto therapy operations, was only an occasional visitor to the farm, and at no time privy to its managerial discussions. He appears to have interviewed mostly fellow therapists trained in Lea's first training group, Hypno 1. He created plausible but not necessarily exact summaries of events on the basis of the accounts and documents available, leaving the way open for many who were in the community to dispute his interpretations. Complicating his task was the contradictory nature of Therafields as both a therapy business and a community. Most members imagined themselves members of a communal project that aimed to deliver a more psychologically healthy way of living. But there could be no democracy in this community. The therapy operation required treatment decisions and financial

decisions for which Lea — whose money and reputation were initially most at risk — was ultimately accountable. Among those who mistrust Goodbrand's portrayal of Therafields is Ellie Nichol, who has suggested to me that he knew little about the farm, about Barrie's work as vice president, about the relationships between Barrie and the others whom Lea entrusted with Therafields administration, or about the viewpoints of the younger therapists-in-training, those in house groups or those operating the farm. Where relevant, I will be noting aspects of Goodbrand's account that she or others doubt or dispute.

4. Doyle writes, "When Lea managed to give administrative control of the developing organization to her son and his friend, Barry [sic] in 1967, she was claiming it as her own business, ultimately, her family business. Doubtless she did not articulate this to herself at the time but in essence that is what happened. She was not able to trust the senior, more mature members of her seminar to nurture and care for the assets that were accruing. She had to maintain personal control. Before long that control was utilized to manipulate resources in ways unknown to the seminar and certainly to the average Therafields member" ("Thoughts," November 19, 2010).

Chapter 10: Psychotherapy Poetics

1. Ellie Nichol strongly disagrees that there is any significant connection between Barrie's experiences and employment in psychotherapy and his writing. She suggests that the two activities were merely parallel, or that therapy was a background to his writing much like the fact that he lived in Toronto, rather than somewhere else, was a background. The view that Barrie strictly partitioned the writing, psychotherapy, and family parts of his life is fairly common among his friends, and one that I partly shared until I encountered the evidence of his notebooks and the writing he did for internal Therafields publications. On reflection, however, it is quite odd to have once thought that someone as intellectually curious as Barrie could have refused to employ in one area of his life the concepts and methodologies he was learning in another — particularly when both psychotherapy and poetry are language-based endeavours.

2. Paul Dutton has the following recollection of Lea's use of "deep relaxation": "I recall Lea quite explicitly stating, in one large group gathering — a deep group, I think, or perhaps a learning group . . . that the term 'deep relaxation' was employed instead of 'hypnosis' simply because it was illegal in Ontario at the time (and maybe still) to practise hypnosis without being certified (or licensed, or something). She made no bones about it being hypnosis, nor about the [alternative] term hypnotherapy."

3. Ellie Nichol wonders whether Niechoda may have mistranscribed when she

quotes Barrie here as saying "my ma was depressed all the time because we were moving" and whether he may have said, or meant to say, "my ma was depressed because we were moving all the time" (email September 15, 2011). After Barrie's death, Ellie lived in the same city as his mother and saw her frequently. She remembers her as lively, energetic, and witty and as a frequent storyteller from whom Barrie may have acquired his childhood interest in writing stories.

4. While it is possible that Barrie could have encountered a similar statement about releasing one's voice in a European poetry magazine of this period, such as Zurbrugg's *Stereo Headphones* (there is strong possibility but no specific evidence that he did), he would most likely have read it in the context of his earlier Therafields liberationist understandings of the voice in abreactive therapy — the understandings that he implicitly references here.

5. Barrie explains how in Hopi mythology Palongawhoya's "job" was to sing to the creator and thereby bring "harmony" to the cosmos, and that later others had cheapened such singing by using their voices for utilitarian tasks including social deception. For Barrie the story had illuminated such differences as between writing poetry for the sake of the language or writing it for self-aggrandisement as a "wise" or "talented" person, or between using language as a poet and using it to get a sexual partner, complete a business deal, or get elected to political office.

Chapter 11: Beginning *The Martyrology*

1. That is, "Comics as Myth" should probably be read as indicating that there were no saints in Barrie's imagination, and quite possibly no well-defined Cloudtown, until his discovery with David Aylward of "St Ranglehold." The essay seems fairly clear that in Barrie's recollections the fantasy figures of his childhood — Tracy, Catchem, Junior, Pat Patton — segued first into his Bob de Cat, then into Captain Poetry, Madame X, and Blossom Tight and only after that into the saints of his *Scraptures*. "These saints grew out of a comic strip milieu" (Peters 81) is perhaps as much a personal history statement as one about composition.

Chapter 12: Friends Much More Than Footnotes

1. Others from the Therafields community suggest that Goodbrand overgeneralizes when he characterizes his fellow therapists as so widely disliking Visvaldis. Ellie Nichol has suggested to me that how he was viewed had depended on who you were speaking with, and when, and that Goodbrand's book is not the only "truth" about him and Therafields that various people currently assert. Doyle

quotes an unidentified woman who cooked for seven years at Lea Hindley-Smith's opulent home on the farm, a house known as "The Willow," as having told her "A lot of the men in Hypno 1 looked down on him. On the other hand he was treated by some others as if he was a god" ("Thoughts," February 7, 2011).

2. Goodbrand's dichotomous view here of Therafields is also not entirely accepted by the ex-Therafields community. Doyle in her blog writes that many people involved had "different locations within the community, often with very differing experiences," and that she herself — present from 1966 to 1983 — had "intuited changes that were happening in the broader context of the organization as a whole but was unable to fully understand or articulate them" (October 18, 2010). Ellie Nichol, who was in the same learning group as Doyle, the "Character Analysis Group," also suggests that different parts of the community could experience Therafields quite differently from those in Hypno 1 or in management.

3. About these money-consuming projects, Doyle comments that "though many of the improvements enhanced living and working conditions in the environment, much of Lea's urge for driving the literally incessant construction and renovation rolled out from 1967 to the mid-1970s was to give Visvaldis a focus and a sense of purpose within the community" ("Thoughts," February 9, 2011).

4. Ellie has told me more than once that because Lea did not care for conventional family living arrangements, there were few — if any — set mealtimes for her to hold administrative meetings at.

5. The ideas of "The Paranoid and the Paranee" are almost certainly entirely Lea's, with Barrie's co-authorship restricted to sentence structure and word choice. Doyle remarks that "the paranoid/paranee issue" was one of "the things that Lea incessantly talked about through the early 1970s" ("Thoughts" November 9, 2010).

6. Ellie recalls that "Terry" was Lea's pet dog, that it was accidentally run over by one of the farm workers, and that the incident thus had emotional ramifications far beyond those that Barrie addresses in the poem. It is a good example of how incomplete, fragmented, or selective Barrie's recollections of events in his work can be, and how autobiographical incidents — while remaining "autobiographical" — can be shaped by the movement of language and form within his writing. An extreme example of this is his 1969 "novel" "For Jesus Lunatick."

7. In reading this chapter Ellie Nichol tends to discount some of the anxieties Barrie portrayed himself as having. She tells me that she was unaware that Barrie was experiencing discomfort over the prospect of sharing a domestic space with her, or that he viewed this discomfort as a limitation that he should overcome.

Living together as couples was not a Therafields practice or goal, she points out, and, as Goodbrand notes, Lea characterized many, if not most, live-in relationships as parasitic and victimizing of the weaker partner (98–99). She suspects that some of Barrie's self-deprecating jests may have been his way of coping with the expectations of non-Therafields friends who were committed to conventional live-in relationships. She tells me that my phrases "bear living under the same roof" and "endure sharing the same floor" do not reflect any situation or issue that she can recall.

8. My personal guess is that Barrie may have kept the strength of the fears he had about closeness to women somewhat secret from Ellie because of his anxiety and insecurity about jeopardizing their relationship — as expressed in this "Some Description of Her" narrative.

9. See his essays "Language Writing: From Productive to Libidinal Economy" (*North of Intention* 143–58) and "Writing as a General Economy" (201–21). McCaffery dedicated *North of Intention* to bpNichol.

Chapter 13: The Meanings of Crocuses

1. The social dimension of Barrie's therapy with Lea Hindley-Smith and its influence on how Barrie's understandings of humanity and culture developed should, once again, not be underestimated. The following passage about Lea in the unedited manuscript of Goodbrand's book could be easily adapted to describe Barrie's own view in the later *Martyrology* of the cosmic context in which the human species laboured.

> Lea couldn't see how we could be adult and not address the question of the health of our environment of all kinds. Moreover, she was of the Kleinian school, which insisted on the necessity of reparation to mend the world in order to counteract the inherent destructiveness that is a large part of our species. She didn't believe that we could just take care of ourselves, putting ourselves right, and ignore the context. (127)

2. See also Barrie's attempt to gloss these lines in Multineddu's interview, 26.

3. Although the robe was definitely humorously appropriate for the award ceremony context, it also resembled more questionable clothing being worn at the time by Lea and Visvaldis, clothing that contributed to their being spoken of by some in the Therafields community as "the royal family" (McGeachy 7), or to Lea being spoken of sardonically as "queen of the universe, queen of Therafields" (Brenda Doyle, quoted in McGeachy 9). Visvaldis tended to wear a "robe"

routinely whenever in public, and Lea fancied showy dresses and beehive hair-styles, prompting their cook at the Willow to tell Doyle that at some mealtimes "Visvaldis in his robes and Lea in her fancy clothes and her false crown were like the king and queen" ("Thoughts," February 2, 2011). Four of the photographs of Visvaldis in the photo section of Goodbrand's book show him in a robe not dissimilar from the one he designed for Barrie.

Chapter 14: Expository Turns

1. Hansjörg Mayer (born Stuttgart, 1943) is a German visual poet and arts publisher who spent much of his life in Britain, teaching graphic design at the Corsham College of Visual Arts. He is presently based in London.

Chapter 15: Me & We

1. Ellie Nichol is emphatic in counselling against viewing Barrie's parents as being "bad," "limited," or "lesser" than a "good" and "worldly" Lea Hindley-Smith, and Barrie as being first damaged by his parents and then "saved" by Lea. Her argument is that Avis and Glen Nichol were normal good parents of their time, and that Barrie's childhood difficulties had arisen more from his perceptions than from their actions. Glen was a typical 1940s father who saw his family responsibilities mostly in financial terms and, because of his heavy workload, got little practice in interacting with his children. He and Avis had little way of understanding possible careers for their children except in terms of occupations they were familiar with. That these did not include the arts or psychotherapy was a product of the small-town Canadian prairie culture they had grown up in, not of any personal failure. It is very possible that Barrie shared Ellie's view — even while writing the letter his mother responds to. I again think of that 1965 notebook entry that I mentioned in Chapter 1, an entry made near the beginning of his therapy, in which he records that he is reading Edmund Bergler's *Parents Not Guilty of Their Children's Neuroses*.

Chapter 16: Working Together

1. McCaffery's remark in an essay on sound poetry, "Voice in Extremis," about "the antisocial lyricism of individual composition" (2001 184) suggests that he might have been substantially in agreement with Barrie about the Horsemen had he openly expressed his dismay.

2. In an email to me on January 9, 2012, Dutton describes the difficulties of the Horsemen in much the same terms: "the interpersonal relations proceeded through

a steady decline over years, like a marriage gone sour — or, to employ psycho-
logical terms, an unconscious acting out of interlocking neurotic patterns, which,
let me hasten to add, I believe that Beep managed to keep pretty much out of. . . ."

3. Dutton wrote to me on August 5, 2011, "As well, it should be known that bp
was the glue that held the group together. David McFadden wasn't far off the mark
when he quipped, at a Horsemen trio performance during the couple of years that
Beep absented himself from the group, that we were 'the headless Horsemen.' We
in fact did function well as a trio through those years, maintaining and expanding
the group's reputation and repertoire, but the quartet's very first readings were
either Nichol engagements that he turned over to the Four Horsemen, or were
ones got because of his reputation. And in its latter days, the only performances
everyone agreed to do were those that came in through Beep."

4. Nichol's story about Coleman's role is quoted by Niechoda in note 27 of part
II of her introduction, 48.

5. I offer a much longer narrative of the conflicts that engulfed Barrie and others
at Coach House between 1975 and 1988 in "The Beginnings of an End to Coach
House Press," *Open Letter*, Ninth Series, Number 8 (Spring 1997): 40–77. Coleman's
continuing fierceness about Coach House is reflected in "The Coach House Press:
The First Decade. An Emotional Memoir," published in the same issue, 26–35.

6. It's noteworthy that Barrie uses the same "dream world" name for Cloudtown
in the "Friends as Footnotes" section of *The Martyrology, Book II* as his brother
Don had given to his fantasy life when bringing him to Toronto in 1964. Barrie
had then seen his "task" to be to dump that "dreamworld," but it wasn't until
1971 that he could dump, or declare dead, the dream world of saints that his
childhood comic book fantasies had evolved into.

Chapter 17: Russian Roulette

1. Doyle challenges Goodbrand's characterization of Lea both as urging the
building of a community and as having a "European" understanding of psy-
choanalysis. On October 10, 2010, Doyle writes that first of all there was no
effective community: "he [Goodbrand] says that 'In 1974 the community com-
mitted itself to finding sufficient land to feed a community of a thousand. A
fourth one hundred acre farm was purchased . . .' Pg 135. 'The community' — if
he is speaking here of the several hundred who were then members — had not
only no forum to discuss such a project, but no knowledge of the purchase until
after the fact. Even then it became known only gradually as people heard of it
while up at the farm. Decisions of this nature were made by a small group, by

Lea with Rob, Barry [sic], and Visvaldis. Rik would be involved as he handled financial details. [. . . .] These decisions and their implementation happened only at the top." Lea herself, Doyle argues, often held the Hypno 1 therapists, who had bought the first farm, responsible for the "community" concept. "Her own ambivalence [was] stated periodically in seminar groups, about the developing community. 'It was you people who wanted this, not me,' she would direct at the former religious" ("Thoughts," October 10, 2010). As for community and social justice being specific to European schools of psychoanalysis, Doyle writes, "The Europeans of whom Lea spoke most often were Freud, Klein, and Reich. Each had his or her own followers and detracters. [. . . .] The gossip and in-fighting within that rarified air was as intense as in any professional arena. To my knowledge (though I would be happy to be contradicted) none established or advocated a community based on psychoanalytic principles or as an outgrowth and extension of therapeutic resolution" ("Thoughts," November 16, 2010).

2. Goodbrand quotes Therafields member and therapist Father Jim Conlon as telling him that "[p]eople had real trust in bp. He was the balance wheel. He settled things whenever he was around. He let people find their own lives. He had no agenda for anyone. He had no expectation of how their lives would unfold. Lea could be interfering, sometimes to great benefit," Goodbrand adds, "Everyone on occasion, distrusted Lea, Rob or Visvaldis, but not Barrie" (106).

3. The *A Publication* editorial had given the general members of Therafields the illusion of democracy, or at least of being consulted. But the actual decisions were made by management, as Doyle indicates in note 1 above. Goodbrand argues that even the senior therapists of Hypno 1 felt ignored during such decision-making. One of the ex-Therafields responders to Doyle's blog wrote to her, "This is the stuff of cults," and quoted Howard Adelman, a philosopher and co-founder of Rochdale College, as having told him, "It's like a giant wedding cake with Lea and Visvaldis on top, then her children, Josie, Rob, Malcolm and Barrie, too. The next tier was Hypno 1, then CAG [the Character Analysis Group], then the Brunswick Group, then everyone else in the house groups. Finally, everyone else receiving therapy. The communication and feedback went from the top down-ward" (Comment posted July 22, 2011).

4. The lines also recall his thoughts about the psychic suicide his fantasy life had constituted, and in their gun imagery echo from 1971 his lines toward the end of *The Martyrology II*:

> the one thing always i have feared
> my own rashness
> killing myself on whim
> i carry shotgun shells in my pocket

blow my brains out in a department store
shocked faces my own surprise
folding slowly on the floor
silent as i had never been in life

Chapter 18: Strange Years

1. In Multineddu's interview with Barrie, Multineddu asks why so much of the middle books of *The Martyrology* seem to have been written while he is travelling. "You travel a lot," Multineddu exclaims. Barrie replies, "Well, I tend to write a lot when I travel, that's all [laughing]. . . . It's actually the other way around, that very often the time I had free to write was when I was travelling. [. . . .] I would sit with my notebook and I would write for like five, six, eight, ten hours, just pausing to sleep, or eat a bit . . ." (27).

2. Lea's books were all novels, which she seems to have based on idealizing reconstructions of her own life. She intended them as instructive examples of the kinds of psychoanalytic problems and solutions that an individual could encounter, and viewed them as more useful than academic description of cases and methodologies. In a sense she was using her life as an extended Freudian case study. This approach echoed the one she took in her seminars, which was to teach through anecdote and through doing analysis with some of those present rather than on the basis of a curriculum with assigned topics and readings. The language in these novels was often simple and repetitive, a style she may have been encouraged to continue by Barrie because of its distant reminders of the style of Gertrude Stein. It is possibly no accident that all three writers — Lea, Barrie, and Stein, author of *Everybody's Autobiography* and *The Autobiography of Alice B. Toklas* — were deeply engaged by the challenges of autobiography. It is also likely, considering Barrie's co-authorship of Lea's two short essays, that he advised her editorially on these novels. Goodbrand believes that he did, and that he also wrote a chapter of her first book (email, November 3, 2011), though neither of us have encountered documents that confirm this. However, in general there is almost no documentation of Barrie's relationships with people he saw routinely in his Toronto and Mono Township activities; their communication was usually oral.

3. Lea's novels were almost as elaborately inter-related as Barrie's *Martyrology* was with his other published and unpublished books. "The Summonsa Tapestries" at this point were projected to contain two trilogies, one titled "Ronald" and containing the novels *Ronald and Susan* (1975), *The Way It Might Have Been* (1977), and the uncompleted "Suron," and the second titled "La Covenir" and containing *Secret Places* (1976), *Not for You Tea in the Afternoon* (19), and "Threshold," also uncompleted. Barrie's review "for the Easily Defensive" reflected resentment

in the general Therafields community about being expected to purchase and read books that many considered to be at best awkwardly written. (They probably would not have enjoyed a Stein novel either!) It also echoed Lea's now routine rebuffing of any criticism by suggesting that the dissenter was suffering from unconscious limitations — such as paranoia, mother-hatred, or mistrust of "the matrix." Doyle suggests that this change in Lea reflected her own need for more therapy, writing "The identified 'paranoid' others became for her a present day embodiment of the until then successfully repressed terrors that she had held since a young child. It is likely that these terrors centred around her father as it was primarily men that Lea began to identify as paranoid. She declared herself no longer willing to work with them. The men who had worked with her as clients, as learners, and as colleagues on the development of the farm became divided into two groups: those who were with her, that is, who didn't challenge her centrality and those who held opinions contrary to her own." Barrie, it would seem, was at this point still one of the former. See also Goodbrand 212.

4. The book that resulted in part from Marlatt's visit to Avebury is her *How Hug a Stone*. For a survey of critical responses to Marlatt's "mother goddess" suggestions see my article "Words and Stones in *How Hug a Stone*," in my book *Canadian Literary Power*, 167–96.

5. One can speculate that Barrie's understanding of his relationship to his parents, including that he had transferred his devotion to his mother from her to his writing — to "Mother Tongue" — and was still waiting for a meaningful communication from his father, has left him inhabiting any possible female deity as he writes and thus without need to acknowledge her further, while also repeatedly addressing a usually silent "Lord" or "father."

6. Again, it should be noted that Ellie Nichol says that she was unaware that Barrie may have been experiencing discomfort over the prospect of sharing a domestic space with her, and is puzzled by the humorous and self-deprecating remarks he made about the matter in his correspondence — here to his cousin Donna, and to his sister Deanna in the next paragraph — believing that he probably made them more to make himself appear "normal" to his family and non-Therafields friends than to express his actual feelings.

7. Ellie may also have been unaware of Barrie's irritation about what he perceived as his mother's deliberate shunning of her — or possibly saw it as unreasonable. She remembers his mother fondly as independent, cheerful, and hospitable, and given their similar Saskatchewan backgrounds, may have identified with her. She has suggested that it would be unfair for her to be unfavourably remembered no matter what comments Barrie may have made about her.

Chapter 19: Blown Away

1. At least three of the songs referred to specific psychoanalytic issues Barrie himself had grappled with. "Ordinary Man" recalled his "ho-ho-ho" habit of not taking himself seriously (something he lamented in his very first notebook), of pretending that he didn't have important thoughts, anxieties, or — in the Four Horsemen's case — contributions that he wished to make. "Australopithecus," with its lines "And when I find a man / It makes me so mad / Because he always starts / to remind me of dad" echoed Barrie's Oedipal attachment to his mother, as — more obviously — did the song "I am Obsessed with My Mother's Breasts." Therafields insiders who knew something of Barrie's past had an additional reason to laugh.

2. In a letter to Daphne Marlatt, who was co-editing with John Marshall the Island Writing Series, Barrie described his concern about whether publication of this "hour" might distress Ellie. He had thus checked with her about it, and got her approval. She'd said that she could never see why Zelda had gotten angry unless Fitzgerald had lied. Barrie went on to write that Ellie'd also told him she was comfortable with anything he wrote about her appearing, as long as he wasn't lying, and that this had been the only occasion on which he'd "bothered" to ask anyone in advance about something he'd written about them. But in this instance, he wrote, it seemed important to do so because the events were still raw to both of them.

Chapter 20: Eric Von Daniken Meets Kurt Schwitters

1. McCaffery however mistakenly assigns the decision to dissolve Therafields and end Barrie's role in it to 1987 rather than 1982.

2. Barrie evidently never did, in his own mind at least, entirely rid himself of the "ho, ho, hoing" "cheerful lad" defence mechanism that made it easy during his childhood and adolescence for his parents and friends to regard him as easy-going and untroubled. In the case of the Four Horsemen it is very possible that the other three could have little idea of the distress that their wit and stubbornness around written collaboration could cause him. Dutton recalls Barrie's preference for harmony and aversion to conflict as good things — "It was he who most effectively resolved conflicts, who most often solved tactical problems, who gave direction and inspired loyalty. And he did it all with a light hand . . ." (email January 11, 2012). Even someone as close to Barrie as Ellie could have been misled into perceiving him as much less prone to anxiety than he has recorded himself as being. Defence mechanisms, of course, are ways of fictionalizing ourselves.

1. "Tracks" was based on the story of the building in the 19th century of a railroad from Cobourg through the Rice Lake area to Peterborough. Barrie's interest in story was thus partly derived from his father's CNR employment and the numerous resulting family journeys by rail.

2. His lawyer was my partner, Linda, who had previously been his agent under her maiden name, Linda McCartney. She was also our colleague on the Coach House editorial board.

3. *First Screening* is presently viewable on the internet at http://vispo.com/bp/ in various reconstructed versions. See also Geoff Huth's article "First Meaning: The Digital Poetry Incunabula of bpNichol," and "Introduction to bpNichol's *First Screening*" by Jim Andrews, Geoff Huth, Lionel Kearns, Marko Niemi, and Dan Waber, both published in *Open Letter* 13:5, Spring 2008.

4. Len McGravey, an ex-Basilian who joined Lea Hindley-Smith's Catholic Group in 1968 and who in 1973 became a member of the Therafields "Gemini 2" learning group (along with Mary Barton, Howard Gerhard, Rafael Baretto-Rivera, John Ligoure, and Paul Dutton, among almost 40 others), and continued in the Therafields community until 1980, recalled in his 2007 blog that a close Therafields friend in the early 1970s had died from excessive fasting. He wrote that in this period "Lea Hindley-Smith and some of her therapists often experimented with various fasting fads, following the dietary systems of current gurus. [. . . .] She believed that natural healing was the blessed way to wholeness, recommending to her followers organic remedies, including various extreme combinations of diets and fasting for long periods of time. She also insisted that this process must be strictly supervised by alert qualified personnel. For that, I'll give her credit as is her due. Kurt first experimented with the short fast of a few days. Shortly afterwards, he adopted Lea's belief in the 'long fast,' sipping only water of [sic] juice over the prospected period. He and others believed that the long fast would 'clear up the accumulated toxins in the body.' This 'purification process' was also intended for healing the body organs and bringing balance to any emotional turbulence" ("A Brief History of Therafields, Part Six").

5. Dutton recalls that one of Barrie's York students had been amazed by "his stocking up on junk food during class breaks — potato chips and candy, Diet Coke and tea, and apparently all of those in the same break," and suggests that Barrie's "oral needs were enormous." He adds that he "was often startled by some of his food choices (wieners and chicken-skin and the aforementioned junk food), given all the healthy-food info he was exposed to, both within and outside of Therafields." Barrie himself writes in "The Mouth," in *Selected Organs*, "When I

went into therapy my therapist always said I had an oral personality" and mentions his fixations on oral sex, oral gratification, and the "oral reality of the poem" (15) — all of these very likely related to his Oedipal preoccupations that mark the opening poems of *Selected Organs*, "The Vagina," "The Mouth," and "The Tonsils."

6. The dedication is somewhat mysterious. Bernstein was not at the festival and does not appear to be even implicitly alluded to within the text. There is very little correspondence between Barrie and him. He recalls that although he had met Barrie at one or two conferences that he never once, to his regret, heard Barrie read.

7. Dutton considers *The Gargoyle* "one of the most memorable of Nichol's lyricist-composer collaborations" and worthy of production to larger audiences. Barrie, however, considered it a peripheral work, written, like his television scripts, mainly for money. While he was enjoying the collaboration that both theatre and television require, much as he had enjoyed and supported collaboration and cooperation at both Therafields and in the Four Horsemen, he would rather have been spending his time expanding *The Martyrology*, extending his various 'pataphysical collections or trying to finish the ever-present "bpNichol by John Cannyside."

Chapter 22: The Waste of My Words

1. Barrie appears to have made this decision to change the title while Coach House Press was designing the book. The change allowed the cover to be a kind of visual poem in that the "6" did double-duty by signifying both that this was *Book 6* and that *Book 6* contained "6 books."

2. The only published remnant of "The Bard Project" so far is "'IM: mortality play," which appeared in 1990 in *Line* 25:2, 7-10.

3. On Barrie's death Juhl may have been one of the most generous responders, sending the family a reported $10,000, most likely in recognition of the precarious income and benefit situation of a freelance writer.

4. This is the only act of overt self-censorship that I have found Barrie to have committed, one that is in a sense negated by the earlier magazine publication.

5. The inclusion of Dewdney, Fawcett, and Bromige, however, did support Barrie's allegation that the writers in the collection were too diffuse in their aims and assumptions to form a group. Barrie's own writing was light-years closer to the Language goal of valuing words "for what they are themselves" rather than as

"instrumentalities leading us to a world outside or beyond them" (Andrews and Bernstein, x) than that of either Dewdney or Fawcett.

6. There may have been more at play in Barrie's outburst against the "Language group" than McCaffery was aware of. Andrews had written to Barrie several times in the spring and summer of 1977 urging him to contribute to the magazine he and Charles Bernstein were about to launch. But it is unclear whether Barrie answered the first two of these letters. Andrews seemed interested more in Barrie writing a short article about McCaffery than in his sending $L=A=N=G=U=A=G=E$ some of his own poetry. Barrie could have sent poetry from among his current manuscripts, but an article would have required new reading and writing. It's also possible that Barrie could have been offended by the specificity of Andrews's request and its implications for how he might comparatively view his and McCaffery's writing. In 1998 McCaffery commented that Barrie's "response to Language Writing" had been "surprisingly little," and speculated that he may have disagreed with its "connected critique of the sign, reference and narrative" while also having "cultivated (briefly) some stylistic affinities with Language Writing" (Jaeger, 86–87).

7. When Mann was doing the final editing of the film in the spring of 1988 Barrie would also make frequent visits to his studio to view and advise. Mann remembers that he would not sit but would stand with the aid of a wooden cane.

8. Dutton describes "MEME" as calling "for two male and two female poets (sound poets, actually), two solo singers, three dancers, a choir, a marching band and an electronic ensemble. The language the poets speak is one of Nichol's own invention, comprising a limited vocabulary of eleven root words, with various prefixes and suffixes of a mainly prepositional nature. The words, which signify a few objects and elements in nature, some personal pronouns, and a few basic emotional states, serve the purposes of the simple drama that gradually unfolds. The choir, which functions as a Greek chorus, mixes English with the language Nichol invented" (1989).

Chapter 23: Unbound

1. Reluctant to publish the poems in a now obsolete technology — the Apple IIe had now been replaced by the Apple Macintosh, which used a different operating system — Red Deer waited until 1993 to publish a Macintosh Hypercard version of *First Screening* that had been created by University of Calgary student J.B. Holm. That type of Macintosh in turn became obsolete in 2004.

2. The surgeon also regretted that the tumour had not been detected much

earlier, which in his opinion it should have been. Later a check of an x-ray taken before Barrie's 1985 surgery, one apparently centered on the L5-S1 spinal area, revealed that the tumour was visible at the bottom.

Chapter 24: The Afterlife of bpNichol

1. It is noteworthy that Ellie did not write about the requested topic, "The Influence of Therafields on bp's Writing" (113), although she did write about Therafields and some of Barrie's experiences there. As mentioned earlier, she does not perceive much connection between his therapy, or his work as a psychoanalyst, and his writing, and is skeptical about the soundness of the connections that I make here — while also clearly realizing that without Lea's help it's unlikely that he would have become the writer that we know. As Barrie wrote at the beginning of *The Martyrology, Book 5*, "still / for Lea / still." It is also noteworthy that in Barrie's musical comedy *Group*, from which Ellie gets her substitute title, "The Ordinary Man," the phrase "ordinary man" is heavily (and amusingly) ironized — see *An H in the Heart* 68–9.

2. This is Steve McCaffery's recollection, in his interview by Peter Jaeger. Considering the question of whether Barrie would have "approved" being published by McClelland & Stewart, McCaffery tells Jaeger, "Absolutely not. Leaving aside Nichol's own convictions never to be published by a mainstream press such as M&S, and his commitment to small press publication till the day he died (we spoke about this on our last day together as he drove me from his home on Lauder Avenue to the St. Clair subway station)" (Jaeger 84). McCaffery also regrets here that he was not consulted about the collection by Ellie Nichol or the editors, and says that he considers it an "insult" that work he had co-authored with Nichol was included by them without acknowledgement, adding, "I was told by Barrie in the late 1970s that I was designated in his will as his literary executor" — a will that in 1983 was replaced because of Barrie and Ellie's marriage. After Barrie's death, he continues, he was told by someone that "Barrie's revised will specified me as executor in the event of both their [Ellie and Sarah Nichol's] deaths" (84–85). However, Barrie's 1979 will had not named him as literary executor, but only as a member of an advisory committee of him, Julia Keeler, and Rob Hindley-Smith to be consulted by the will's executor, Renwick Day. His final will, signed in November 1983, and probated in December 1988, names Ellie as executor, Renwick Day as alternate executor, gives his executor sole power to deal with his published and unpublished works and his copyrights, and makes no mention of McCaffery. Quite possibly the frosty relations between McCaffery and Ellie, so evident in the Jaeger interview, were already cool at the time of the will.

works cited

Works by bpNichol

Nichol, bp. *ABC: The Aleph Beth Book*. Ottawa: Oberon Press, 1971.

___. *Ad Sanctos: The Martyrology, Book 9*. Musical score by Howard Gerhard. Toronto: Coach House Press, 1993.

___. *Aleph Unit*. Toronto: Seripress, 1973.

___. *The Alphabet Game: A bpNichol Reader*. Ed. Darren Wershler-Henry and Lori Emerson. Toronto: Coach House Books, 2007.

___. *Alphabet/Ilphabet*. Toronto: Seripress, 1978.

___. *Art Facts: A Book of Contexts*. Tucson: Chax Press, 1990.

___. *As Elected*. Vancouver: Talonbooks, 1981.

___. *Beach Head*. Sacramento: Runcible Spoon, 1971.

___. *bp*. Toronto: Coach House Press, 1967.

___. *bpNichol Comics*. Ed. Carl Peters. Vancouver: Talonbooks, 2002.

___. *The Captain Poetry Poems*. Vancouver: blew ointment, 1971.

___. *Continental Trance*. Lantzville, B.C.: Oolichan Books, 1982.

___. *Dada Lama*. London: Tlaloc, 1968.

___. *A Draft of Book IV of The Martyrology*. Edmonton: bpNichol, 1976.

___. *Familiar*. Toronto: Eleanor and bpNichol, 1980.

___. *First Screening*. Toronto: Underwhich Editions, 1984.

___. *Ganglia Press Index*. Toronto: Ganglia, 1972.

___. *Gifts: The Martyrology Book(s) 7&*. Ed. Irene Niechoda. Toronto: Coach House, 1990.

___. *An H in the Heart: A Reader*. Ed. George Bowering and Michael Ondaatje. Toronto: McClelland & Stewart, 1994.

___. "Interview (en anglais) Raôul Duguay/bpNichol." *Open Letter*. Second Series, No. 6 (Fall 1973): 65-73.

___. *Journal*. Toronto: Coach House Press, 1978.

___. *Konfessions of an Elizabethan Fan Dancer*. London: Writer's Forum, 1967.

___. *Lament*. Toronto: Ganglia Press, 1969.

___. "The Lily." *Writing* 5 (Spring 1982): 12.

___. *Love: A Book of Remembrances*. Vancouver: Talonbooks, 1974.

___. *The Martyrology, Book I*. Toronto: Coach House Press, 1972.

___. *The Martyrology, Book II*. Toronto: Coach House Press, 1972.

___. *The Martyrology, Books 1 & 2*. Toronto: Coach House Press, 1977.

___. *The Martyrology, Books 3 & 4*. Toronto: Coach House Press, 1976.

___. *The Martyrology, Book 5*. Toronto: Coach House Press, 1982.

___. *The Martyrology, Book 6 Books*. Toronto: Coach House Press, 1986.

___. *Monotones*. Vancouver: Talonbooks, 1971.

___. *Nights on Prose Mountain*. Toronto: Ganglia Press, 1969.

___. Notebooks. There are at least 31 Nichol notebooks at Simon Fraser University's Special Collections, datable by the dates of their entries. Ten of these are from the 1963–71 period and part of SFU's first acquisition of Nichol papers. Barrie began numbering his notebooks in 1969, numbering the fourth one number "III" and the seventh one number IV, while naming the fifth "Tegnikal Notes." In 1972 he began naming his principal notebooks while numbering smaller concurrent ones, of which he accumulated five, including two marked "fourth short notebook." There are 15 clearly named notebooks at Simon Fraser. In July 1981 in his "Title Notebook," he attempted to draw up a list of his 1972–80 notebooks, with dates, "for handy ref." He noted that he had lost his "Blue Jean Yes" notebook of April–November 1979. Most of the listed notebooks are identifiable in the SFU collection. Because of the ambiguities of their naming and numbering I have usually referenced these only by the date of the entry I have cited.

___. *The Other Side of the Room*. Toronto: Weed/Flower Press, 1971.

___. *Portrait of David*. Toronto: Ganglia Press, 1966,

___. "Prelude." *Axis*. Vol 1. December 24, 1969.

___. *Selected Organs: Parts of an Autobiography*. Windsor: Black Moss Press, 1988.

___. "some words on the martyrology march 12 1979." In Michael Ondaatje, ed., *The Long Poem Anthology*. Toronto: Coach House Press, 1979. 335-37.

___. *Still Water*. Vancouver: Talonbooks, 1970.

___. *The True Eventual Story of Billy the Kid*. Toronto: Weed/Flower Press, 1970.

___. *Truth: A Book of Fictions*. Ed. Irene Niechoda. Toronto: Mercury Press, 1993.

___. *Two Novels*. Toronto: Coach House Press, 1969.

___. *Unit of Four*. Toronto: Seripress, 1973.

___. *Zygal: A Book of Mysteries and Translations*. Toronto: Coach House Press, 1985.

___, ed. *The Cosmic Chef: An Evening of Concrete*. Ottawa: Oberon, 1970.

___, and Brian Dedora. *A B.C. Childhood*. Toronto: grOnk, 1982.

___, and Adam Crabtree. "Communication and Armouring." *Axis*, Vol 3, May 15, 1980: 323–29.

___, and Lea Hindley-Smith. "Notes on Milieu Therapy." *Axis*, Vol 1.1 December 24, 1969.

___, and Lea Hindley-Smith. "The Paranoiac and the Paranee." *Axis*, Vol 1:88 July 9, 1970.

___, Lea Hindley-Smith, Stan Kutz, and Philip McKenna. "Therafields." *The Canadian Forum,* January 1973: 12-17.

Works by other authors

Andrews, Bruce, and Charles Bernstein. *The L=A=N=G=U=A=G=E Book.* Carbondale, IL: Southern Illinois UP, 1984.

Andrews, Jim, Geoff Huth, Lionel Kearns, Marko Niemi, and Dan Waber. "Introduction to bpNichol's *First Screening.*" *Open Letter*, Thirteenth Series, Number 5 (Spring 2008): 40-43.

Bayard, Caroline, and Jack David. *Out-Posts/Avant-Postes.* Erin, ON: Press Porcepic, 1978.

Bök, Christian. "Nickel Linoleum." *Open Letter*, Tenth Series, No. 4 (Fall 1998): 62.

Davey, Frank. *Earle Birney.* Toronto: Copp Clark, 1971.

___. Interview with Deanna Robb, February 5, 2011. The MP3 recording is in my private possession.

___. Interview with Don ("D.J.") Nichol, October 26, 2010. The MP3 recording is in my private possession.

___. "This Gentleman, bpNichol." In Jean Baird and George Bowering, ed., *The Heart Does Break: Canadian Writers on Grief and Mourning.* Toronto: Random House Canada, 2009. 99-112.

Doyle, Brenda. "Thoughts on Therafields." http://thoughtsontherafields. blogspot.com/ 2010/10/in-fall-of-1997-i-began-series-of.html. Accessed February 9, 2011, March 7, 2011, and September 19, 2011. Web.

Dudek, Louis. *Atlantis.* Montreal: Delta Canada, 1967.

Duncan, Robert. "Ideas of the Meaning of Form." *Kulchur* 1:4 (1961), 60-74.

Dutton, Paul. "bp Anecdotingly." *Open Letter*, Thirteenth Series, No. 8 (Spring 2009): 77-91.

Eagleton, Terry. *Sweet Violence.* Oxford: Blackwell, 2003.

Four Horsemen. *Horse d'Oeuvres.* Don Mills, ON: PaperJacks, 1975.

Freud, Sigmund. "Analysis terminable and interminable." *The Standard Edition of the Complete Psychological Works of Sigmund Freud.* Ed. James Strachey. Vol. 23. New York: Vintage, 1999. 209–53.

Frye, Northrop. *The Great Code: The Bible and Literature.* New York: Harcourt Brace & Jovanovitch, 1981.

Godard, Barbara. *Canadian Literature at the Crossroads of Language and Culture.* Edmonton: NeWest Press, 2008.

Goodbrand. Grant. *Therafields: The Rise and Fall of Lea Hindley-Smith's Psychoanalytic Commune*. Toronto: ECW Press, 2010.

Hancock, Geoff. "The Form of the Thing: An Interview with bpNichol on Ganglia and grOnk." *Rampike* 12:1 (Fall 2001). Also excerpted in Miki, *Meanwhile*, 396–409.

Hindley-Smith, Lea. *Ronald and Susan*. Toronto: Therafields, 1975.

___. *Secret Places*. Toronto: Therafields, 1978.

___. *The Way It Might Have Been*. Toronto: Therafields, 1977.

Huth, Geoff. "First Meaning: The Digital Poetry Incunabula of bpNichol." *Open Letter* Thirteenth Series, No. 5 (Spring 2005): 49–58.

Jaeger, Peter. "An Interview with Steve McCaffery on the TRG." *Open Letter*, Tenth Series, No. 4 (Fall 1998): 77–96.

Jarry, Alfred. *Gestes et opinions du docteur Faustroll, pataphysicien*. Paris: Gallimard, 1972 [1911].

Kroetsch, Robert. *Creation*. Toronto: new press, 1970.

Lacan, Jacques. *Encore: Le Seminaire livre XX*. Paris: Éditions du Seuil, 1974.

___. *L'envers de la psychanalyse. Le Séminaire livre XXVII*. Texte établi par Jacques-Alain Miller. Paris: Éditions du Seuil, 1991.

Lind, Loren. Carbon typescript of an interview with Nichol, December 11, 1968. Filed at Simon Fraser University Special Collections among Nichol's correspondence.

Lindquist, Sven. *Exterminate All the Brutes*. London: Granta, 1992.

McCaffery, Steve. "The Martyrology as Paragram." *Open Letter*, Sixth Series, Nos. 5–6 (Summer-Fall 1986): 191–206.

___. "The Silent Punster: Nichol's Semiology of the Saints." *Open Letter*, Thirteenth Series, No. 5 (Spring 2008): 97-109.

___, ed. *Rational Geomancy: The Kids of the Book Machine: The Collected Research Reports of the Toronto Research Group 1973–1982* by Steve McCaffery and bpNichol. Vancouver: Talonbooks, 1992.

___, and bpNichol. *In England Now that Spring*. Toronto: Aya Press, 1979.

McElroy, Gil. *St. Art: The Visual Poetry of bpNichol*. Charlottetown: Confederation Centre Art Gallery & Museum, 2000.

McGeachy, Matt. "Therafields: Toronto's (Nearly) Forgotten Therapeutic Community." *Columbia Undergraduate Journal of History* II:1 (Spring 2009). http://cujh.columbia.edu/2009/ 02/matt-mcgeachy-therafields-torontos. html. Web. Accessed October 23, 2011.

Miki, Roy. "Turn this Page: Journaling bpNichol's *The Martyrology* and the Returns." *Open Letter*, Tenth Series, No. 4 (Fall 1998): 116–33.

Miki, Roy, ed. *Meanwhile: The Critical Writings of bpNichol*. Vancouver: Talonbooks, 2002.

___, ed. *Tracing the Paths: Reading . . . Writing The Martyrology*. Vancouver: Talonbooks / West Coast Line, 1988.

___, and Fred Wah, ed. *Beyond the Orchard: Essays on the Martyrology*. Vancouver: West Coast Line, 1997.

Multineddu, Flavio. "An Interview with bpNichol in Torino, May 6 & 8, 1987." *Open Letter*, Eighth Series, No. 7 (Summer 1993): 5–35.

Nichol, Eleanor. "An Ordinary Man." *West Coast Line*, 16 (29:1), (Spring-Summer 1995): 113–18.

Niechoda, Irene. "Additor's Note." In Nichol. *Truth: a Book of Fictions.* 1993. 172–75.

___. "Gift / Gifts / Giving: An Afterward." In Nichol. *Gifts.* 1990. N.p.

___. *A Sourcery for Books 1 and 2 of bpNichol's The Martyrology.* Toronto: ECW Press, 1992.

Perreault, Donna. "What Makes Autobiography Interrogative?" *Biography*, 13, No. 2 (Spring 1990): 130–42.

Poirier, Richard. *The Performing Self.* New York: Oxford UP, 1971.

Rosenberg, David. "Body by Nichol." *Open Letter*, Fourteenth Series, No. 1 (Fall 2009): 7–40.

Rothenberg, Jerome. "Je est un autre." http://poemsandpoetics.blogspot.com/2010/09/ je-est-un-autre-ethnopoetics-poet-as.html. Web.

Scobie, Stephen. *bpNichol: What History Teaches.* Vancouver: Talonbooks, 1984.

Shives, Arnold. Unpublished statement written to accompany letters he had received from Nichol in 1964–66. Simon Fraser University, Bennett Library, Special Collections.

Spenst, Kevin. "Ken Norris" (interview). May 11, 2011. http://kevinspenst .com/?p=558. Web.

___. "Kevin Spenst Talks to Ken Norris." *Prism International* June 13, 2011. http://prismmagazine.ca/2011/06/13/interview-kevin-spenst-talks-to-ken-norris/. Web.

Starnino, Carmine. "Does bpNichol's once-revolutionary wordplay have staying power?" *Maisonneuve.* July 5, 2011. http://maisonneuve.org/press-room/article/2011/jul/5/captain-poetry/. Web.

Swail, Christopher. "Reading to the Limits: Space-Time and *The Martyrology.* In Miki, *Beyond the Orchard*, 1997. 171–83.

Swift, Jonathan. *Gulliver's Travels and Other Writings.* Boston: Riverside Press, 1960. This is the edition Barrie would have been asked to read in his English 200 course at the University of British Columbia.

Turner, Michael. *Three Readings.* Vancouver: Western Front Media Arts, 2011.

Wershler-Henry, Darren. "Argument for a Secular *Martyrology.*" *Open Letter*, Tenth Series, No. 4 (Fall 1998): 37–47.

index

bissett, bill, VII, VIII, 62, 69, 70, 75, 76, 77, 78, 80, 81, 83, 88, 89, 91, 92, 110, 143, 144, 146, 149, 204, 206, 226

Black Moss Press, 235, 243, 267

Blaser, Robin, 296, 298

blew ointment, 62, 70, 80

Blizzard Island, 266, 268, 270, 275, 276, 280, 281

Bök, Christian, 291, 293

Bolt, Carol, 250, 259

bory, jean françois, 78, 147, 171

Bourne, Lesley-Anne, 275–76

Bowering, George, 43, 62, 72, 73, 76, 77, 78, 106, 142, 148, 173, 188, 235, 238, 261, 282, 285, 289, 290

Bromige, David, 173, 270, 319N

Brossard, Nicole, 236

Burnham, Clint, 257, 259

Caruso, Barbara, 172, 173, 250, 251, 252, 290, 294

Chopin, Henri, 188, 206, 296

Claire, Paula, 188, 282

Clark, Thomas A., 207, 211, 215

Clarke, Arthur C., 211

Clifford, Wayne, 80

Clinton, Martina, 78

Coach House Books, 289, 290, 304N

Coach House Press, x, 66, 73, 80, 81, 85, 90–91, 127, 138, 144, 148, 172, 173–77, 194, 198, 206, 209, 214, 221, 223, 236, 238, 241, 244–45, 249–50, 251, 259, 263–64, 266, 267, 270, 272, 276, 288, 289, 312N, 317N, 318N

Cobbing, Bob, 81, 83, 90, 188, 206, 262, 306N

Coleman, Victor, x, 62, 71, 72, 78, 110, 148, 173–76, 301N, 312N

Colombo, John Robert, 84, 130

Copithorne, Judith, 41, 48, 75, 76, 78, 244–45, 259

Coupey, Pierre, 14, 102

Cowper, William, 178

Cox, Kenelm, 78

Crabtree, Adam, 107, 227

Creeley, Robert, 41, 43, 173, 226, 293, 304N

Cull, David, 43, 47, 48, 84

Dada, 41–44, 63, 131, 142, 221, 253, 269, 287, 301N

Davey, Linda, 148–49, 191, 175, 176, 183, 188, 317N

David, Jack, VIII, 64, 72, 75, 84, 103–05, 106, 180, 202, 204, 216

Dawson, David, 43

At ECW Press, we want you to enjoy this book in whatever format you like, whenever you like. Leave your print book at home and take the eBook to go! Purchase the print edition and receive the eBook free. Just send an email to ebook@ecwpress.com and include:

→ the book title
→ the name of the store where you purchased it
→ your receipt number
→ your preference of file type: PDF or ePub?

A real person will respond to your email with your eBook attached. And thanks for supporting an independently owned Canadian publisher with your purchase!